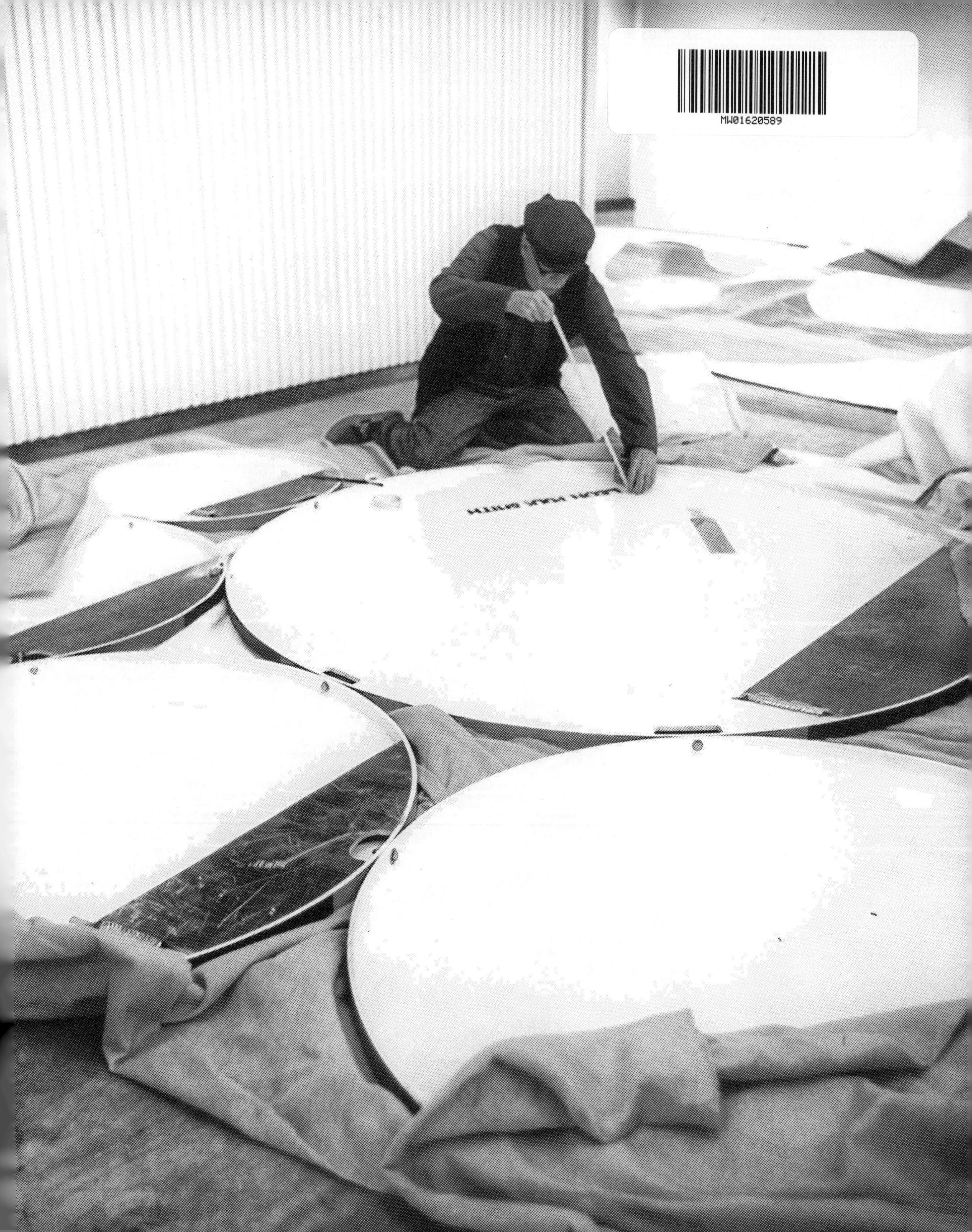

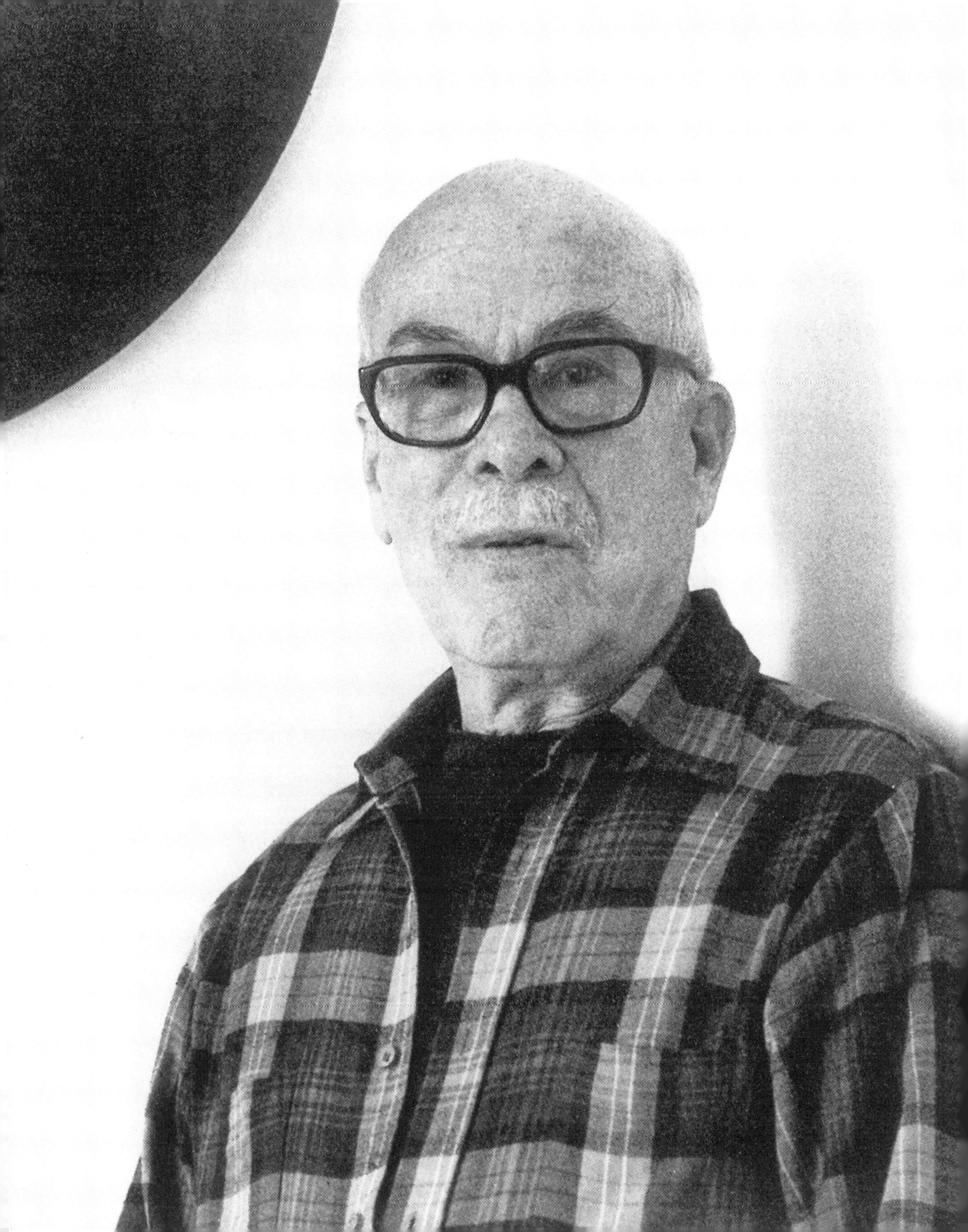

Leon Polk Smith

haus konstruktiv

Leon Polk Smith
Going Beyond Space

Herausgegeben von | Edited by
Sabine Schaschl, Stiftung für konstruktive, konkrete und konzeptuelle Kunst, Museum Haus Konstruktiv, Zürich

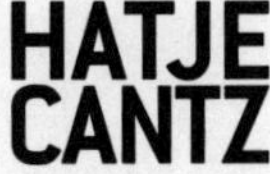

Vorwort und Dank

Mit der Ausstellung *Going Beyond Space* lädt das Museum Haus Konstruktiv zu einer ebenso erhellenden wie inspirierenden Wiederentdeckung der Werke von Leon Polk Smith ein – mehr als zwanzig Jahre nach seiner letzten institutionellen Ausstellung in Europa und mit der ersten musealen Präsentation in der Schweiz überhaupt.

Leon Polk Smiths künstlerische Position kann aus heutiger Sicht als ein «Missing Link» in der Kunstgeschichte verstanden werden. Sein Werk verbindet über Referenzen zur Malerei Piet Mondrians die europäische Avantgarde mit der amerikanischen Abstraktion der 1940er/1950er-Jahre. Smiths Vorreiterrolle im Hard-Edge-Stil und seine Shaped Canvases sind wiederum Errungenschaften, die aus dem amerikanischen Wirkkreis auf Europa ausstrahlten. Mit der einzigartigen Werkgruppe der *Constellations* erreichte Smith einen Höhepunkt in seiner künstlerischen Karriere und wurde über die Grenzen Amerikas hinaus bekannt. In den letzten Jahren erlangte sein Werk vor allem in den USA dank zahlreicher Ausstellungen neue Sichtbarkeit. Es bleibt zu hoffen, dass die Ausstellung im Museum Haus Konstruktiv zu seiner lange überfälligen Neurezeption in Europa beiträgt.

Die Zürcher Präsentation ist retrospektiv angelegt und umfasst in exemplarischer Weise nahezu alle Werkgruppen. Wir freuen uns ausserordentlich über die grosse Anzahl hochkarätiger Leihgaben, die uns zur Verfügung gestellt wurden, und sind der Leon Polk Smith Foundation, die das Vorhaben stets unterstützte, zutiefst dankbar. Mein persönlicher Dank gilt den Vertretern der Stiftung Patterson Sims und John Koegel sowie Greg Hilty und Jeannie Freilich von der Lisson Gallery. Die Ausstellung bringt Werke zusammen, die über Jahrzehnte nicht gemeinsam gezeigt wurden. Dafür möchte ich allen Leihgeber:innen aus Europa und den USA meinen grossen Dank aussprechen.

Mein ergebenster Dank geht an die Art Mentor Foundation, die das Museum Haus Konstruktiv bereits in der Vergangenheit bei ausgewählten Projekten mit substanziellen finanziellen Mitteln unterstützt hat. Ihre Voraussicht und Hingabe an das Ausstellungsvorhaben schufen die Basis für dessen Realisierung, wofür ich allen Vorstandsmitgliedern der Art Mentor Foundation danke. Persönlich möchte ich mich von Herzen bei Evelyn Kryst bedanken, die mit ihrer Liebe zur Kunst und ihrer Fürsprache so vieles möglich macht.

Mein herzlicher Dank geht auch an alle Autor:innen, die in ihren Beiträgen das Werk des Künstlers, seine Positionierung innerhalb der Kunstgeschichte und den Einfluss seiner Herkunft auf sein Schaffen neu beleuchten – Smith wuchs in einem vornehmlich von der Kultur der Chickasaw und Choctaw Native Americans geprägten Umfeld auf.

Meinem grossartigen Team und allen Mitarbeitenden an der Ausstellung und Publikation möchte ich von Herzen danken. Ich bin sehr stolz auf unseren Zusammenhalt und die Leidenschaft, mit der wir alle das Bestmögliche für die Vermittlung der Inhalte und Werte unserer Institution leisten. Vielen herzlichen Dank.

Sabine Schaschl
Direktorin Museum Haus Konstruktiv

Preface and Acknowledgements

With the illuminating and inspiring exhibition *Going Beyond Space,* Museum Haus Konstruktiv is offering the chance to rediscover Leon Polk Smith's works presented more than twenty years after his last institutional exhibition in Europe and shown for the first time ever in a Swiss museum.

From a present-day perspective, Smith's artistic position can be seen as a "missing link" in art history. Through references to Piet Mondrian's paintings, Smith's oeuvre connects the European avant-garde to American abstraction in the 1940s–50s, while his pioneering role in the Hard-edge style and his shaped canvases are achievements that radiated from the American sphere of influence to Europe. With his unique group of works entitled *Constellations,* Smith reached a high point in his artistic career and became known beyond the borders of the US. In recent years, his oeuvre has gained new visibility, especially in the US, thanks to numerous shows. We hope that the exhibition at Museum Haus Konstruktiv will contribute to his long-overdue new appreciation in Europe.

Our presentation is a retrospective encompassing examples from almost all his series. We are extremely pleased that a large number of high-caliber works have been made available to us on loan, and we are deeply grateful to the Leon Polk Smith Foundation, which supported the project throughout. My personal thanks go to the Foundation's representatives Patterson Sims and John Koegel, as well as Greg Hilty and Jeannie Freilich at Lisson Gallery. The exhibition combines works that have not been shown together for decades, and I would like to express my immense gratitude to all the lenders from Europe and the US who have made this possible.

My sincerest thanks also go to the Art Mentor Foundation, which has supported Museum Haus Konstruktiv in the past with substantial funding for selected projects. I thank all the board members at the Art Mentor Foundation for their foresight and their dedication to this exhibition project, thereby providing the basis for its realization. From the bottom of my heart, I would like to personally thank Evelyn Kryst, whose love of art and whose advocacy make so much possible.

My deepest gratitude to all the authors, whose contributions shed new light on the artist's oeuvre, his positioning within art history, and the influence of his background on his work, having been raised in an environment imbued with the culture of the Chickasaw and Choctaw Native American people on the high plains of Oklahoma.

I would like to wholeheartedly thank my magnificent team and everyone who worked on the exhibition and publication. I am very proud of our team spirit and the passion with which we all do our best to convey the substance and values of our institution. Thank you very much.

Sabine Schaschl
Director Museum Haus Konstruktiv

Die Leon Polk Smith Foundation: Geschichte und Dank

Die Leon Polk Smith Foundation ist hocherfreut, dass das Museum Haus Konstruktiv diese ambitionierte Übersichtsausstellung und Publikation zur Kunst von Leon Polk Smith organisiert hat. Die grosse europäische und internationale Anerkennung, die darin zum Ausdruck kommt, hätte Smith zutiefst befriedigt.

Smith wurde 1906 als achtes von neun Kindern im damaligen «Indian Territory» geboren, ein Jahr bevor Oklahoma zum 46. Bundesstaat der USA wurde. Er bestritt den Lebensunterhalt für sich und seine Familie zunächst mit Viehwirtschaft und Bauarbeiten. Smith studierte in Oklahoma und gehörte damit zur ersten Generation derer, die eine College-Ausbildung genossen. Auf die Kunst und auf Kunstschaffende stiess er erstmals 1934, in seinem letzten Studienjahr. Sein Leben veränderte sich und er fing an, Kunst zu machen. Nach dem College arbeitete er als Grund- und Sekundarschullehrer. In Oklahoma blieb er bis zu seinem dreissigsten Lebensjahr, dann ging er nach New York, um an der Columbia University ein Aufbaustudium im Fach Pädagogik zu absolvieren. In New York begann er ein bemerkenswert urbanes und fortschrittliches Leben, doch seine Kunst baute er auf den Grundlagen seiner ersten Jahrzehnte in der eindrucksvollen Landschaft Oklahomas und der Kultur der indigenen Gemeinschaften auf, mit denen er dort zu tun hatte.

Zu seinen Lebzeiten wurde Smith von einer Reihe progressiver New Yorker Galerien und Kunsthändler:innen vertreten, darunter die Egan Gallery, Betty Parsons, Eleanor Wards Stable Gallery, Madeleine und Arthur Lejwas Galerie Chalette, Denise René, Susan Caldwell und Joan Washburn. Die meisten seiner Ausstellungen fanden in Amerika statt, doch gewann Smiths Werk auch in Europa eine beträchtliche Anhängerschaft; Galerie- und Museumsausstellungen in den späteren Lebensjahrzehnten und die Vertretung durch deutsche Galerien Mitte der 1960er- und Ende der 1980er-Jahre zeugen davon.

Als er auf die Neunzig zuging, plante und initiierte Smith gemeinsam mit seinem Lebensgefährten Robert Mead Jamieson die Leon Polk Smith Foundation als gemeinnützige Stiftung zum Erhalt und zur Förderung seiner Kunst und seines Vermächtnisses. Zusammen mit ihrem Anwalt wählten Smith, Jamieson und Robert T. Buck, der damalige Direktor des enzyklopädischen New Yorker Brooklyn Museums, das eine Retrospektive mit Smiths Gemälden und Zeichnungen organisierte, den ersten Vorstand der Stiftung aus. Smith hinterliess der Leon Polk Smith Foundation sämtliche Kunstwerke, die sich zum Zeitpunkt seines Todes in seinem Besitz befanden, sowie finanzielle Mittel, die durch Verkäufe seiner – der Stiftung vermachten – Kunstwerke aufgestockt wurden. Binnen sechs Jahren nach seinem Tod Ende 1996 wurden sein Nachlass und sein Archiv in die Archives of American Art überführt. Mit Mitteln der Smith Foundation und der Terra Foundation for American Art wurden diese Quellen geordnet und digitalisiert, um sie einer breiten Öffentlichkeit zugänglich zu machen. Siehe: https://www.aaa.si.edu/collections/leon-polk-smith-papers-6162

Die Hauptaufgabe der Smith Foundation besteht darin, Galerien, Museen, Wissenschaftler:innen und Bildungseinrichtungen zu unterstützen und zu ermutigen, Smiths Leben und Kunst zu studieren, zu erforschen, darüber zu schreiben und Ausstellungen zu organisieren. Ein wichtiges Projekt war die Einrichtung einer – auf den von Smith und Jamieson geführten Inventarbüchern basierenden – Online-Datenbank mit Bildern und Aufzeichnungen zu sämtlichen bekannten Werken von Smith. Diese Datenbank ist für Forschende mit Genehmigung der Stiftung zugänglich. Überdies ist die Stiftung immer daran interessiert, mehr über die Werke von Leon Polk Smith zu erfahren.

The Leon Polk Smith Foundation: History and Acknowledgments

It is deeply gratifying to the Leon Polk Smith Foundation that this ambitious survey of and publication on the art of Leon Polk Smith has been organized by the Museum Haus Konstruktiv. It signals a level of European and international recognition that would have been profoundly satisfying to Smith.

The eighth of nine children, Smith was born in what was still Indian Territory in 1906, the year before Oklahoma became the forty-sixth state of the US. He initially supported himself and his family with ranching and construction work. Educated in Oklahoma, Smith was a first-generation college student. In 1934, he encountered art and artists for the first time in his final year of college. His life was transformed, and he began making art. After college, he supported himself as a primary and secondary school teacher. He remained in Oklahoma until he was thirty, when he moved to New York City to pursue graduate studies in education at Columbia University. In NYC, he began a notably urbane and forward-thinking existence while building his art upon his first decades in rural Oklahoma's striking landscape and the culture of the Nativ American communities he came in contact with there.

Smith was represented in his lifetime by a series of progressive New York City galleries and art dealers, including the Egan Gallery, Betty Parsons, Eleanor Ward's Stable Gallery, Madeleine and Arthur Lejwa's Galerie Chalette, Denise René, Susan Caldwell, and Joan Washburn. While the majority of his exhibitions have been in America, Smith's work has had a significant following in Europe, with gallery and museum shows in the later decades of his life and representation in the mid-1960s and late 1980s by German galleries.

As he was approaching ninety, Smith planned and initiated with his life partner, Robert Mead Jamieson, the Leon Polk Smith Foundation as a charitable trust to preserve and promote his art and legacy. Together with their lawyer, Smith and Jamieson—with Robert T. Buck, then Director of New York's encyclopedic Brooklyn Museum, which was organizing a retrospective of Smith's paintings and drawings—selected its original board of directors. Smith left all of the art in his possession at the time of his death to the Leon Polk Smith Foundation, along with funding that has increased from the sales of his art bequeathed to the Foundation. Over a six-year period following his death at the end of 1996, his papers and archives were transferred to the Archives of American Art. With funds from the Smith Foundation and the Terra Foundation for American Art, these resources were organized and digitized for broad public use and availability. See: https://www.aaa.si.edu/collections/leon-polk-smith-papers-6162.

The Smith Foundation's main roles have been to assist and encourage galleries, museums, scholars, and educational institutions to study, research, organize exhibitions, and write about Smith's life and art. A major undertaking has been the creation of an online database with images and records of all of Smith's known artworks using ledger inventory books of Smith's art kept by Smith and Jamieson. This database is accessible to scholars by permission from the Foundation. Furthermore, the Foundation is always eager to learn about works by Leon Polk Smith.

The Smith Foundation has donated paintings, drawings, and prints to over thirty museums and public collections. The largest donation has been 756 works on paper and small paintings to the Oklahoma State University Museum of Art in Stillwater. This repository was chosen for its location, its focus on Oklahoma-connected artists, and its commitment to art education for the University's students and community.

Die Smith Foundation hat Gemälde, Zeichnungen und Drucke an über dreissig Museen und öffentliche Sammlungen gestiftet. Die grösste Schenkung umfasste 756 Arbeiten auf Papier sowie kleine Gemälde und ging an das Oklahoma State University Museum of Art in Stillwater. Dieses Museum wurde aufgrund seines Standorts, seiner Fokussierung auf Künstler:innen mit einer Verbindung zu Oklahoma und aufgrund seines Engagements in der Kunstvermittlung für die Studierenden und Angehörigen der Universität ausgewählt.

In dem Bestreben, das Wissen über die Kunst und das Leben Smiths zu vertiefen und seine öffentliche Wertschätzung zu steigern, hat die Foundation den Aufbau und die Pflege einer umfangreichen Website organisiert, die unter anderem seine Lebensgeschichte, seine Ausstellungsgeschichte, Werke in öffentlichen Sammlungen, eine Bibliografie sowie Interviews umfasst. Siehe: leonpolksmithfoundation.org

Fördergelder der Stiftung wurden dem Oklahoma State University Museum of Art gewährt, damit es die von der Foundation übereigneten Kunstwerke aufarbeiten, weitere Forschungen unterstützen und Ausstellungen organisieren kann. Im Einklang mit Smiths Identifikation mit den Native Americans hat die Foundation Beiträge zu verschiedenen Initiativen entsprechender Kunst- und Kulturorganisationen geleistet.

Die Leon Polk Smith Foundation ist vor allem Sabine Schaschl, der Direktorin und leitenden Kuratorin des Museum Haus Konstruktiv, sowie ihren Kolleginnen, der Kuratorin und Sammlungsleiterin Evelyne Bucher und der Kuratorin Eliza Lips, zutiefst dankbar für ihr Engagement für dieses Projekt und dafür, dass sie Smiths Kunst in so erheblichem Umfang und in einem so passenden Kontext nach Europa zurückgebracht haben. Dankbar sind wir auch der Lisson Gallery unter der Leitung von CEO Alex Logsdail, dem kuratorischen Direktor Greg Hilty und der leitenden Direktorin Jeannie Freilich. Die Lisson Gallery präsentierte 2018 eine Ausstellung von Smiths Gemälden und Zeichnungen in London. Sie sorgte massgeblich für den Erfolg dieses Projekts und ein erweitertes Publikum für Smiths Kunst in Europa und anderswo.

Leon Polk Smith Foundation
John Koegel, Vorstand
Patterson Sims, Präsident

Among its core efforts to increase knowledge and public appreciation of Smith's art and life, the Foundation has overseen the creation of and maintains an extensive website that covers his life, exhibition history, public collections, bibliography, and interviews, among other topics. See: leonpolksmithfoundation.org

Grants from the Foundation have been given to the Oklahoma State University Museum of Art, so that they can process their gift of art from the Foundation, support further research, and organize exhibitions. In keeping with Smith's identification with Native Americans, the Foundation has made contributions to several Native American arts and cultural organizations' initiatives.

The Leon Polk Smith Foundation is, above all, deeply thankful to Sabine Schaschl, Director and Head Curator of Museum Haus Konstruktiv, and her colleagues Evelyne Bucher, Curator and Head of the Collection, and Eliza Lips, Curator, for their commitment to this project and for bringing Smith's art back to Europe in such a substantial way and fitting context. We are also grateful to the Lisson Gallery led by CEO Alex Logsdail with Greg Hilty, Curatorial Director, and Jeannie Freilich, Senior Director. Lisson presented an exhibition of Smith's paintings and drawings in London in 2018, and the gallery has been crucial for this project's success and expanding the audience for Smith's art in Europe and elsewhere.

Leon Polk Smith Foundation
John Koegel, Chairman
Patterson Sims, President

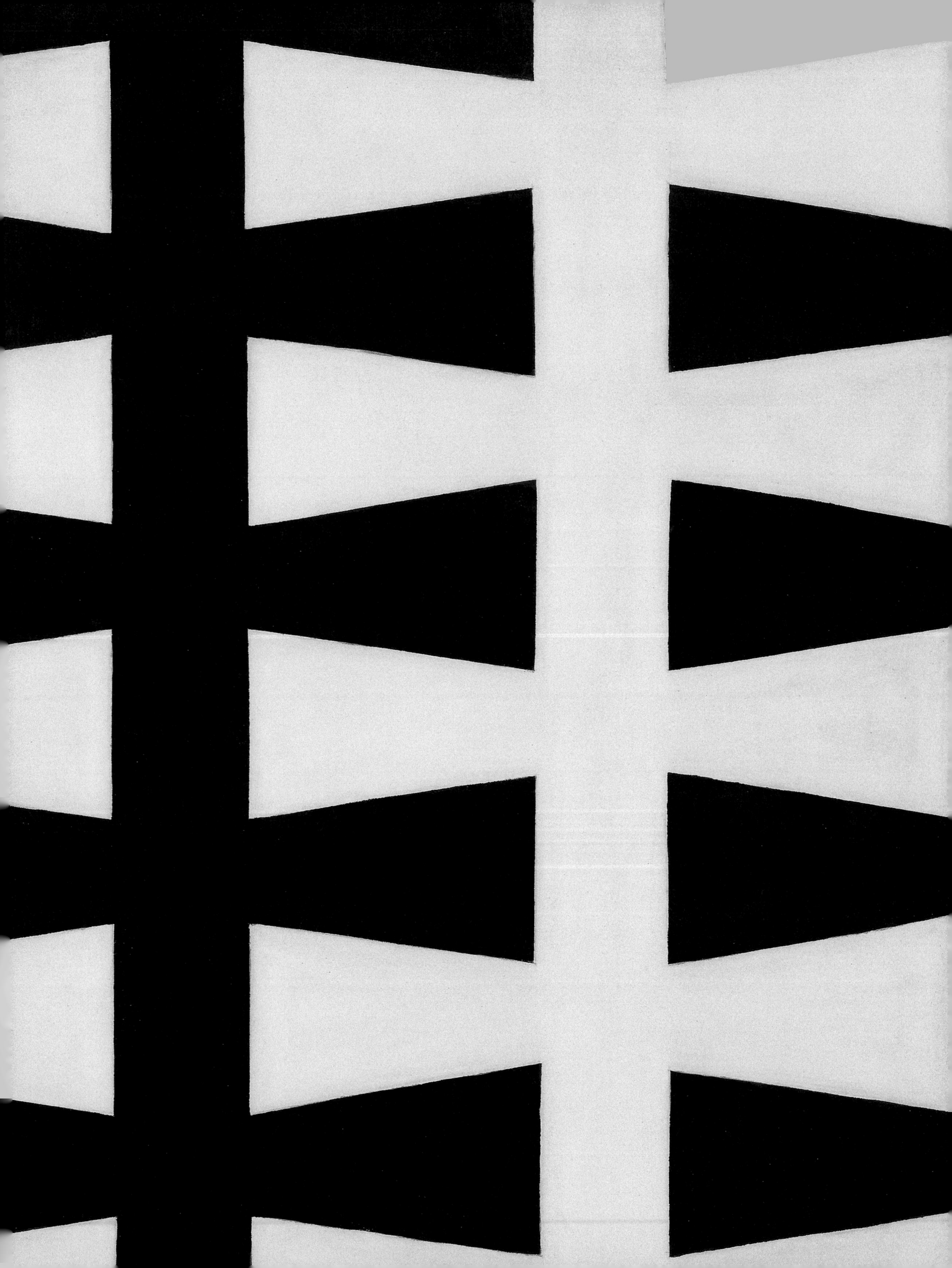

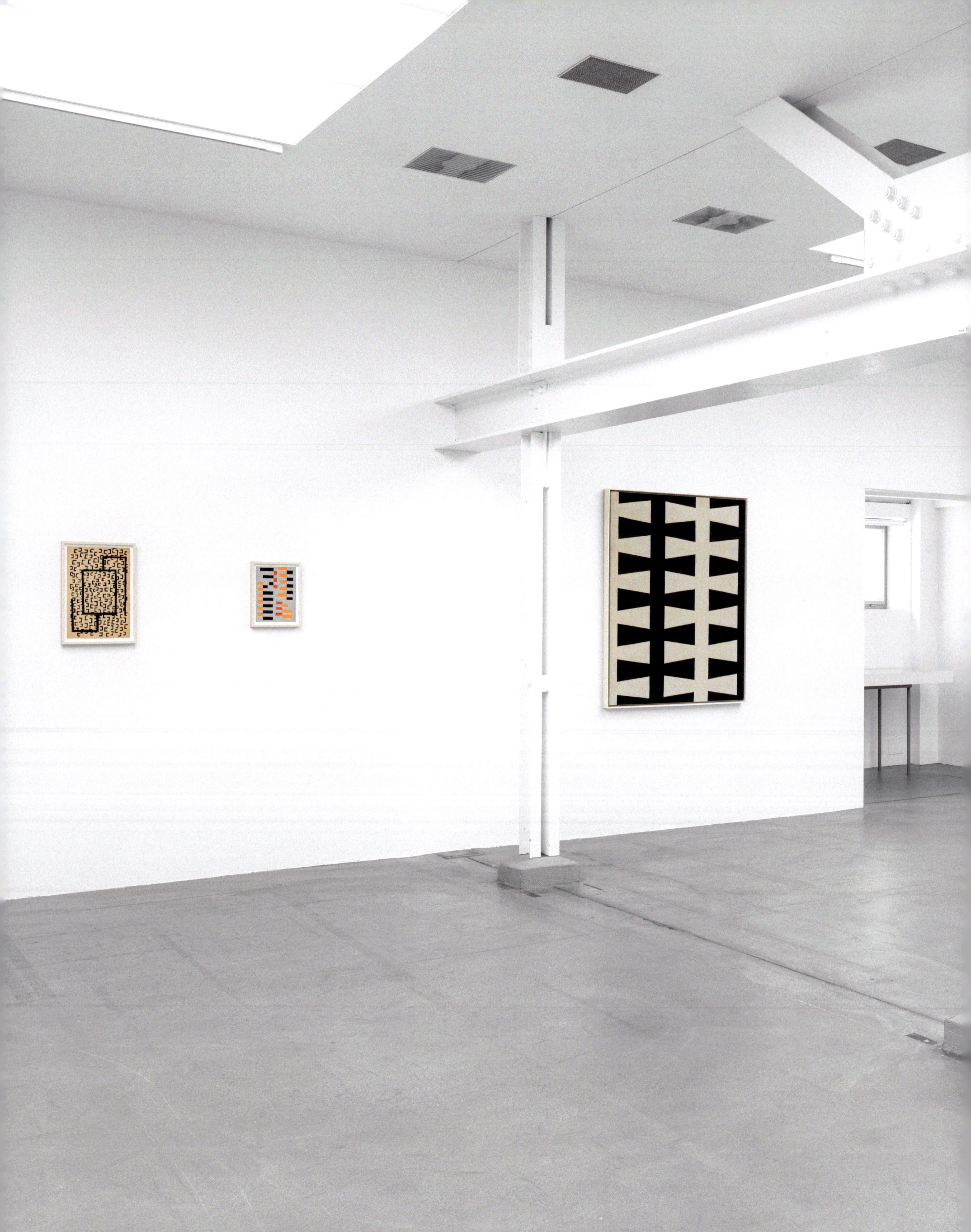

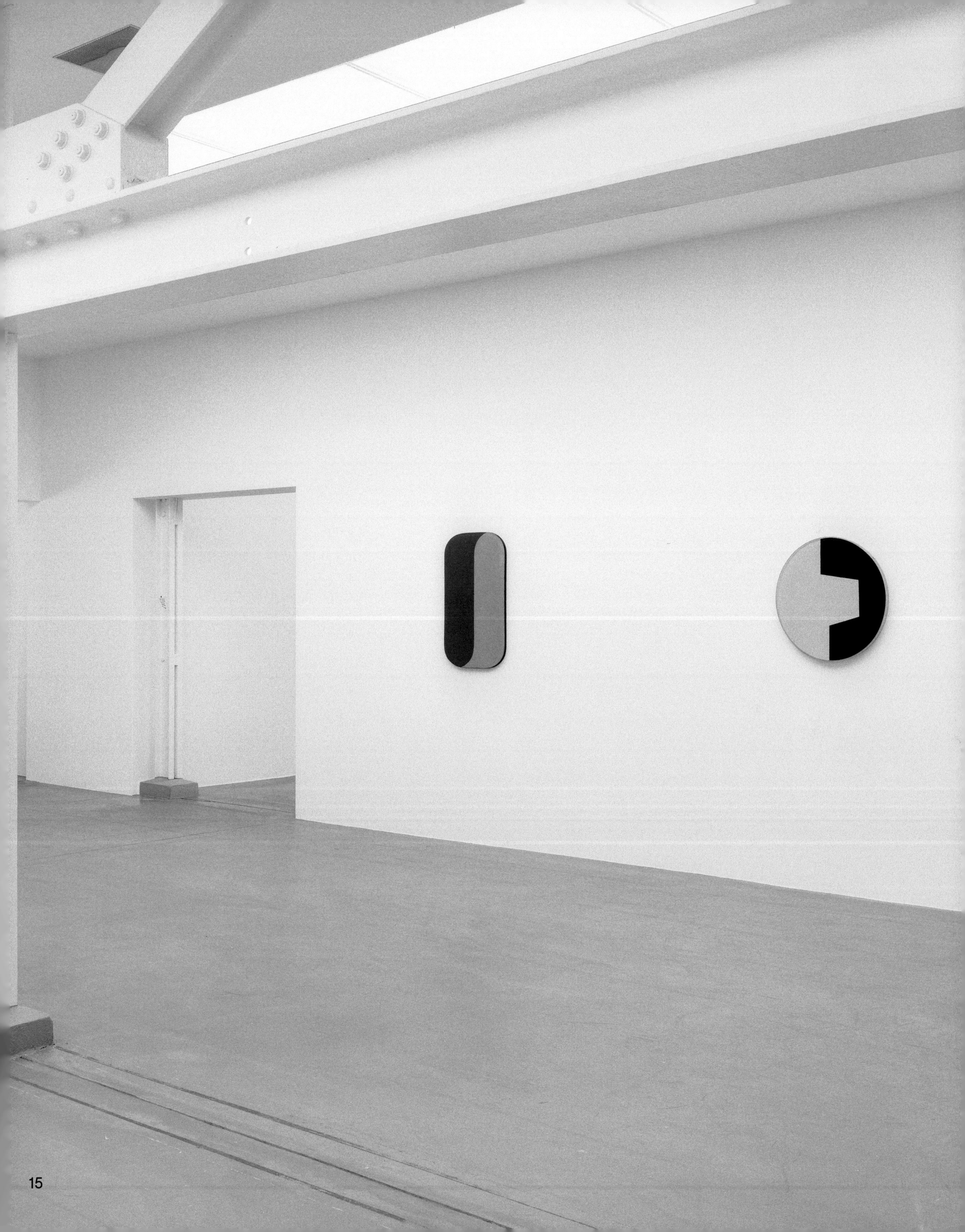

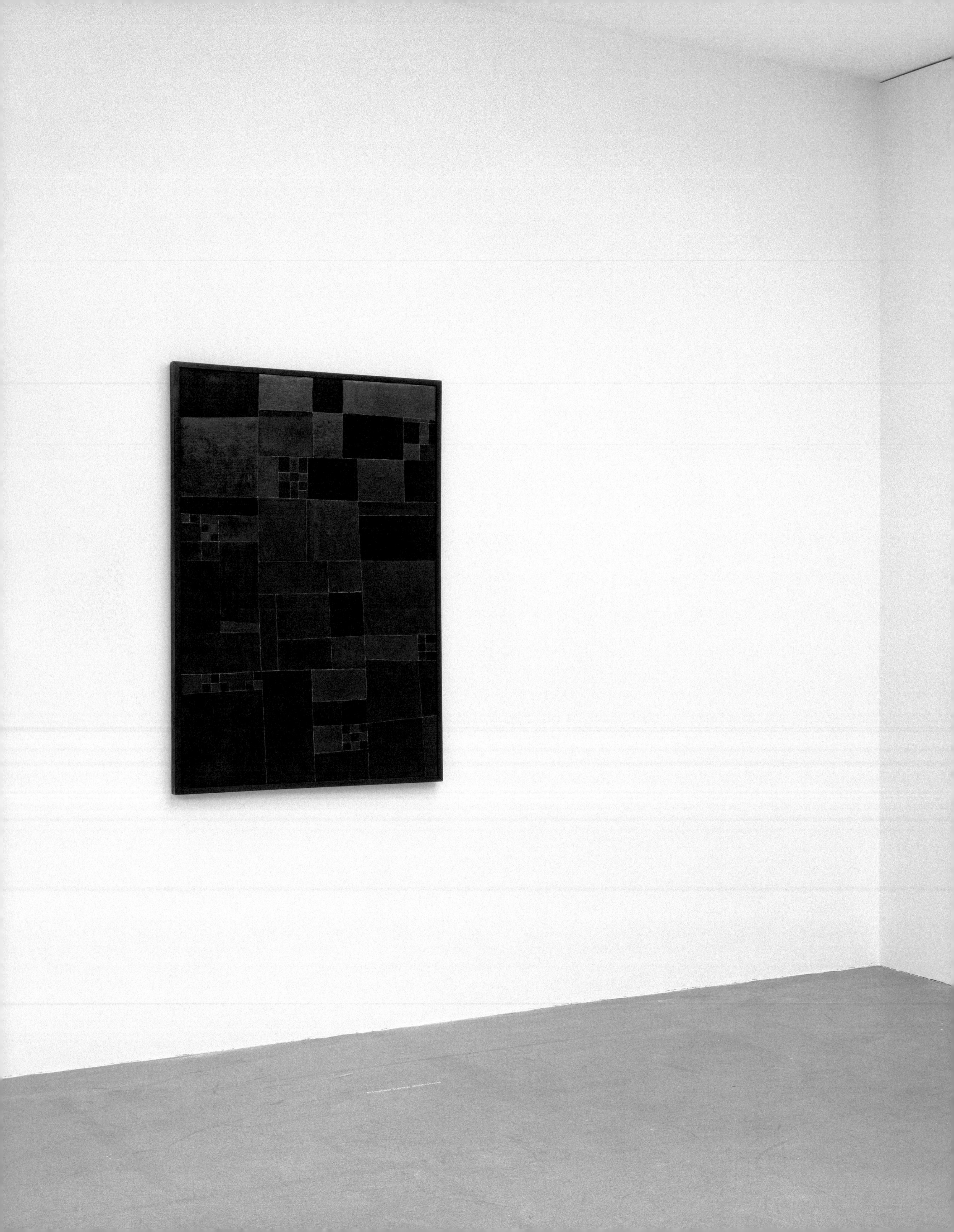

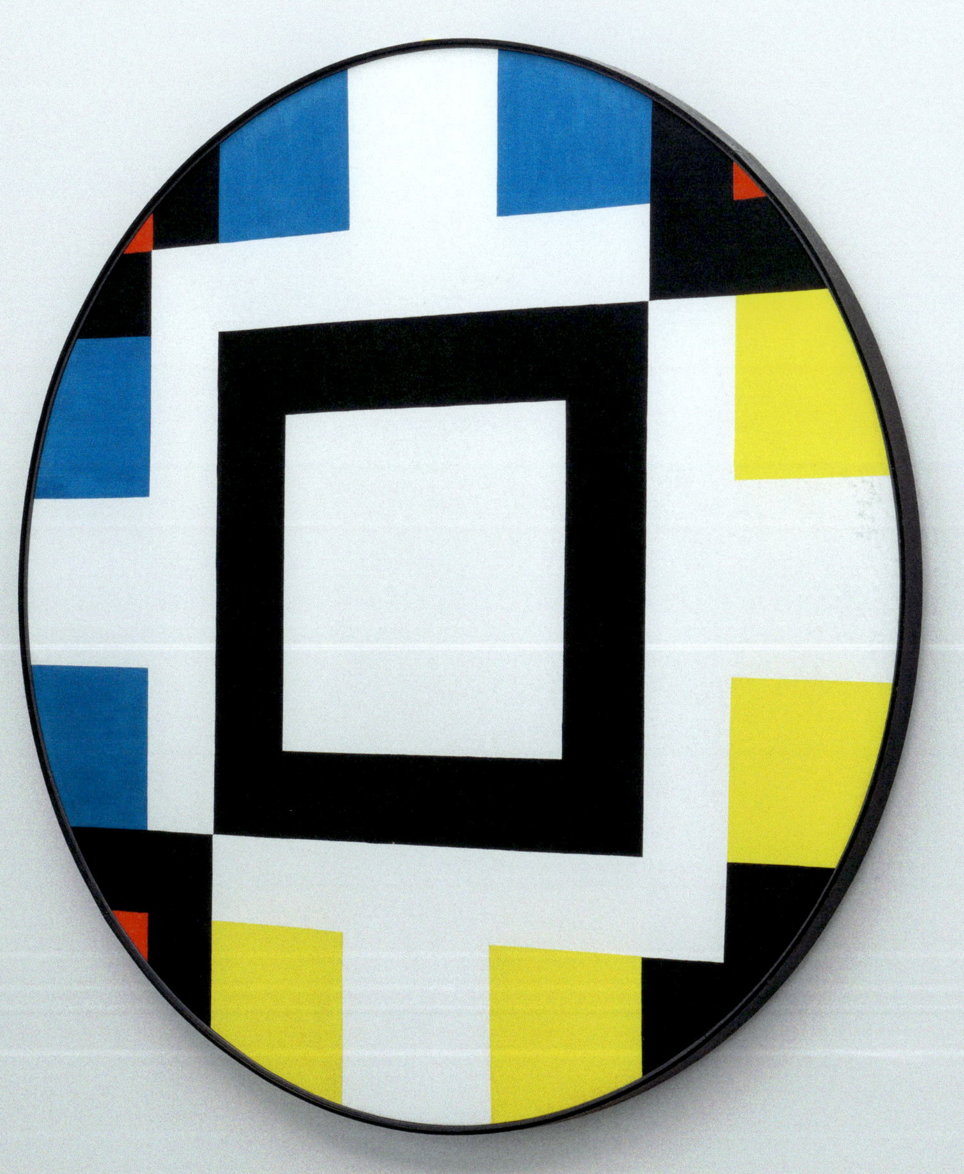

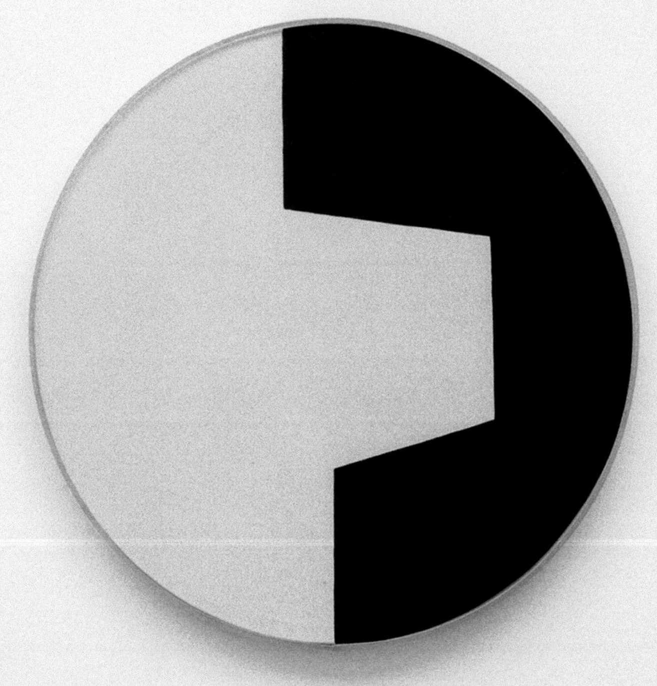

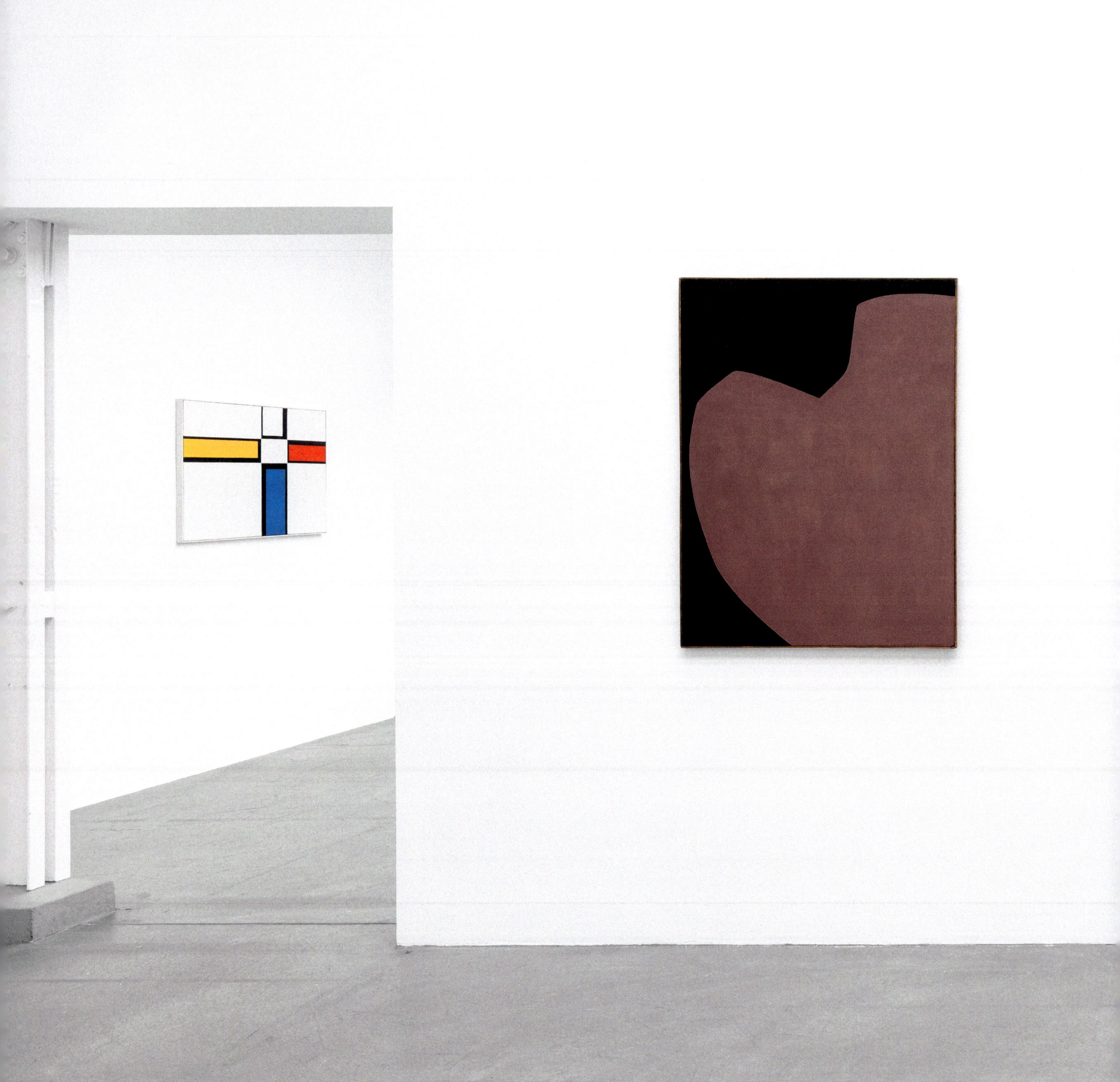

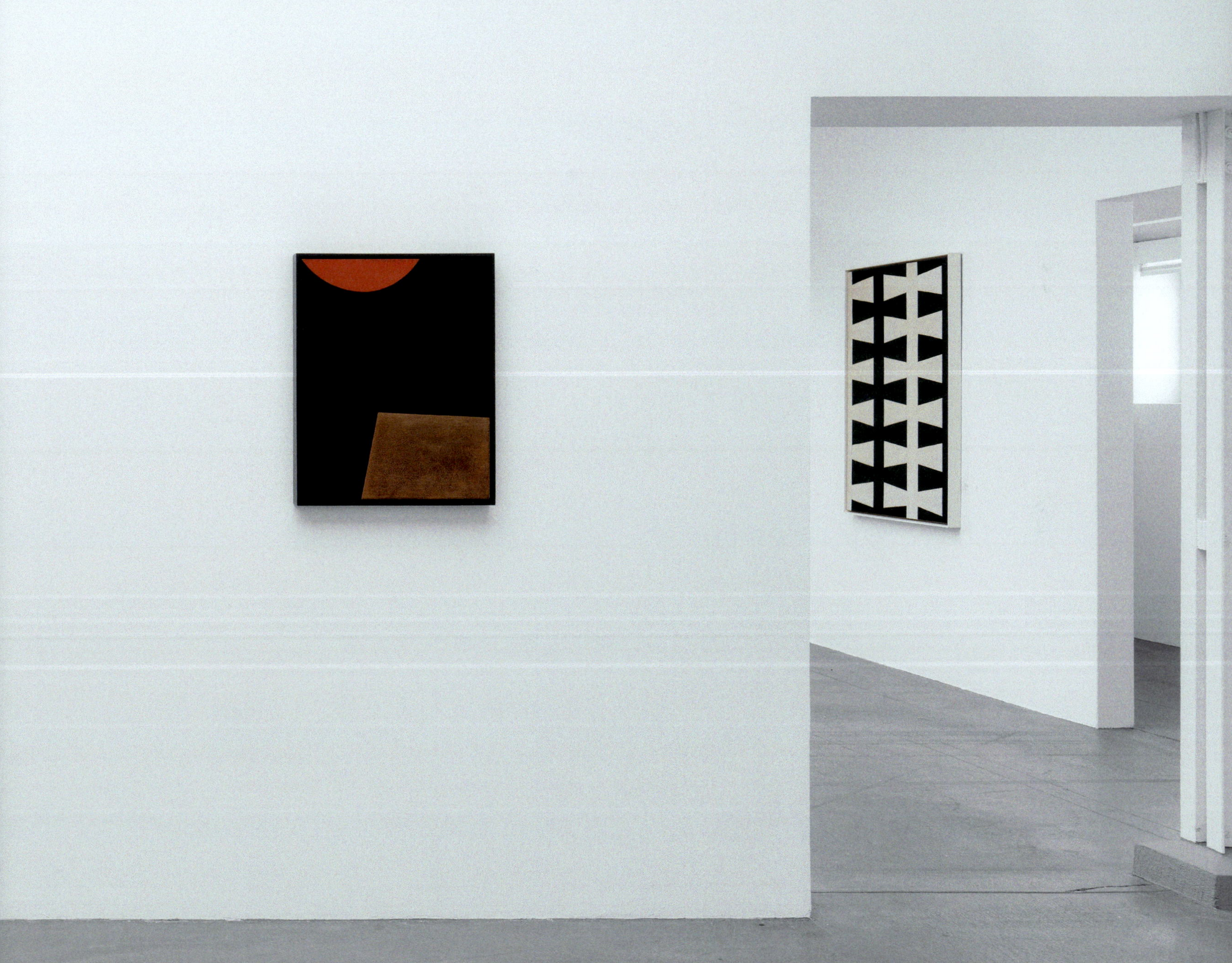

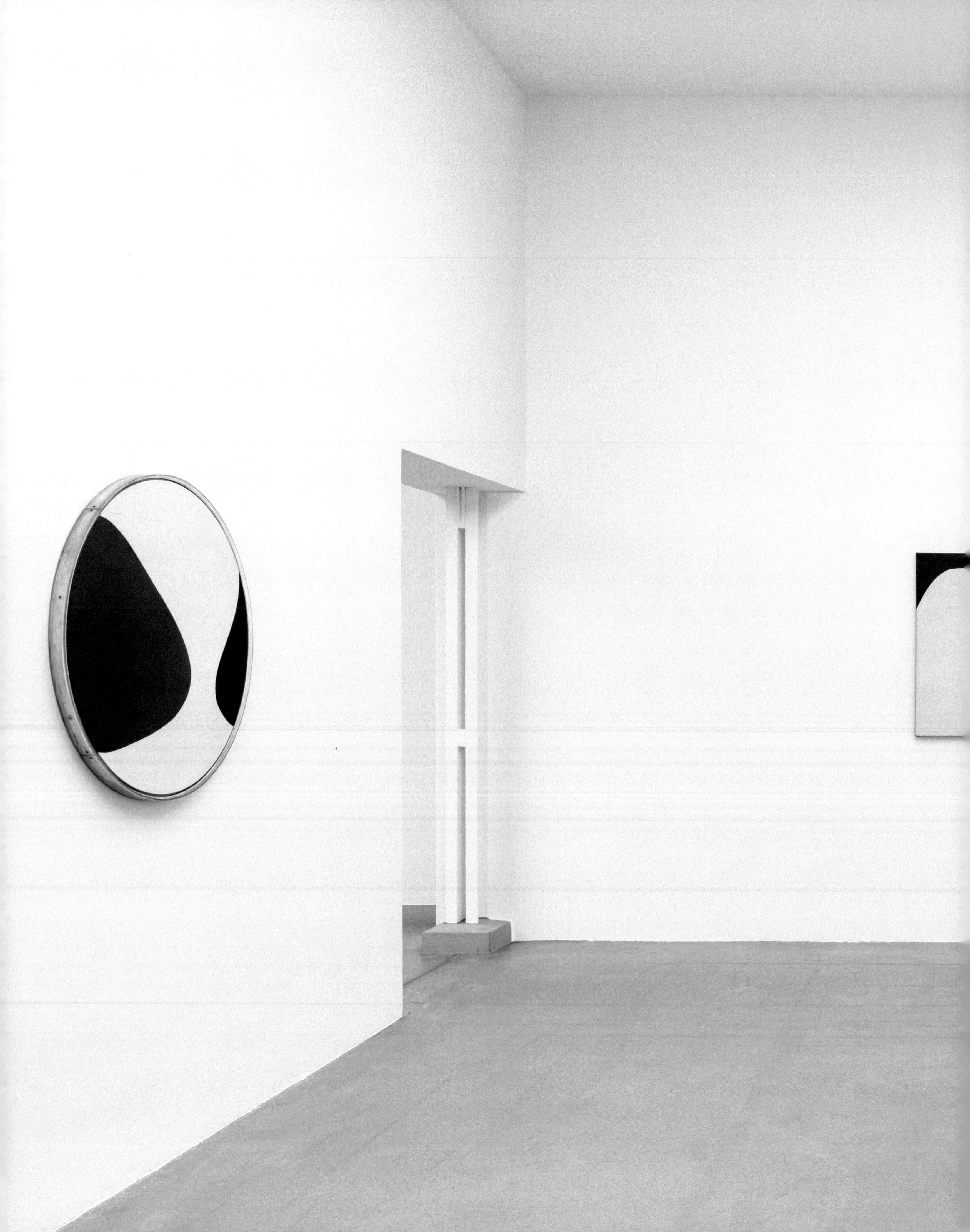

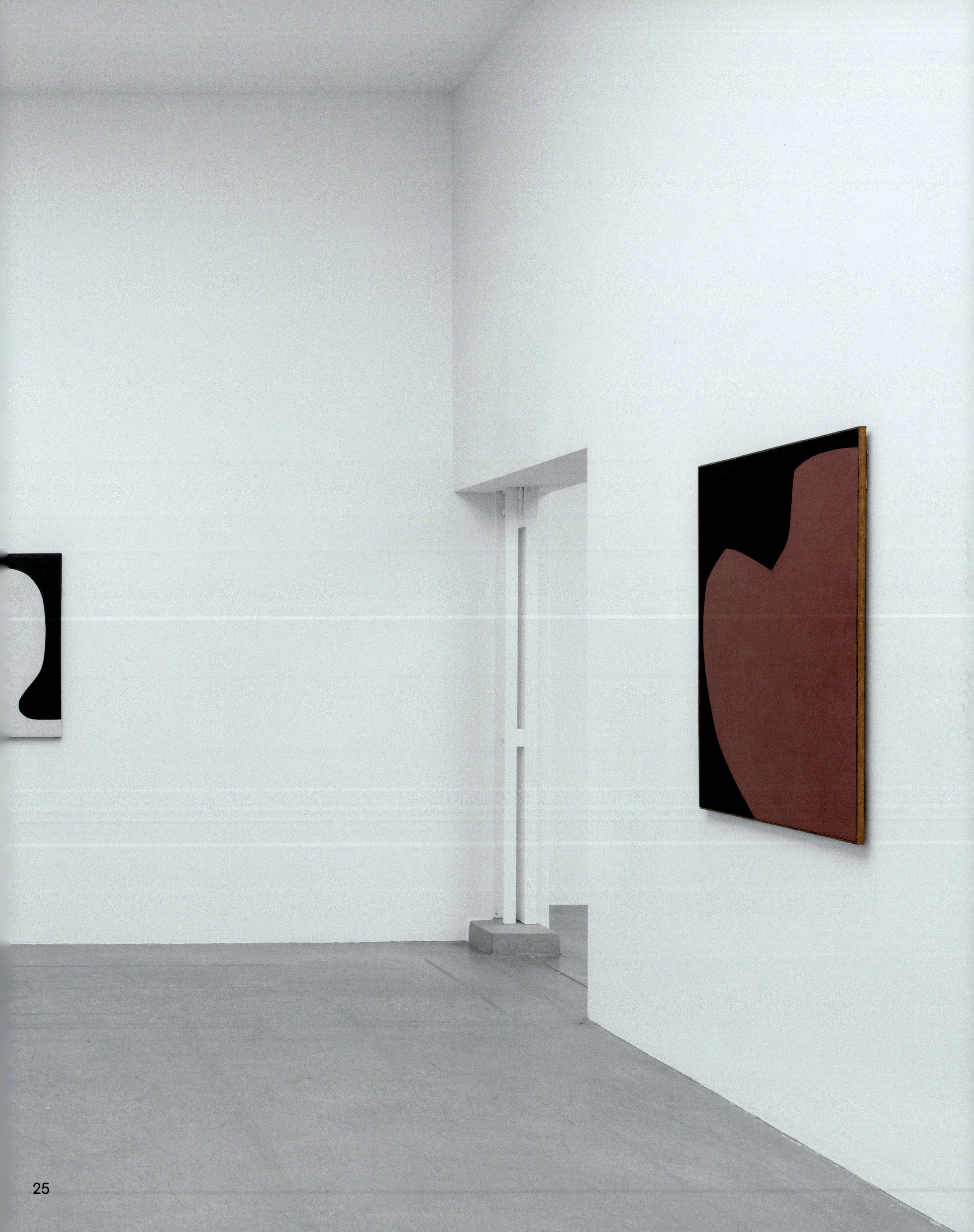

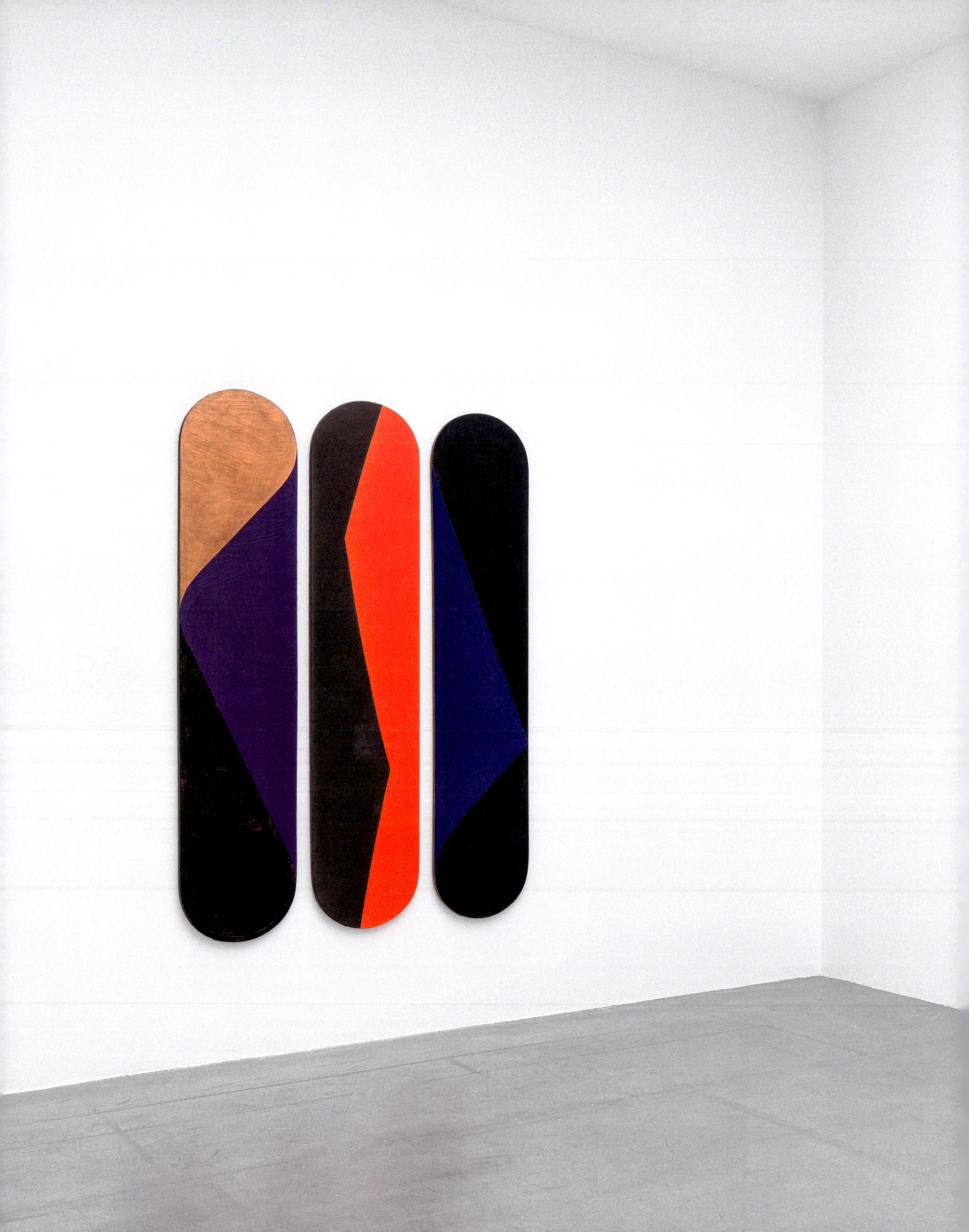

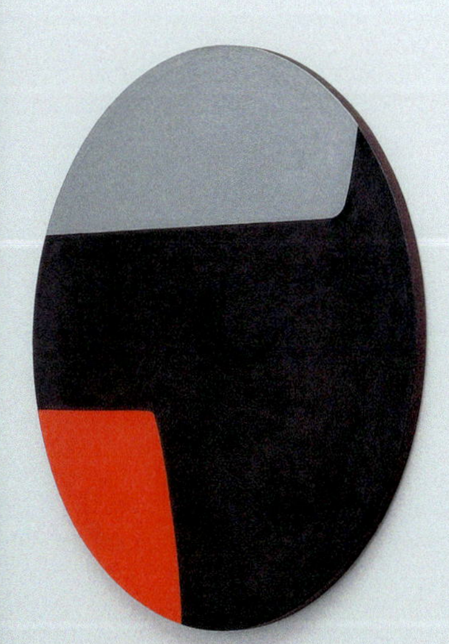

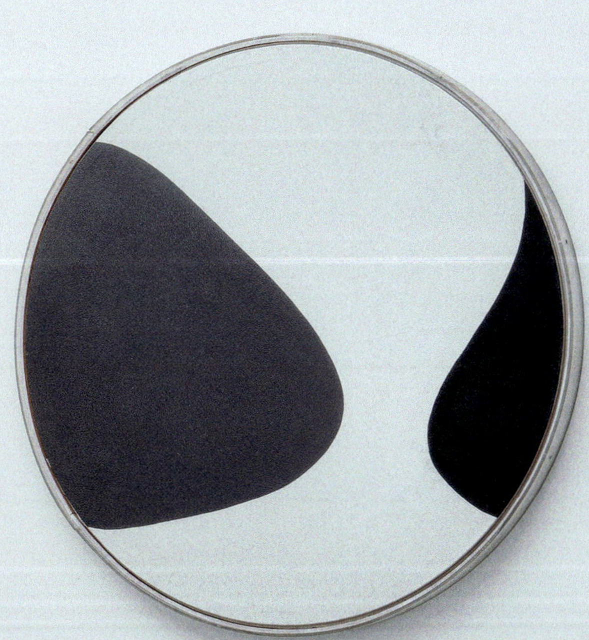

Going Beyond Space

Leon Polk Smith im Museum Haus Konstruktiv

Leon Polk Smith at Museum Haus Konstruktiv

29

Sabine Schaschl

D Es ist ein besonderes Momentum in der Ausstellungsgeschichte des Museum Haus Konstruktiv, wenn die erste Schweizer und – nach mehr als zwanzig Jahren auch die erste europäische – Einzelpräsentation von Leon Polk Smith in unserer Institution stattfindet. Das Haus Konstruktiv widmet sich seit über fünfunddreissig Jahren den Errungenschaften der konstruktiv-konkreten und konzeptuellen Kunst und richtet dabei sein Augenmerk immer wieder auf die Zürcher Konkreten. Eines der permanent präsentierten Sammlungswerke ist der *Rockefeller Dining Room*[1] des 1899 in Zürich geborenen Künstlers Fritz Glarner ❶/❷, der trotz seiner Auswanderung 1936 in die USA zu den Vertretern der Zürcher Konkreten gezählt wird. Bereits in den 1920er-Jahren fand Glarner, damals in Paris lebend, Anschluss an die avantgardistische Kunstszene und lernte Piet Mondrian kennen. Nach einer kurzen Rückkehr nach Zürich, wo er an der viel beachteten Ausstellung *Zeitprobleme in der Schweizer Malerei und Plastik* im Kunsthaus Zürich teilnahm und unter anderem auf Max Bill traf, übersiedelte er nach New York und schloss sich dort der Künstlervereinigung American Abstract Artists an. Zu einem Zeitpunkt, als Amerika unter einer starken ökonomischen Depression litt und Ausstellungs- und Auseinandersetzungsmöglichkeiten mit Kunst limitiert waren, boten die American Abstract Artists eine wichtige Plattform für Künstler:innen. Zu den zahlreichen Gründungsmitgliedern zählten beispielsweise Josef Albers, Ilya Bolotowsky, Burgoyne Diller und Harry Holtzman.

Wie viele europäische Künstler:innen in den Kriegsjahren emigrierte auch Piet Mondrian 1940 in die USA und fand in New York einen Sammler- und Künstler:innenkreis vor, der ihn als Wegbereiter einer gegenstandsfreien Kunst feierte und seine neuen, «Neoplastizismus» genannten Gestaltungsprinzipien lebhaft diskutierte und weiterentwickelte. Mondrian fand umgehend Aufnahme in die Künstlervereinigung und traf dort auch seinen Freund Fritz Glarner wieder. Angesichts der guten Vernetzung Glarners in den avantgardistischen Kunstszenen in Europa und den USA muss sich Smith, der sich trotz einiger Anfragen der American Abstract Artists nie dieser Vereinigung anschloss, eine Begegnung mit Glarner als äusserst negativ eingeprägt haben: In einem Gespräch am 12. Juli 1993 berichtete Smith der Kunsthistorikerin Brooke Kamin Rapaport[2] von einem Besuch von Fritz Glarner und Charmion von Wiegand[3], bei dem ihn die beiden dazu bringen wollten, gemeinsam den Galeristen Sidney Janis zu einem Ausschluss dreier Künstler aus seiner Ausstellung *Post-Mondrian Painters in America*[4] von 1949 zu bewegen.

> Sie waren sehr streng in der Frage, was Mondrian sei und was nicht. [...] Und bei dieser Ausstellung erklärten sie Sydney [sic!], dass sie ihre Bilder zurückziehen würden, dass sie zurücktreten und nicht mitmachen würden, wenn er nicht drei der Künstler herausnähme. Und sie wollten, dass ich mit ihnen zu Sydney gehe, und ich sagte: «Nein, das werde ich nicht. Das ist Sydneys Ausstellung.» [...] Und sie sagten: «Nun, das ist alles gegen Mondrian. Mondrian würde das nicht machen. [...] Wir werden in Zukunft gegen dich arbeiten, wenn du jetzt nicht mit uns zusammenarbeitest.»[5]

Diese Episode ist eine unter vielen, die von den Anschauungs- und Überzeugungskämpfen zwischen Künstler:innen der Moderne zeugen. Sie schildert aber auch, wie sich Leon Polk Smith seine Eigenständigkeit bewahrte, allen – ihm zufolge dann auch wahrgemachten – Androhungen zum Trotz. Mögen die persönlichen Begegnungen zwischen Glarner und Smith von Differenzen geprägt gewesen sein, so gab es doch manches, was die beiden Künstler einte: gemeinsame Ausstellungsbeteiligungen, ihr Interesse an Mondrian und die Auseinandersetzung mit einer neuen Kunstsprache, die sich von den gängigen Kunstvorlieben der Zeit unterschied. Vor diesem Hintergrund kann die Ausstellung im Museum Haus Konstruktiv auch als versöhnliche, die vernachlässigte Rezeption des Werkes von Leon Polk Smith korrigierende Präsentation verstanden werden – und das an einer Stelle Wand an Wand mit Glarners *Rockefeller Dining Room*.

1936 verbrachte Smith, damals dreissig Jahre alt, sein erstes Sommersemester an der Columbia University in New York und entdeckte auf Anregung seiner Lehrerin Ryah Ludins Werke von Mondrian, von Hans Arp und Constantin Brancusi in Albert E. Gallatins Museum of Living Art an der New York University. In zahlreichen Gesprächen unterstrich der Künstler den nachhaltigen Eindruck, den diese Ausstellung und die von nun an beginnende Auseinandersetzung mit Mondrian bei ihm hinterliess.

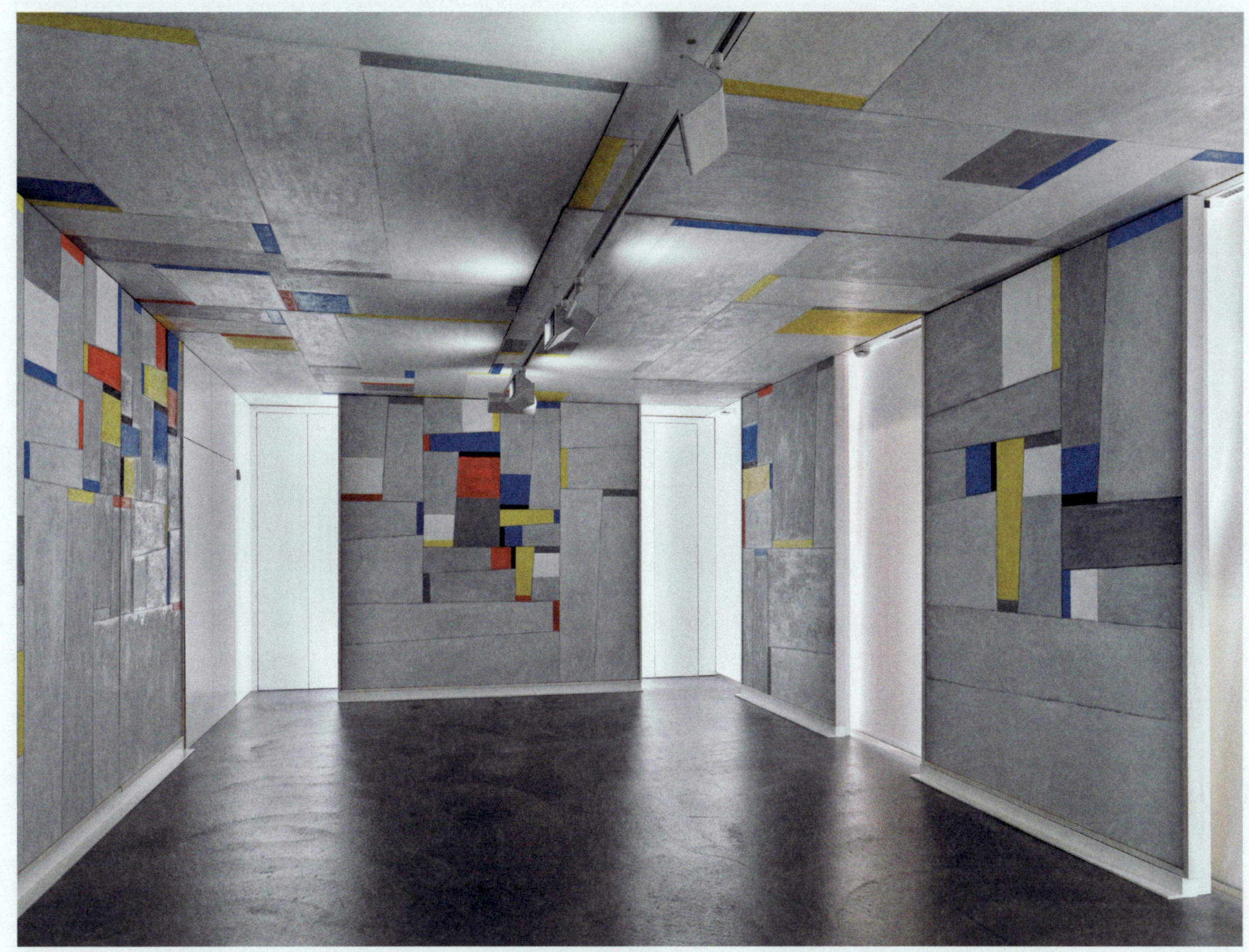

❶ Fritz Glarner, *Rockefeller Dining Room*, 1964/65, Installationsansicht | Installation view, Museum Haus Konstruktiv, 2016
Foto | Photo: Stefan Altenburger

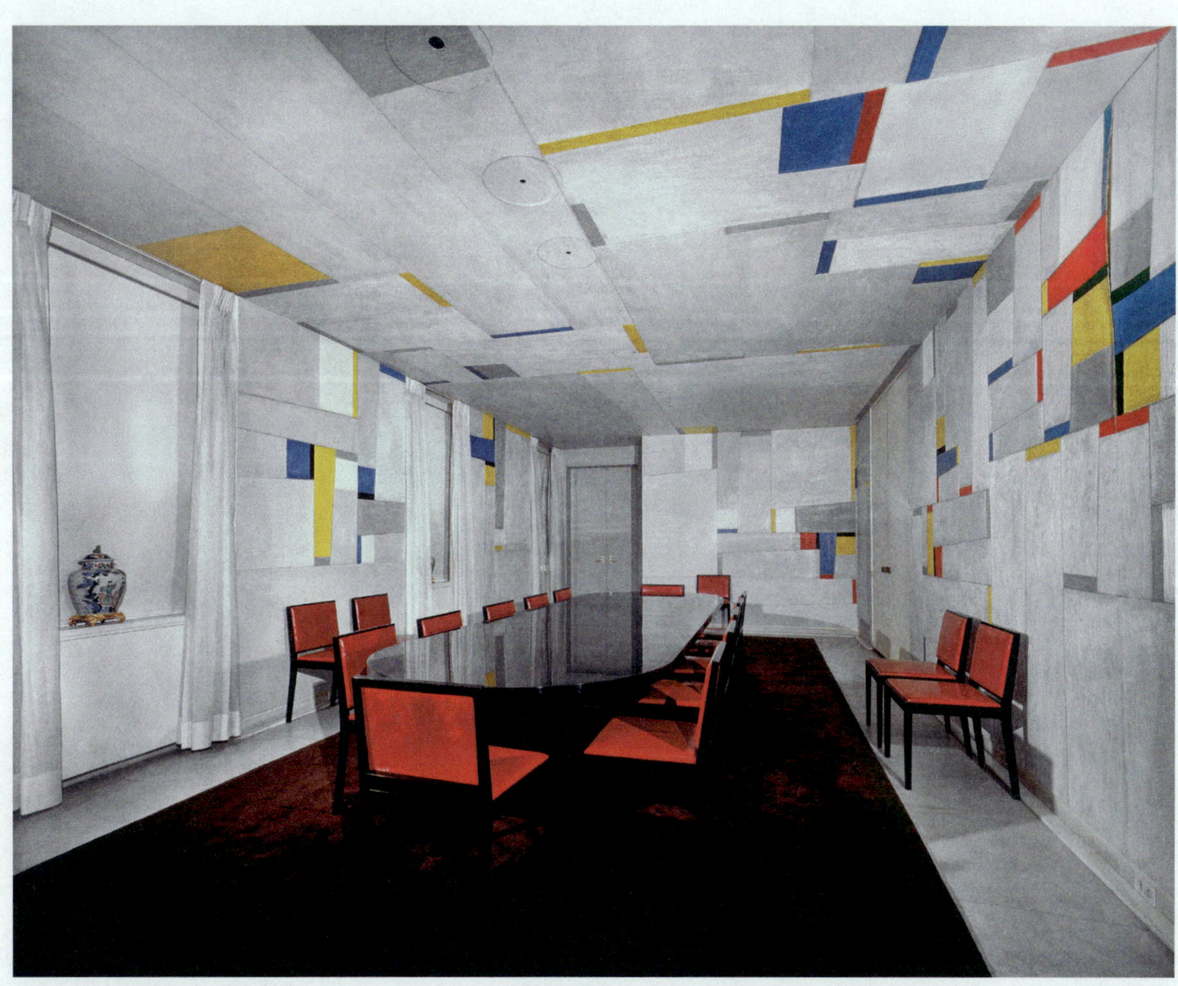

❷ Fritz Glarner, *Rockefeller Dining Room*, 1964/65, Originalzustand um 1980 | Original condition from around 1980

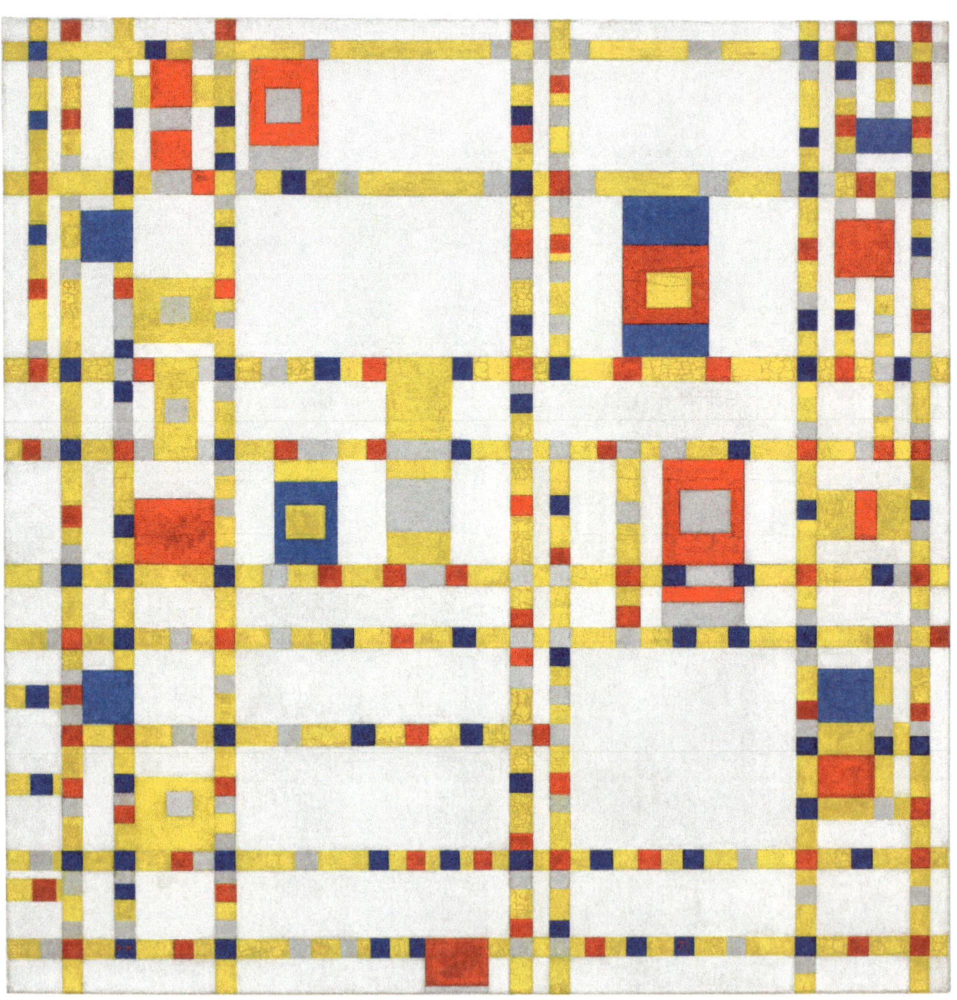

❸ Piet Mondrian, *Broadway Boogie Woogie*, 1942–1943, Öl auf Leinwand | Oil on canvas, 127 × 127 cm, anonyme Schenkung | Given anonymously, The Museum of Modern Art, New York | Scala, Firenze

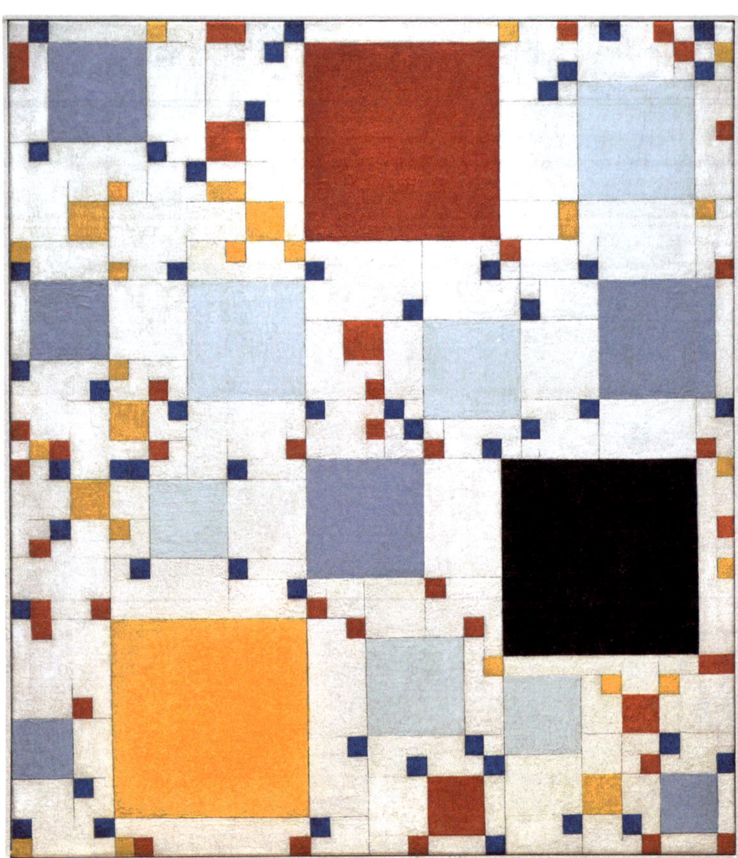

❹ Leon Polk Smith, *Homage to Victory Boogie Woogie #1*, 1946, Öl auf Leinwand | Oil on canvas, 107 × 94 cm, Dallas Museum of Art, DMA League Purchase Fund, 2000.391, © 2023, ProLitteris, Zürich

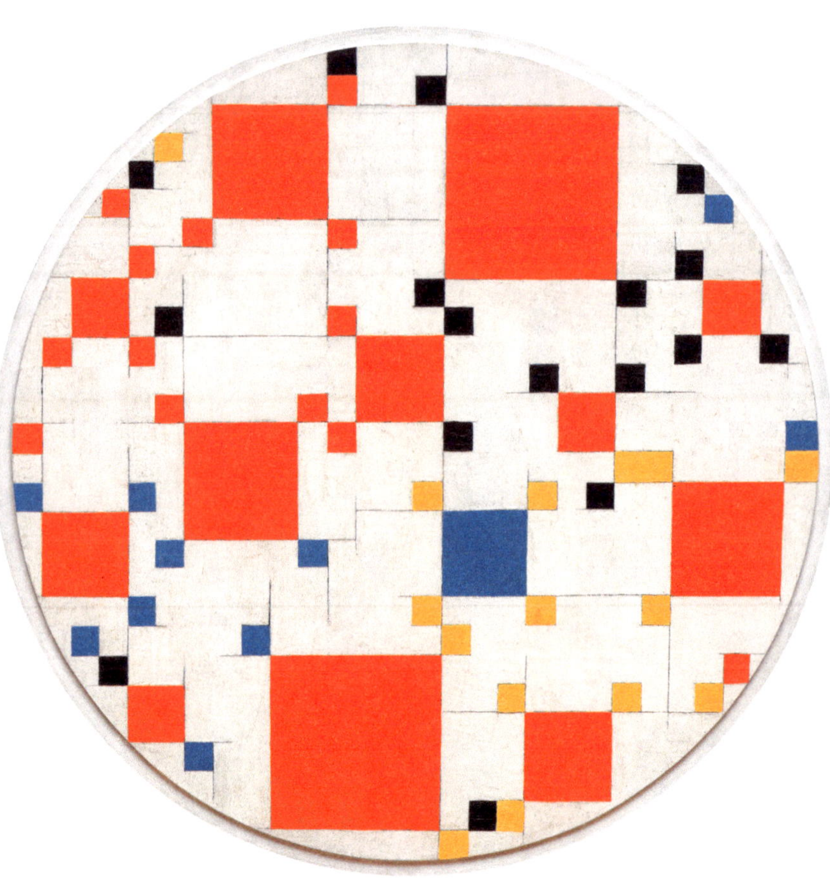

❺ Leon Polk Smith, *Homage to Victory Boogie Woogie #2*, 1946/47, Öl auf Holz | Oil on wood, Ø 74,9 cm, Modern Art Museum of Fort Worth, Schenkung von Dr. Arthur Leiwa und Frau | Gift of Dr. and Mrs. Arthur Lejwa, New York, © 2023, ProLitteris, Zürich

E Switzerland's first-ever solo presentation on Leon Polk Smith, and the first in Europe for over twenty years, is taking place at Museum Haus Konstruktiv, thus marking a special moment in our institution's exhibition history. For over thirty-five years, Haus Konstruktiv has devoted itself to achievements in Constructivist-Concrete and Conceptual Art, repeatedly turning its attention to the Zurich Concretists. From the in-house collection, one work that is constantly on display is the *Rockefeller Dining Room* by artist Fritz Glarner ❶/❷, who was born in Zurich 1899, who was considered a representative of the Zurich Concretists despite his emigration to the US in 1936.[1] Already in the 1920s, while living in Paris, Glarner connected with the avant-garde art scene and met Piet Mondrian. After a brief return to Zurich, where he took part in the highly regarded exhibition *Zeitprobleme in der Schweizer Malerei und Plastik* (Time Problems in Swiss Painting and Sculpture) at Kunsthaus Zürich and met Max Bill, among others, he moved to New York and joined an artists' association there called American Abstract Artists. At a time when the US was suffering from a severe economic depression and opportunities to exhibit and engage with art were limited, American Abstract Artists provided an important platform for artists. Its numerous founding members included Josef Albers, Ilya Bolotowsky, Burgoyne Diller, and Harry Holtzman.

Like many of the artists during the war years, Piet Mondrian emigrated from Europe to the US in 1940. In New York, he found a circle of collectors and artists who celebrated him as a pioneer of non-representational art and who vigorously discussed his new Neoplasticism design principles, taking them further. Mondrian was immediately accepted into the artists' association, where he was also reunited with his friend Glarner. Leon Polk Smith never joined the American Abstract Artists, despite several requests from the association. One encounter he had with Glarner must have made an extremely unfavorable impression on him, given how well-connected Glarner was in the avant-garde art scenes of Europe and the US. In an interview on July 12, 1993, Smith told art historian Brooke Kamin Rapaport[2] about being visited by Glarner and Charmion von Wiegand,[3] who both tried to persuade him to join them in their attempt to make gallery owner Sidney Janis exclude three artists from his 1949 exhibition *Post-Mondrian Painters in America*, saying:[4]

> They were very strong on what was Mondrian and what's not Mondrian. [...] And in this show, they told Sydney [sic!] that they were going to pull their paintings out, they were going to resign and not become a part of it if he didn't eliminate three of the artists. And they wanted me to go with them to Sydney, and I said, "No. I will not. This is Sydney's show." [...] And they said, "Well, that is all against Mondrian. Mondrian wouldn't do that. [...] We'll work against you in the future if you don't work with us now."[5]

This episode is one of many that bear witness to battles between modernist artists over opinions and convictions. However, it also serves as an example of how Smith maintained his independence in the face of threats, which, according to him, were then carried out. Although the personal encounters between Glarner and Smith may have been marked by differences, the two artists had many things in common: joint participation in exhibitions, their interest in Mondrian, and their engagement with a new artistic language that differed from the prevailing artistic tastes of the day. Against this backdrop, the exhibition at Museum Haus Konstruktiv can also be seen as a conciliatory presentation redressing the neglected reception of Smith's oeuvre, which at one point is just a wall away from Glarner's *Rockefeller Dining Room*.

In 1936, at thirty years of age, Smith attended his first summer semester at Columbia University in New York. At the suggestion of his teacher Ryah Ludins, he discovered works by Mondrian, Hans Arp, and Constantin Brancusi in Albert E. Gallatin's Museum of Living Art at New York University. In numerous interviews, the artist stressed that this exhibition and his engagement with Mondrian, which began at that moment, left a lasting impression on him.

He referred to Mondrian particularly clearly in two works: *Homage to Victory Boogie Woogie #1* (1946) and *Homage to Victory Boogie Woogie #2* (1946/47). These incorporate Mondrian's basic use of color, with the primary colors red, blue, and yellow, along with the non-colors black, white, and gray. While Mondrian consistently maintained the formal structure of horizontal and vertical lines in *Broadway Boogie Woogie* (1942–1943),

In zwei Werken wird die Referenz auf Mondrian besonders deutlich: *Homage to Victory Boogie Woogie #1* von 1946 und *Homage to Victory Boogie Woogie #2* von 1946/47. Die Werke greifen die grundsätzliche Farbverwendung Mondrians mit den Primärfarben Rot, Blau, Gelb sowie den Nichtfarben Schwarz, Weiss und Grau auf. Während Mondrian in *Broadway Boogie Woogie* (1942–1943) den Formaufbau aus horizontalen und vertikalen Linien konsequent beibehält und die Liniengebilde aus verschiedenfarbigen einzelnen und aneinandergereihten rechteckigen Feldern zusammensetzt ❸, sind die Bilder von Leon Polk Smith ausschliesslich aus farbigen Quadraten gebildet, die zwar auch einer horizontalen und vertikalen Grundstruktur folgen, sich aber an den Ecken treffen und so diagonale Formationen bilden ❹/❺.

Mondrian hingegen lehnte die Diagonale vehement ab. In Smiths Serie der *Diagonal Passages* aus den späten 1940er- und frühen 1950er-Jahren stehen Bildkompositionen mit Diagonalen verstärkt im Fokus. *Diagonal Passage with Horizontal* von 1950 beispielsweise zeigt ein gelbes, ein weisses, ein rotes und ein blaues Rechteck jeweils von unterschiedlich breiten schwarzen Linien an drei Kanten umzogen ❻. Die schwarzen Umrandungen deuten unterschiedliche Raumtiefen an und dynamisieren die Komposition, indem sie Raum und Form in eine spannungsgeladene Wechselbeziehung bringen. Die ersten Mondrians, die Leon Polk Smith gesehen hat, waren *Composition with Blue and Yellow* aus dem Jahr 1932 und *Composition with White and Red* von 1936 ❼.[6] In beiden bilden die schwarzen Linien ein Raster, das an ausgewählten Stellen mit Farbe ausgefüllt ist. In Mondrians Kompositionen kreuzen die Linien einander, während Smith die linearen Umrisse der horizontalen und vertikalen Farbfelder diagonal Ecke an Ecke zusammentreffen lässt und zusätzlich Raum für diagonal zueinander stehende weisse Flächen schafft.

Wie Lucius Grisebach schreibt, liegt in der Verwendung von Flächen, die sich an horizontalen und vertikalen Linien orientieren und diese mit ihren Ecken berühren «von vornherein eine andere Räumlichkeit, ein offeneres Prinzip, das für die folgenden Entwicklungsschritte wesentlich wurde».[7] Laut seinen eigenen Aussagen war das Werk Mondrians für Smith ein Ausgangspunkt, von dem aus er sein eigenständiges Werk erarbeitete.

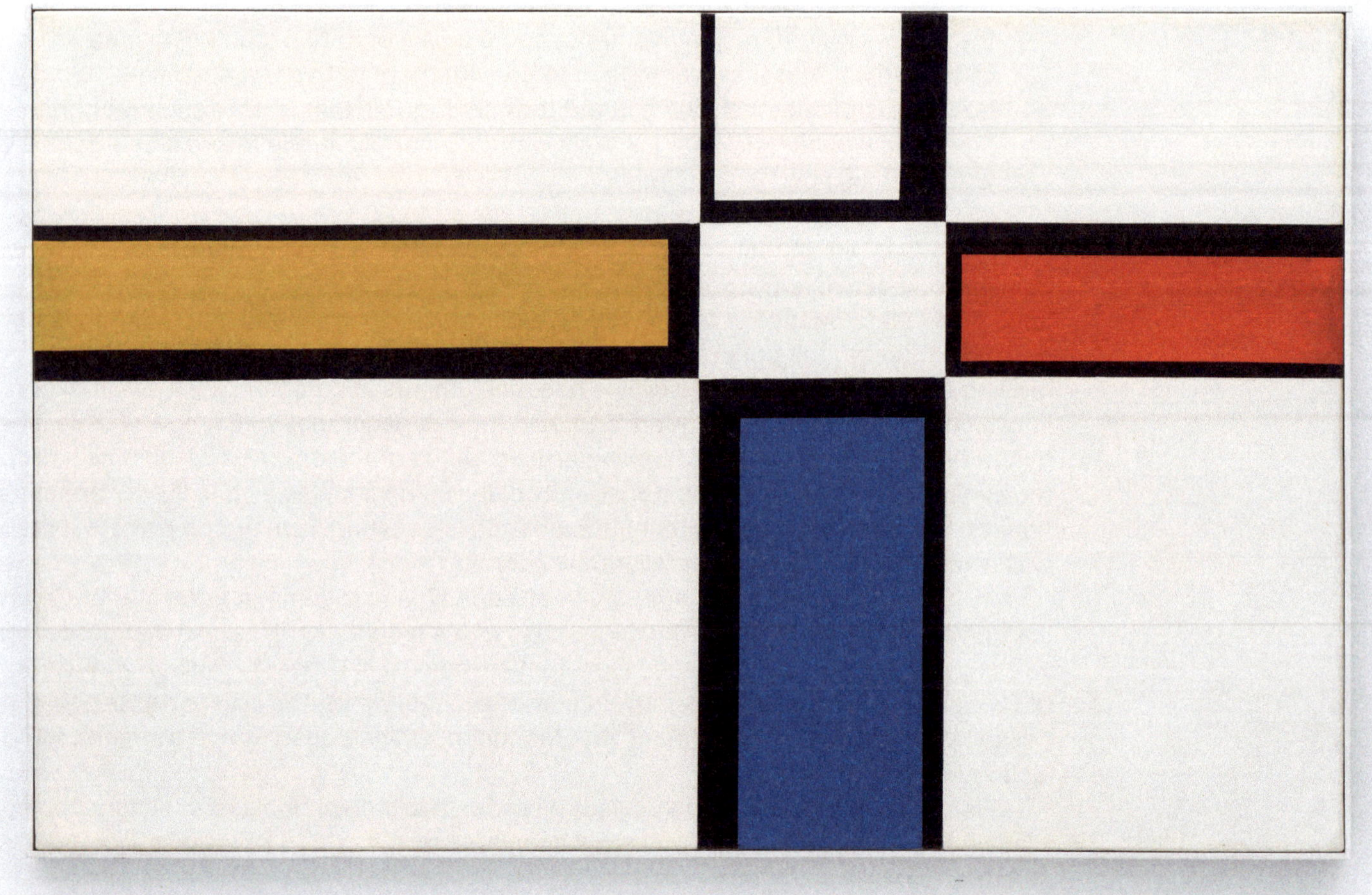

❻ Leon Polk Smith, *Diagonal Passage with Horizontal*, 1950, Öl auf Leiwand | Oil on canvas, 66,7 × 106,7 cm, Leon Polk Smith Foundation, Courtesy of Lisson Gallery, © 2023, ProLitteris, Zürich

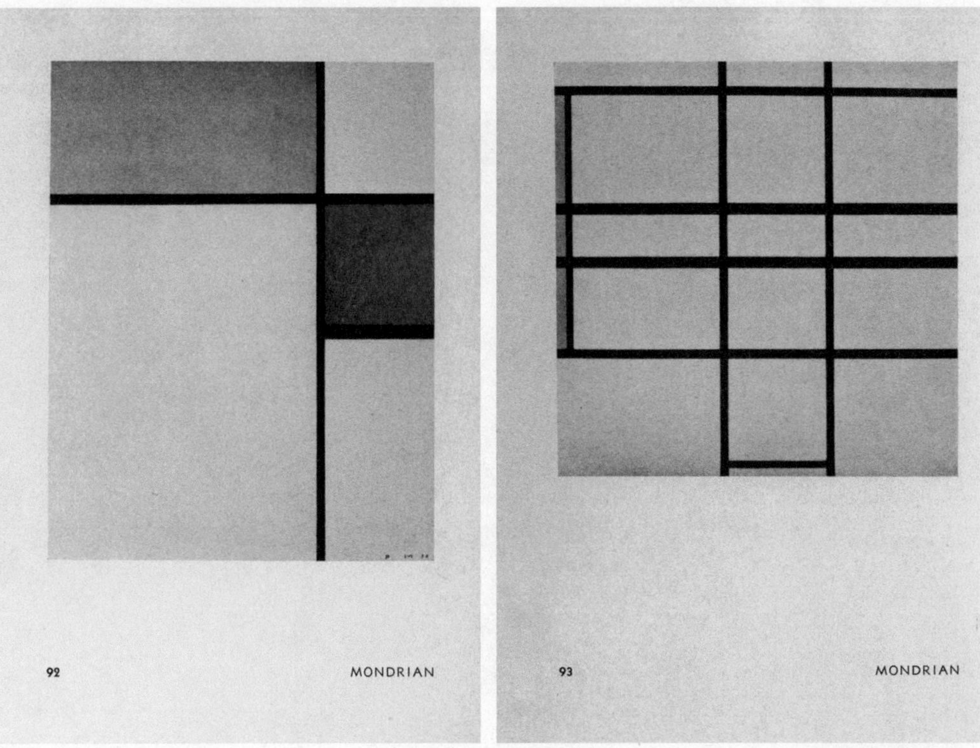

❼ *Museum of Living Art – A. E. Gallatin Collection*, Katalog | Catalogue, New York University, New York, G. Grady press, 1937, Abb. | Figs. 92, 93

assembling linear entities from differently colored individual and lined-up rectangular fields ❸, Smith's paintings exclusively comprise colored squares, adhering to a basic horizontal and vertical structure but touching at their corners, thus creating diagonal formations ❹/❺.

Mondrian, on the other hand, vehemently rejected diagonals. In Smith's *Diagonal Passage* series from the late 1940s and early 1950s, there is a special focus on visual composition using diagonals. For example, *Diagonal Passage with Horizontal* (1950) shows four rectangles in yellow, white, red, and blue, respectively, each surrounded by black lines of varying widths on three edges ❻. The black outlines suggest different spatial depths and dynamize the composition by causing space and form to tensely interact. The first Mondrians that Smith ever saw were *Composition with Blue and Yellow* (1932) and *Composition with White and Red* (1936) ❼.[6] In both of these paintings, the black lines form a grid, which is filled with color in selected places. In Mondrian's compositions, the lines cross each other, whereas Smith lets the linear outlines of the horizontal and vertical color fields meet diagonally, corner to corner, also creating space for diagonally aligned white areas.

As Lucius Grisebach writes, in this use of fields oriented along horizontal and vertical lines, which their corners also touch, there resides "a different spatiality from the outset, a more open principle, which became essential for the subsequent developmental steps."[7] Smith's own statements indicate that, for him, Mondrian's oeuvre was a starting point from which he conceived his independent practice:

> What I was seeking through the 1940s was to find my outlet from this vertical horizontal and to express the same thing that Mondrian had worked with, that is the form-space equilibrium, the interchangeability of form and space. I wanted to find a way of using that in a curvilinear manner, in curved lines, free forms. [...] But I was seven or eight years finding that.[8]

Smith found his way out of Mondrian's design principles, which he considered too narrow, via a sporting goods catalogue that contained drawings of balls for sports, such as basketball and tennis. The seams of the balls, sketched with dotted lines, introduced him to the possibilities of spatial interventions in a picture surface. Smith translated this new discovery into paintings on round canvases in which one or a few curved lines enter into a dynamic relationship with the image's shape. Unlike in his vertically and horizontally arranged visual compositions, Smith now chose smooth, flowing contours, like in *First-One* (1954) ❽, or angular and perpendicular lines, like in *Pontotoc* (1958) ❾.

❽ Leon Polk Smith, *First-One*, 1954, Öl auf Leiwand | Oil on canvas, Ø 100,3 cm, Albright-Knox Art Gallery, Buffalo, NY, Schenkung von | Gift of Natalie & Irving Forman, 2004, © 2023, ProLitteris, Zürich

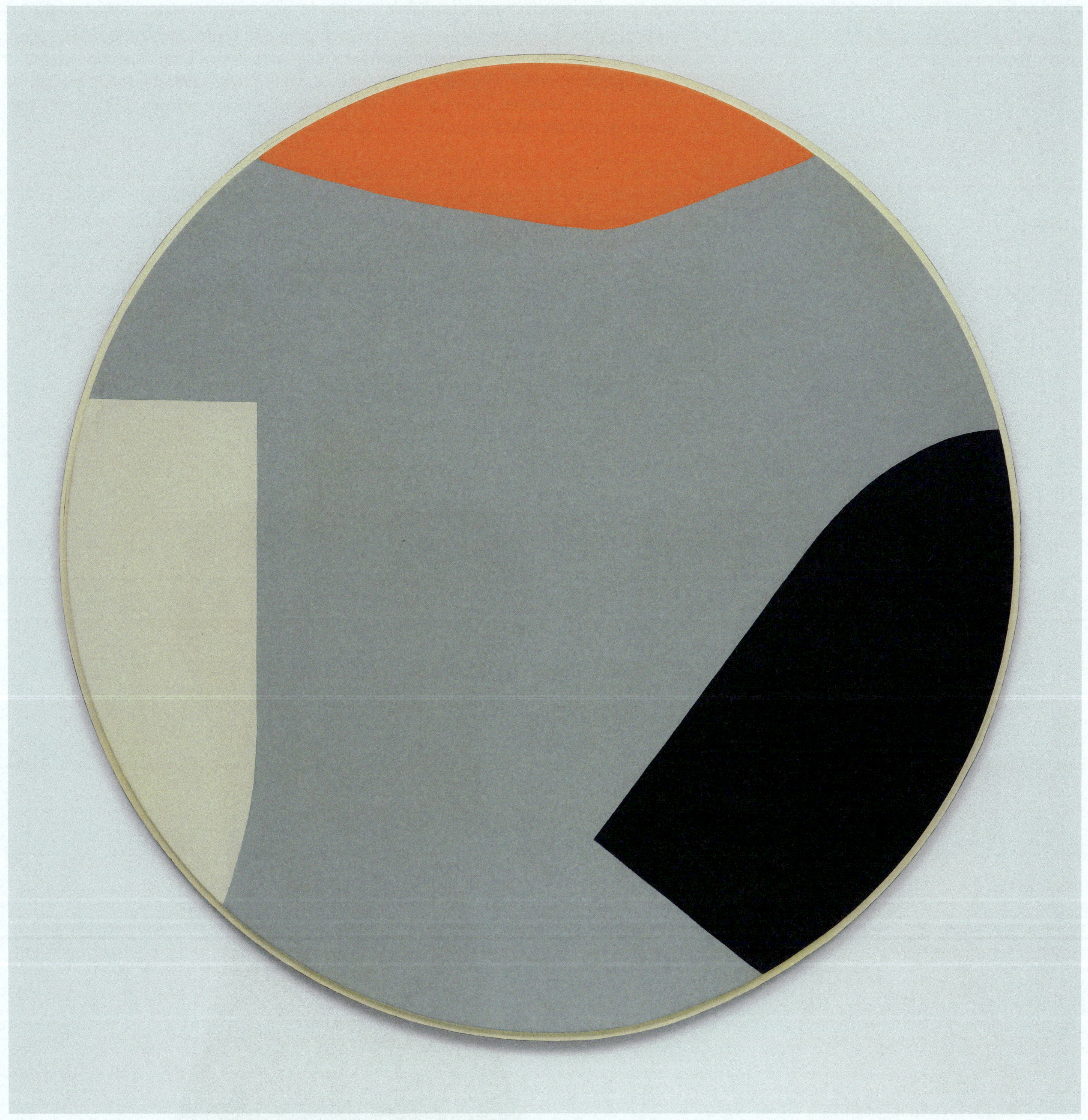

9 Leon Polk Smith, *Pontotoc*, 1958, Öl auf Leiwand | Oil on canvas, Ø 122,5 cm, Leon Polk Smith Foundation, Courtesy of Lisson Gallery, © 2023, ProLitteris, Zürich

> Was ich während der vierziger Jahre versuchte, war einen Ausweg zu finden aus diesem Vertikal-horizontal-System und doch genau das zum Ausdruck zu bringen, womit schon Mondrian gearbeitet hatte, nämlich das Form-Raum Gleichgewicht, die Austauschbarkeit von Form und Raum. Ich wollte einen Weg finden, dies mit Hilfe von gekrümmten Linien zu tun, mit Kurven und freien Formen. [...] Aber es hat sieben oder acht Jahre gedauert, das zu entwickeln.[8]

Den Ausweg aus den als zu eng empfundenen Mondrianschen Gestaltungsprinzipien fand Smith über eine Sportartikelbroschüre, die Zeichnungen von Basket-, Tennis- und anderen Bällen beinhaltete. Die mit gestrichelten Linien skizzierten Nähte der Bälle führten ihm die Möglichkeiten von räumlichen Interventionen auf einer Bildfläche vor Augen. Smith setzte die Neuentdeckung in Malereien auf runden Leinwänden um, in welchen eine oder wenige gekurvte Linien mit der Bildform eine dynamische Beziehung eingehen. Im Gegensatz zu den vertikal und horizontal ausgerichteten Bilkompositionen wählte Smith nunmehr weiche, flüssige Linienführungen wie in *First-One* (1954) ❽ oder kantige und rechtwinkelige Linien wie im Gemälde *Pontotoc* (1958) ❾.

Letzteres wurde in der von Max Bill kuratierten Ausstellung *konkrete kunst – 50 jahre entwicklung* im Helmhaus Zürich 1960 ausgestellt. Wie Bills Witwe, die

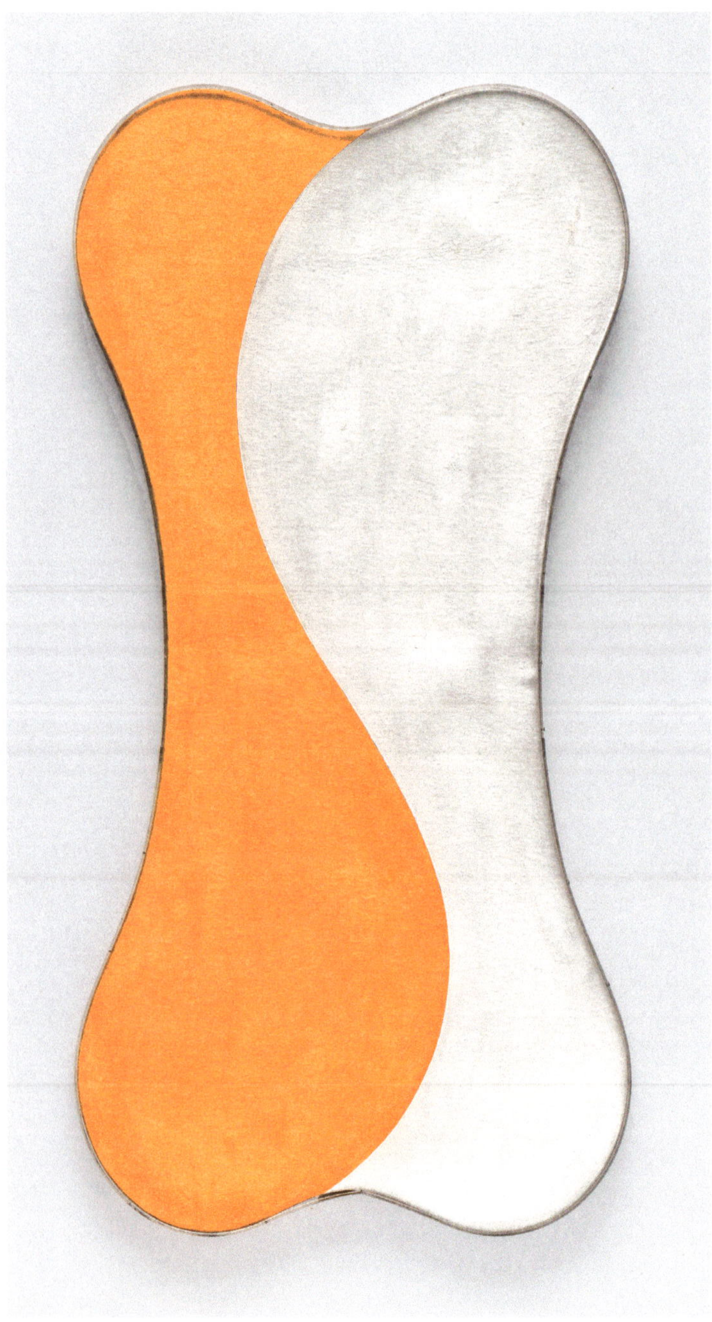

❶❿ Leon Polk Smith, *Yellow White Sun*, 1958–1959, Öl auf Leinwand | Oil on canvas, 198,1 × 96,5 cm, Blanton Museum of Art, The University of Texas at Austin, Schenkung von der | Gift of the Leon Polk Smith Foundation, 2017, © 2023, ProLitteris, Zürich

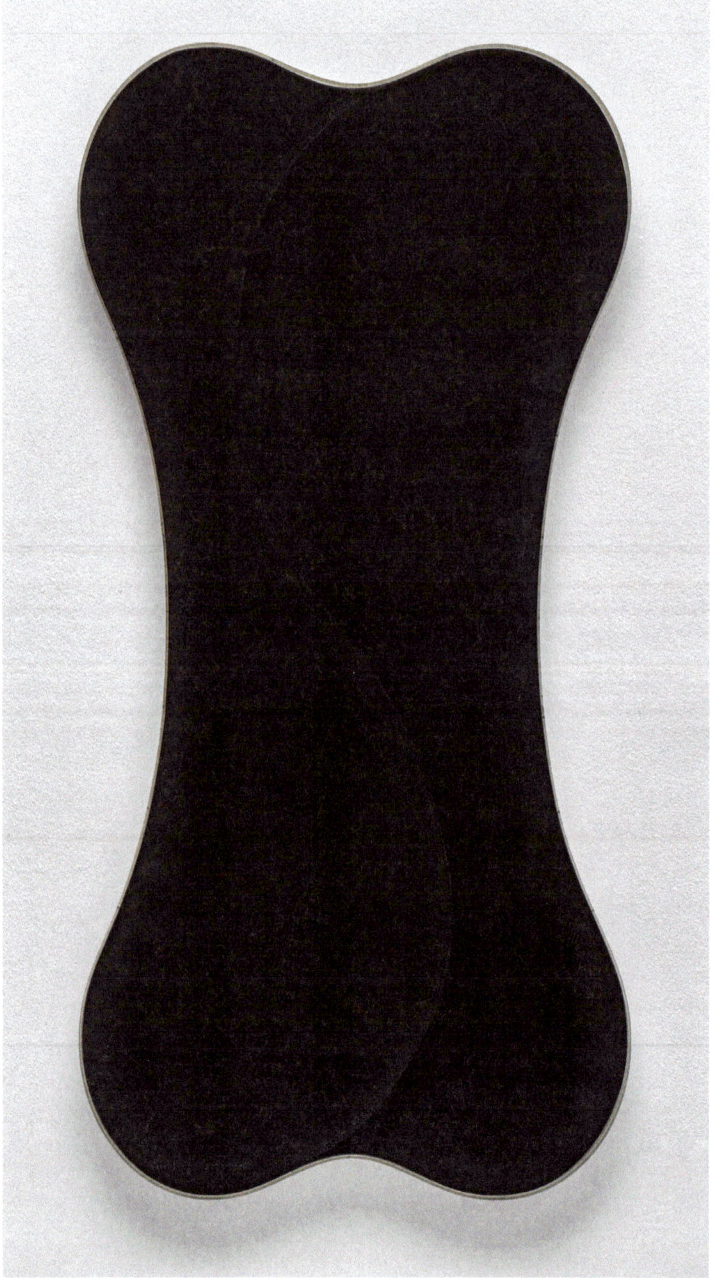

❶❶ Leon Polk Smith, *Moon*, 1958–1959, Öl auf Leinwand | Oil on canvas, 198,1 × 96,5 cm, Blanton Museum of Art, The University of Texas at Austin, Schenkung von | Gift of Jeanne & Michael Klein, 2017, © 2023, ProLitteris, Zürich

The latter was shown in the 1960 exhibition *konkrete kunst – 50 jahre entwicklung* (concrete art: 50 years of development) curated by Max Bill at Helmhaus Zurich. Bill's widow, art historian Angela Thomas Bill, noted that Bill greatly appreciated the oeuvre of his fellow artist from America.[9] In this exhibition, together with numerous renowned avant-garde artists, such as Mondrian, Sophie Taeuber-Arp, László Moholy-Nagy, Robert Delaunay, Wassily Kandinsky, Ad Reinhardt, Georges Vantongerloo, Theo van Doesburg, Ellsworth Kelly, and Agnes Martin, Smith was presented as a Concrete artist. Even though the terms "concrete" and "abstract" have opposite meanings, according to van Doesburg and Bill, who were among the most important Concrete Art theorists, this exhibition was open to both varieties. Whereas abstraction strives to reduce an object to its essential forms—as seen, for example, in Mondrian's early works from the series *Pier and Ocean* (1915) and in his depictions of trees in *The Gray Tree* (1911) and *The Flowering Apple Tree* (1912)—the term concrete denotes artistic production that completely does away with any natural model or reference to an object in the real world and operates only with the means of art—namely, color, form, line, and structure. Even though Smith drew inspiration from the representational world for his 1950s round paintings, the works themselves went beyond mere abstraction of the object. In this respect, it is quite appropriate to describe his art as concrete.

Smith's new line-based concept brought a change of perspective to his oeuvre in terms of content and design, revitalizing the question of the relationship between form and space. In a 1964 interview with author and artist d'Arcy Hayman, Smith described the process of creating his paintings in the following words:

> The proportion, the size of the canvas often suggest a form. I will get up and draw this one line through the canvas which creates two forms, one on either side of the line, and while I am drawing this line, it seems that I am travelling many, many miles in space instead of just fifty inches or sixty inches whatever the canvas happens to be, but it is a great, great distance from one point to the next and around the curve, and I begin to feel the tensions develop and the forces working on either side of this line; there is a color often suggested, usually the color that I am going to use, that comes to me before the line reaches the other side of the canvas.[10]

Swiss artist Hans Jörg Glattfelder, who was friends with Smith in the 1990s and met him regularly during a fellowship in New York, also recalls conversations about the line that can create two fields, two forms, or two worlds with one stroke.[11] In the artistic process, this intellectual dimension, which mentally incorporates the cosmos, is conveyed particularly well by the works *Yellow White Sun* and *Moon* 10/11, both from 1958–1959.

These works show curving lines on the picture surface that correspond to the form of the picture support in a tension-filled manner. The painted line segues into the image's contour line. These are Smith's first shaped canvases. The colors, forms, and titles that he gave them allude to celestial bodies and the vastness of the universe. The brightness of *Yellow White Sun* contrasts with *Moon*, although the constellation of forms is the same in what is certainly an analogy to the real celestial bodies. There is no hierarchy between the picture surfaces; the visual turning of these surfaces, caused by the curved lines, affects the surrounding space. The activation of both pictorial space and real space proved groundbreaking for the *Constellation* (from 1960) and *Correspondence* series, which he began producing in 1967 and which brought the artist recognition, allowing him to give up teaching and devote himself entirely to his artwork.

In his paintings from the *Correspondence* series, the "journey" of the line generates very different forms. For example, a freely drawn zigzag form may emerge, like in *Correspondence Black and Blue* from 1960 12, or a curved form that is transformed into an angular one, like in *Over Easy* from 1958 13, or there might be precisely guided straight lines, like in *Wide Horizon* from 1966 14.

Smith chose the term *Correspondence* to convey an exchange between two forms and fields. The literature on these works repeatedly refers to a balance of energy on one hand, and activation on the other. Even though the point of these works is for color fields separated by clear, hard edges to be brought together without creating foreground or background, the color fields in the *Correspondences* actually generate color spaces of varying depths by means of form and coloring. These characteristics, coupled

Kunsthistorikerin Angela Thomas Bill, festhielt, schätzte jener das Werk seines amerikanischen Künstlerkollegen sehr.[9] Smith wurde in dieser Ausstellung gemeinsam mit zahlreichen namhaften Avantgardekünstler:innen wie Mondrian, Sophie Taeuber-Arp, László Moholy-Nagy, Robert Delaunay, Wassily Kandinsky, Ad Reinhardt, Georges Vantongerloo, Theo van Doesburg, Ellsworth Kelly oder Agnes Martin als «konkret» arbeitender Künstler vorgestellt. Auch wenn die Begriffe «konkret» und «abstrakt» nach den Ausführungen van Doesburgs und Max Bills, die zu den wichtigsten Theoretikern der konkreten Kunst zählten, Gegensätzliches bedeuten, öffnete sich diese Ausstellung für beide Spielarten. Während eine abstrakte Arbeitsweise eine Reduzierung auf die wesentlichen Formen eines Gegenstandes anstrebt, so beispielsweise in den frühen Mondrian-Werken der Reihe *Pier and Ocean* (1915) oder in Mondrians Baumdarstellungen *Der graue Baum* (1911) und *Blühender Apfelbaum* (1912), bezeichnet der Begriff «konkret» die künstlerische Produktion, die gänzlich ohne Naturvorbild, ohne Bezugnahme auf einen Gegenstand der realen Welt auskommt und nur mit den Mitteln der Kunst, also Farbe, Form, Linie, Struktur operiert. Auch wenn Leon Polk Smith die Anregung für seine Rundbilder der 1950er-Jahre der gegenständlichen Welt entnahm, führten die Werke selbst über eine schlichte Abstraktion des Gegenstandes hinaus. Insofern ist der Begriff «konkret» für seine Kunst durchaus passend.

Mit dem neuen Linienkonzept kommt ein inhaltlicher und gestalterischer Perspektivenwechsel in sein Werk, der die Frage nach dem Verhältnis von Form und Raum neu beflügelt. In einem Interview mit der Autorin und Künstlerin d'Arcy Hayman 1964 schilderte Smith den Entstehungsprozess seiner Bilder mit folgenden Worten:

> Aus den Proportionen und dem Maß der Leinwand entsteht eine Form in meiner Vorstellung. Ich stehe auf und zeichne eine Linie über die Leinwand, die zwei Formen kreiert, eine auf jeder Seite der Linie. Während ich diese Linie zeichne, kommt es mir vor, als ob ich viele Meilen im Universum zurücklegen würde und nicht nur ein bis zwei Meter oder wie groß die Leinwand auch ist. Es ist eine sehr große Distanz von einem Punkt zum anderen. Ich fühle die Spannung, die entsteht, und die Kräfte, die auf jeder Seite der Linie wirken. Oft stellt sich dabei eine Farbe ein, gewöhnlich die Farbe, die ich dann auswähle. Das alles entwickelt sich in mir, bevor die Linie die andere Seite der Leinwand erreicht.[10]

Auch der Schweizer Künstler Hans Jörg Glattfelder, der mit Smith in den 1990er-Jahren befreundet war und ihn während eines Atelierstipendiums in New York regelmässig traf, erinnert sich an Gespräche über die Linie, die es vermag, mit einem Strich zwei Flächen, zwei Formen oder zwei Welten zu erschaffen.[11] Die Werke *Yellow White Sun* und *Moon*, beide von 1958–1959, bringen diese geistige, den Kosmos gedanklich mit einbeziehende Dimension des künstlerischen Prozesses besonders gut zum Ausdruck 10/11.

Sie zeigen schwingende Linien auf der Bildfläche, die mit der Form des Bildträgers selbst in spannungsgeladener Weise korrespondieren. Die gemalte Linie geht über in die Linie des Bildkonturs; erste Shaped Canvases entstehen. Mit der Farb-, Form- und Titelgebung spielt Smith auf Himmelsgestirne und die Weite des Weltalls an. Die Helligkeit von *Yellow White Sun* kontrastiert mit *Moon,* wobei die Formenkonstellation – durchaus in Analogie zu den realen Gestirnen – die gleiche ist. Es gibt keine Hierarchie der Bildflächen, und die durch die geschwungenen Linien erzeugte visuelle Drehbewegung der Bildflächen wirkt in den umgebenden Raum. Die Aktivierung sowohl des Bild- als auch des Realraumes erwies sich als wegweisend für die Werkreihen der *Correspondences,* die ab 1960 – und der *Constellations,* die ab 1967 entstanden und dem Künstler jene Anerkennung brachten, die ihm die Aufgabe seiner Lehrtätigkeit und eine ausschliessliche Beschäftigung mit der künstlerischen Arbeit erlaubte.

Die «Reise» der Linie generiert in den Bildern der *Correspondence*-Reihe unterschiedlichste Formen: eine frei gezogene Zickzackform wie in *Correspondence Black and Blue* von 1960 12 kommt ebenso vor wie eine geschwungene Form, die in eine kantige überführt wird wie bereits in *Over Easy* von 1958 13 oder exakt geführte, gerade Linien wie in *Wide Horizon* von 1966 14.

Die Bezeichnung *Correspondence* wählte Smith, um den Austausch zweier Formen und Flächen zum Ausdruck zu bringen. Von energetischer Ausgewogenheit einerseits und Aktivierung andererseits ist in der Literatur über diese Arbeiten immer wieder zu lesen. Auch wenn es bei diesen Werken darum geht, die mit klaren, harten Kanten

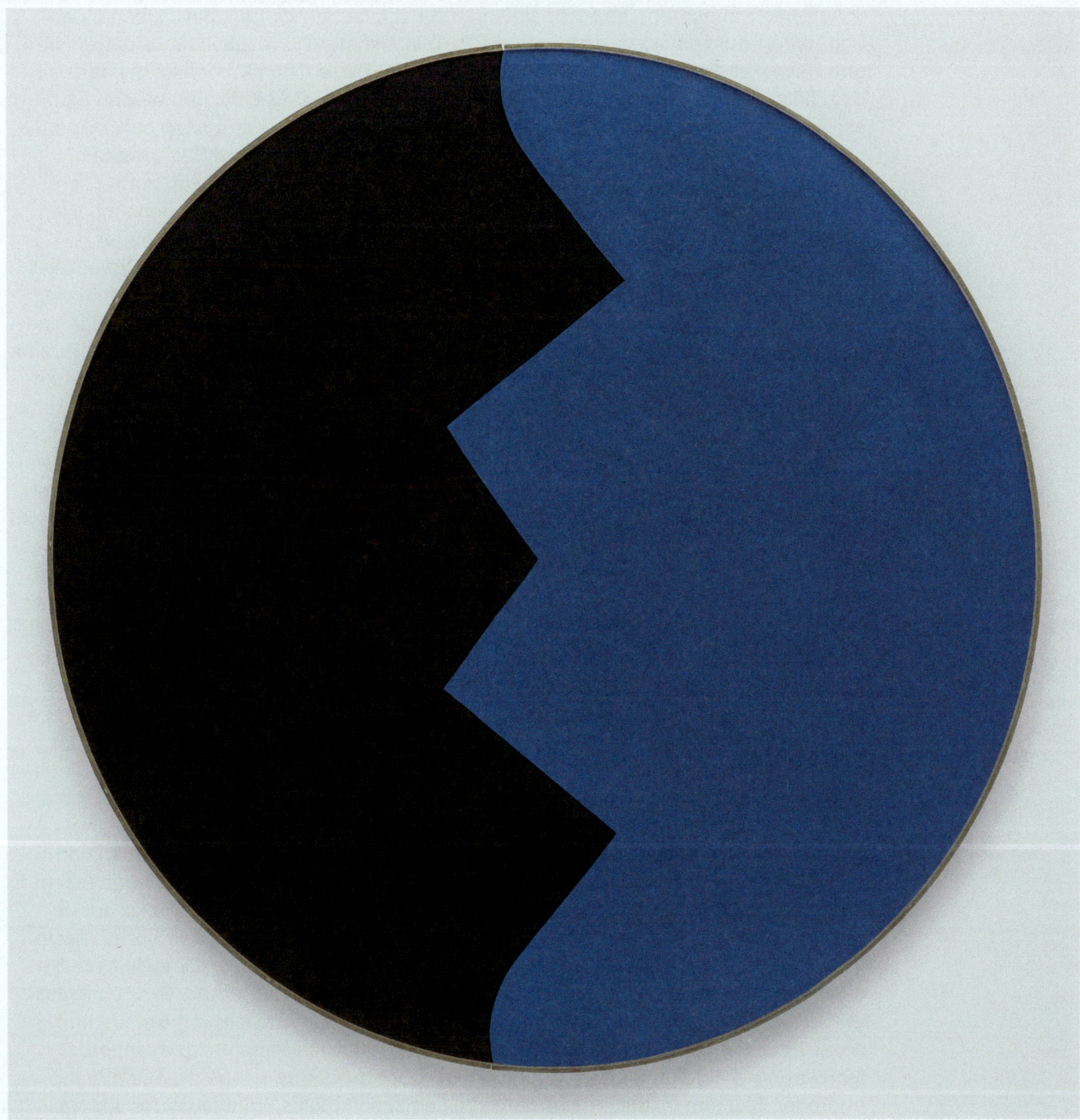

❶❷ Leon Polk Smith, *Correspondence Black and Blue*, 1960, Öl auf Leinwand | Oil on canvas, Ø 120 cm, Leon Polk Smith Foundation, Courtesy of Lisson Gallery, © 2023, ProLitteris, Zürich

with the flat application of paint and the choice of less bold color fields, identify Smith as a representative of Hard-edge painting. He continued to produce *Correspondences* into the early 1970s, sometimes with rectangular picture formats and sometimes with round ones.

In 1967, Smith began to work on his *Constellation* series in which colors and forms extend beyond individual canvases into neighboring ones, creating shared forms and spaces. These multi-part works can be made up of round or oval picture supports, as well as triangles, squares, or rectangles, all with rounded corners. In *Constellation Green-Blue* (1968), a diagonal runs through the round and oval canvases in a manner that causes one green and one blue color space to emerge along this boundary ❶❺. In turn, *Constellation – Lost Horizon*, also produced in 1968, shows two oval canvases touching each other only via their color space ❶❻. Smith developed a wide range of *Constellations*, each comprising two, three, or more picture surfaces in various shapes. In *Constellation Y* (1968), for instance, two rounded triangles and one rounded rectangle are placed in such a way that the weighting of the picture formats, together with the division of the color fields, brings to mind the shape of the letter Y ❶❼.

voneinander abgegrenzten Farbflächen so zueinander zu bringen, dass kein Vorder- und Hintergrund entsteht, erzeugen die Farbflächen der *Correspondences* durch Form und Farbigkeit Farbräume unterschiedlicher Tiefe. Diese Charakteristika, gepaart mit dem flächigen Farbauftrag und der Wahl weniger kräftiger Farbflächen weisen Smith als einen Vertreter der Hard-Edge-Malerei aus. *Correspondences* sollten bis in die frühen 1970er-Jahre entstehen, mal mit rechteckigen, mal mit runden Bildformaten.

Ab 1967 arbeitete Smith an der Werkreihe der *Constellations*. Darin erstrecken sich Farben und Formen über die einzelnen Leinwände hinweg zu den benachbarten Leinwänden, wodurch sie gemeinsame Formen und Räume ausbilden. Die mehrteiligen Werke können aus runden oder ovalen Bildträgern, aber auch aus Dreiecken, Quadraten und Rechtecken mit jeweils abgerundeten Ecken zusammengesetzt sein. In *Constellation Green-Blue* aus dem Jahr 1968 durchzieht eine Schräge die runde und ovale Leinwand so, dass sich entlang dieser Grenze ein grüner und ein blauer Farbraum bilden ❶❺. In der ebenfalls 1968 entstandenen *Constellation – Lost Horizon* wiederum berühren sich zwei ovale Leinwände einzig über ihren Farbraum ❶❻. Smith entwickelte eine grosse Bandbreite an *Constellations*, die sich aus zwei, drei oder mehreren unterschiedlich geformten Bildflächen zusammensetzen. In *Constellation Y* (1968) beispielsweise werden zwei abgerundete Dreiecke und ein abgerundetes Rechteck so platziert, dass die Gewichtung der Bildformate gemeinsam mit der Aufteilung der Farbflächen an die Form des Buchstabens «Y» erinnert ❶❼.

Zu den herausragendsten Beispielen der *Constellation*-Reihe zählt *Constellation Twelve Circles* von 1969 ❶❽. Sieben unterschiedlich grosse runde Leinwände bilden ein Ensemble aus vollständigen und angedeuteten Kreisen, die sich über mehrere Paneele erstrecken und die Wand als Teil der Komposition einbeziehen. «Was erreicht wird, ist die Aktivierung der gesamten Fläche – des Bildraums mit den Zwischenräumen aus Wandfläche – und die Einladung, die Formen in alle Richtungen zu vervielfältigen», beschreibt die Kunsthistorikerin Claudine Humblet die Wirkung des Bildgefüges.[12] Der besondere Stellenwert von *Constellation Twelve Circles* zeigt sich auch darin, dass das Werk 1988 ein weiteres Mal als Direktauftrag des Schweizer Pharmakonzerns Ciba-Geigy[13] (heute Novartis) für die Lobby des Development-Gebäudes in Summit, New Jersey, produziert wurde, nun im grösseren Massstab, auf Aluminiumpaneelen und präsentiert in anderer Ausrichtung an der Wand. Wie Installationszeichnungen belegen, hat Smith mit unterschiedlichen Hängungen von *Constellation Twelve Circles* auf der Wand experimentiert.[14] Wurde das ursprüngliche, mit Acryl auf Leinwand produzierte Werk von 1969 horizontal ausgerichtet, zeigen die Zeichnungen für Ciba-Geigy neben einer horizontalen auch eine im 45°-Winkel angepasste Drehung (Abb. S. 47). Die ausgeführte Hängung wiederum erstaunt durch ihre vertikale Ausrichtung ❶❾. Ein und dasselbe Werk war für den Künstler also in drei möglichen Varianten präsentierbar. Markierungen auf den Bildtafeln von weiteren *Constellations*, die deren Ausrichtung und/oder Zusammenstellung betreffen, zeigen zudem, dass Smith auch für andere Werke aus dieser Reihe alternative Installationsmöglichkeiten vorsah.[15]

Mit den *Constellations* erfährt die räumliche Interaktion der Werkelemente einen Höhepunkt. Smith selbst stellte in seinen späteren Lebensjahren eine Verbindung her zwischen seinen Raumkonzeptionen und seinem Erleben von Raum in den Ebenen Oklahomas, wo er aufwuchs:

> Was mich als Student mit am meisten an Kunst interessierte, war der Raum – und er ist bis heute einer der interessantesten Faktoren in der Kunst für mich geblieben. [...] Natürlich entdeckte ich durch Mondrians Werk eine neue Art, ihn einzusetzen, und das verschaffte mir eine Grundlage für das intensive Gefühl, das ich – aufgewachsen in den Ebenen von Oklahoma – für den Raum hatte.[16]

Einen besonderen Nachhall findet das den Naturerlebnissen seiner Heimat entspringende Raumgefühl in Werken wie *Twilight* (1979) ❷⓿, *New Moon for August* (1983) ❷❶ oder *Sunset Caribe* (1983) ❷❷. Wie die *Correspondences* beruhen sie auf dem Zusammenspiel zweier Farbformen. Anders als diese jedoch sind sie – mit Ausnahme von *Twilight* – Shaped Canvases, und sie sind grossformatig. Einige innerbildliche Linienführungen sind als Spiegelung der Bildform angelegt. In der Grösse der Bildformate treffen die Farbformen in einer stärkeren, für die Rezipient:innen geradezu physisch erfahrbaren Raumwirkung aufeinander. Im Unterschied zu anderen Künstler:innen des Hard Edge

❶❸ Leon Polk Smith, *Over Easy*, 1958, Öl auf Leinwand | Oil on canvas, 109 × 84 cm, Städel Museum, Frankfurt a. M., © 2023, ProLitteris, Zürich

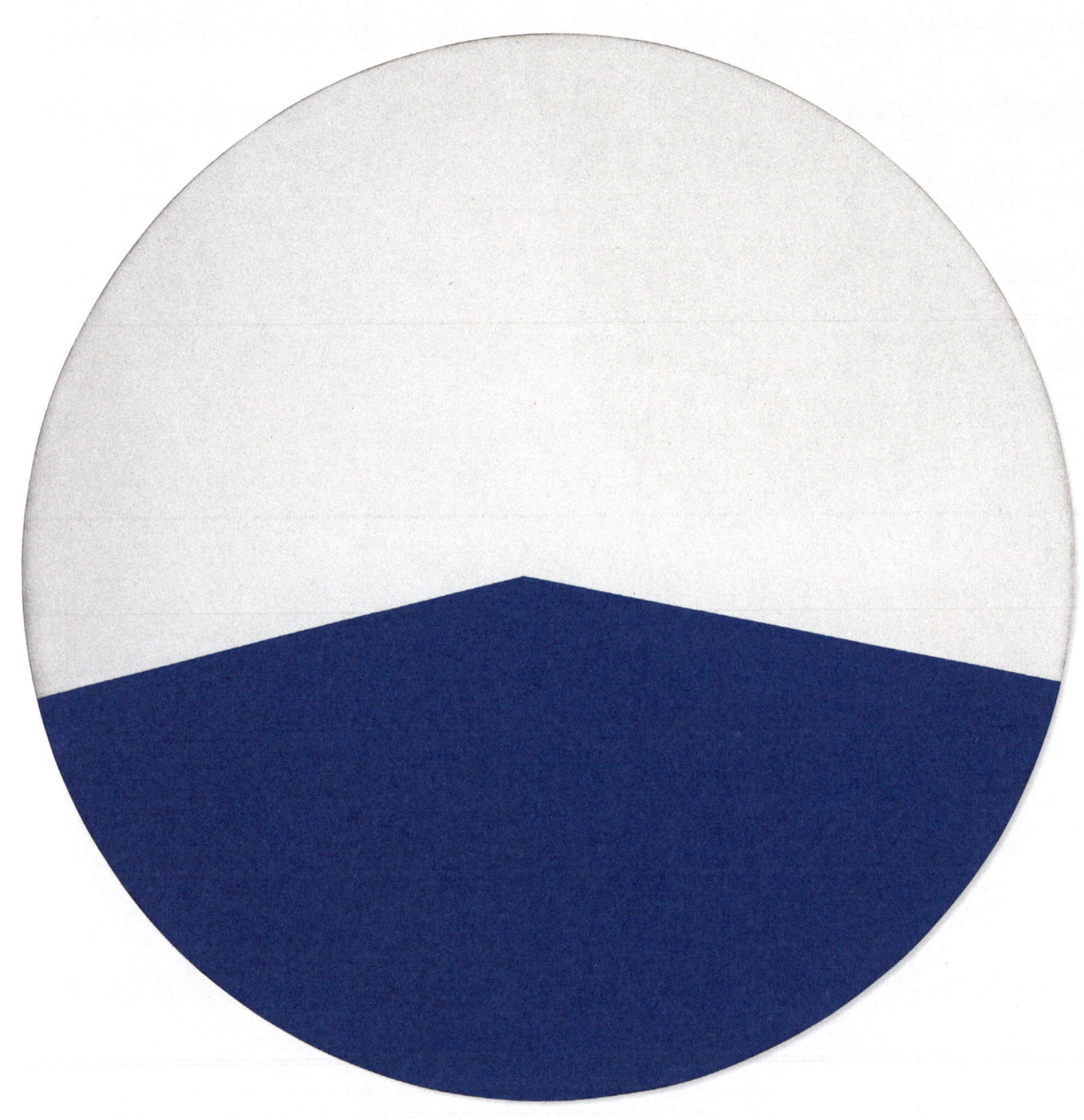

❶❹ Leon Polk Smith, *Wide Horizon*, 1966, Öl auf Leinwand | Oil on canvas, Ø 81,3 cm, Privatsammlung | Private collection, © 2021 Christie's Images Limited, © 2023, ProLitteris, Zürich

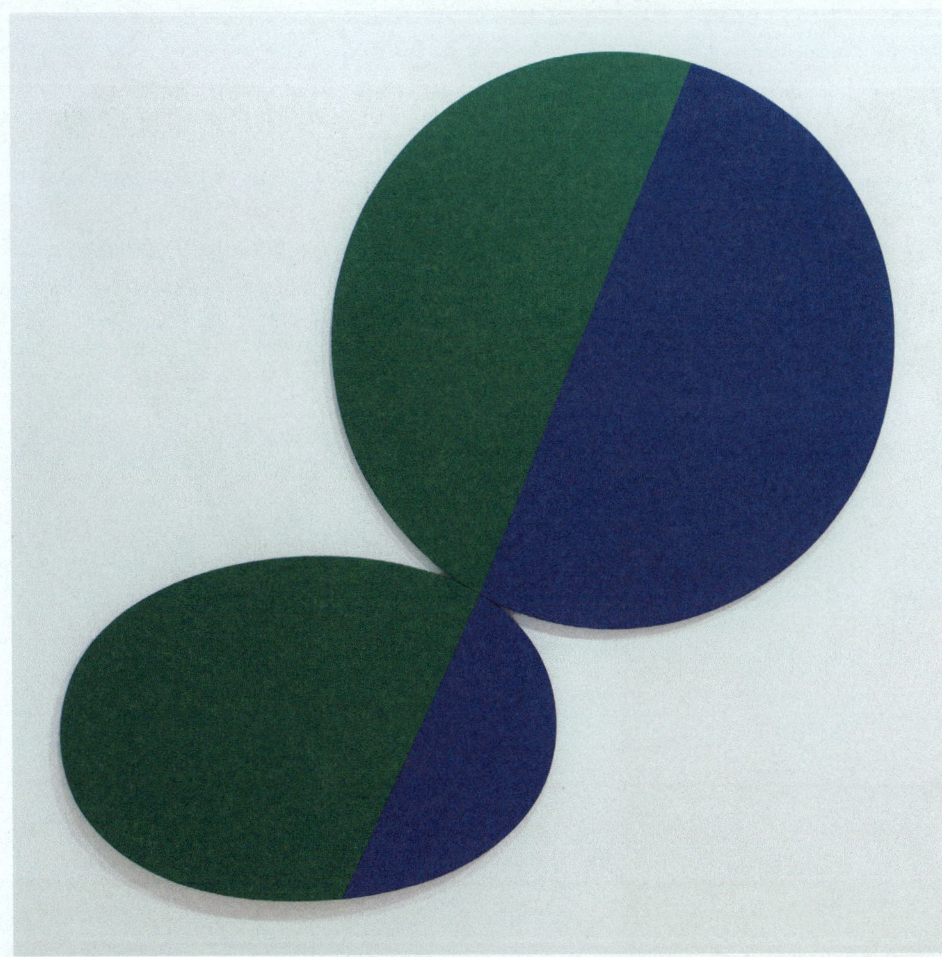

15 Leon Polk Smith, *Constellation Green-Blue*, 1968, Acryl auf Leinwand | Acrylic on canvas, 218 × 218 cm, Galerie Hoffmann, Friedberg, © 2023, ProLitteris, Zürich

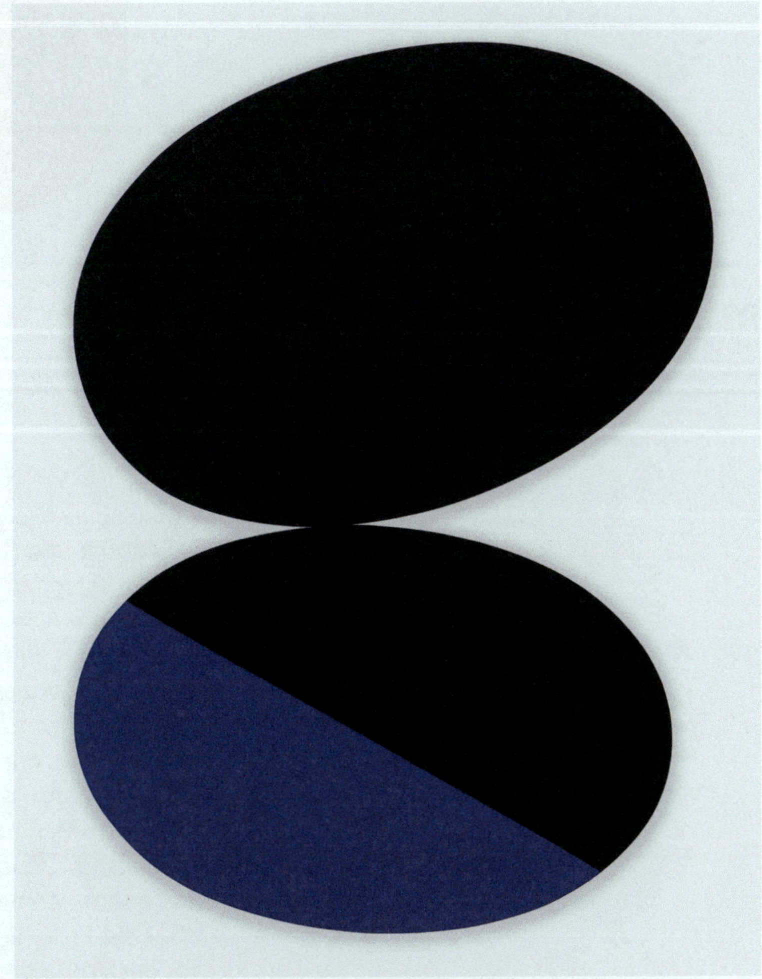

16 Leon Polk Smith, *Constellation – Lost Horizon*, 1968, Farbe auf Leinwand | Paint on canvas, 174,6 × 126,4 cm, Courtesy Gray, Chicago/New York, Foto | Photo: Tom Van Eynde, © 2023, ProLitteris, Zürich

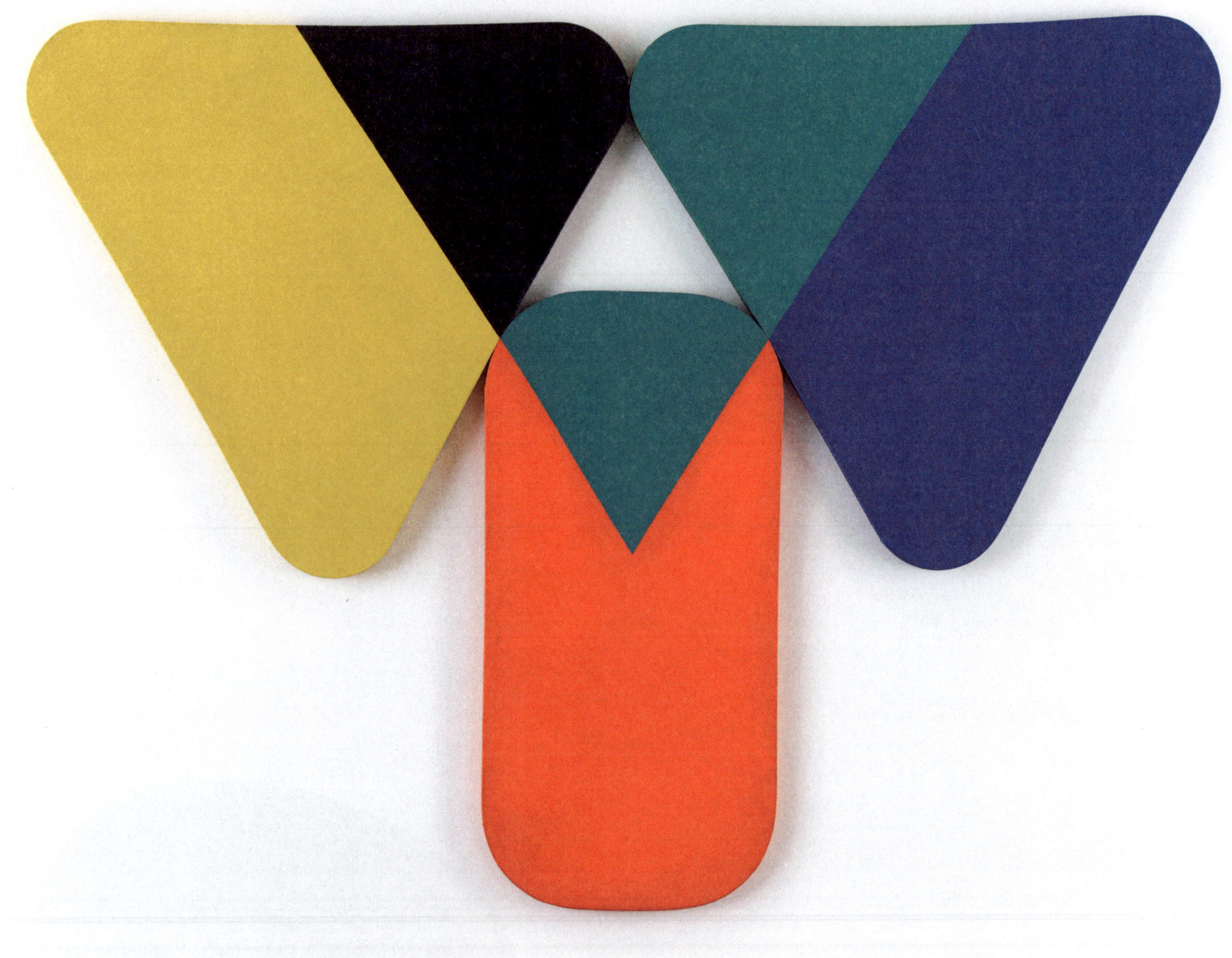

❶❼ Leon Polk Smith, *Constellation Y*, 1968, Acryl auf Leinwand | Acrylic on canvas, 115,6 × 160 cm, Leon Polk Smith Foundation, Courtesy of Lisson Gallery, © 2023, ProLitteris, Zürich

waren seine Werke für Smith eng mit Naturerfahrungen verbunden. *Twilight, New Moon for August* und *Sunset Caribe* erscheinen wie Ausschnitte aus einem kosmischen oder metaphysischen Raum. «Wäre ich nicht in der Prärie geboren und aufgewachsen, ich weiss nicht, wie meine Arbeit zustande gekommen wäre. Es steckt so viel von diesem freien Raum darin und von dem Gefühl eines weiten Himmels, und das ist ein Element, das in den Werken mancher Künstlerinnen und Künstler, die von meinen Gemälden beeinflusst wurden, fehlt», resümierte er selbst.[17] Angesprochen auf die Farbgebung seiner Bilder, die vom klassischen Rot, Blau, Gelb, Weiss und Schwarz der frühen Schaffensjahre bald zu intensiven Farbtönen in Orange, Violett oder Grün wechselte, sagte er: «Man sollte sich von den Farben lösen, die man auf der Erde findet; sie sind limitierend. Ohnehin habe ich die Natur nie als etwas begriffen, das bei unserem Himmel endet. Ich habe meine Bilder immer als über die Erde hinausgehend verstanden.»[18] Über die Erde hinausgehen, über das Sichtbare hinausgehen, sich überwältigt fühlen vor der Weite der Landschaft und des Himmels – Leon Polk Smiths Werke führen von Bildräumen aus Formen und Farben in eine Bildwelt des Sublimen, die uns «beyond space» reisen lässt.

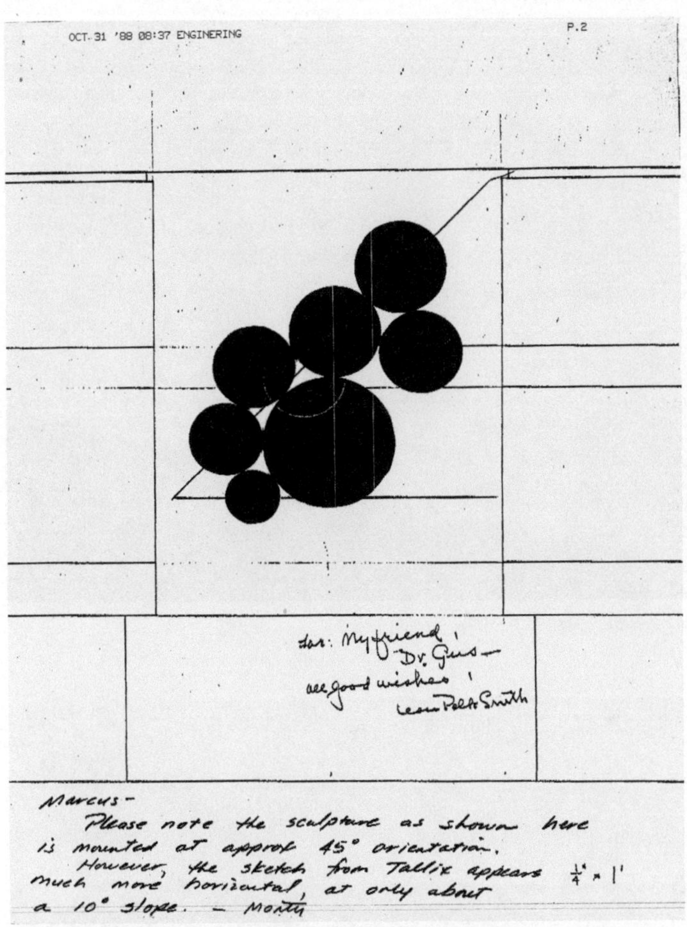

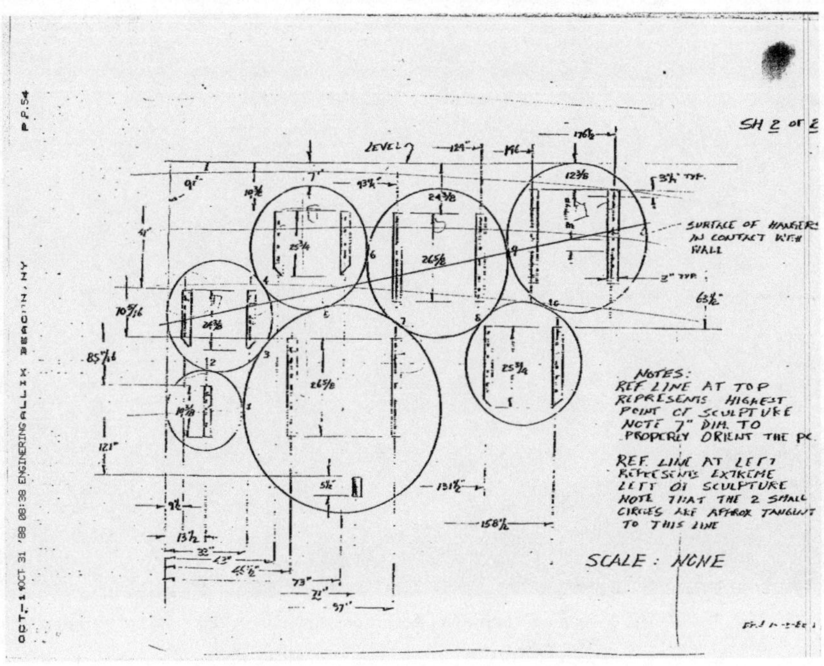

18 *Constellation Twelve Circles:* Installationszeichnungen für den Ciba-Geigy-Werkauftrag | Installation drawings for the Ciba-Geigy commission, 1988

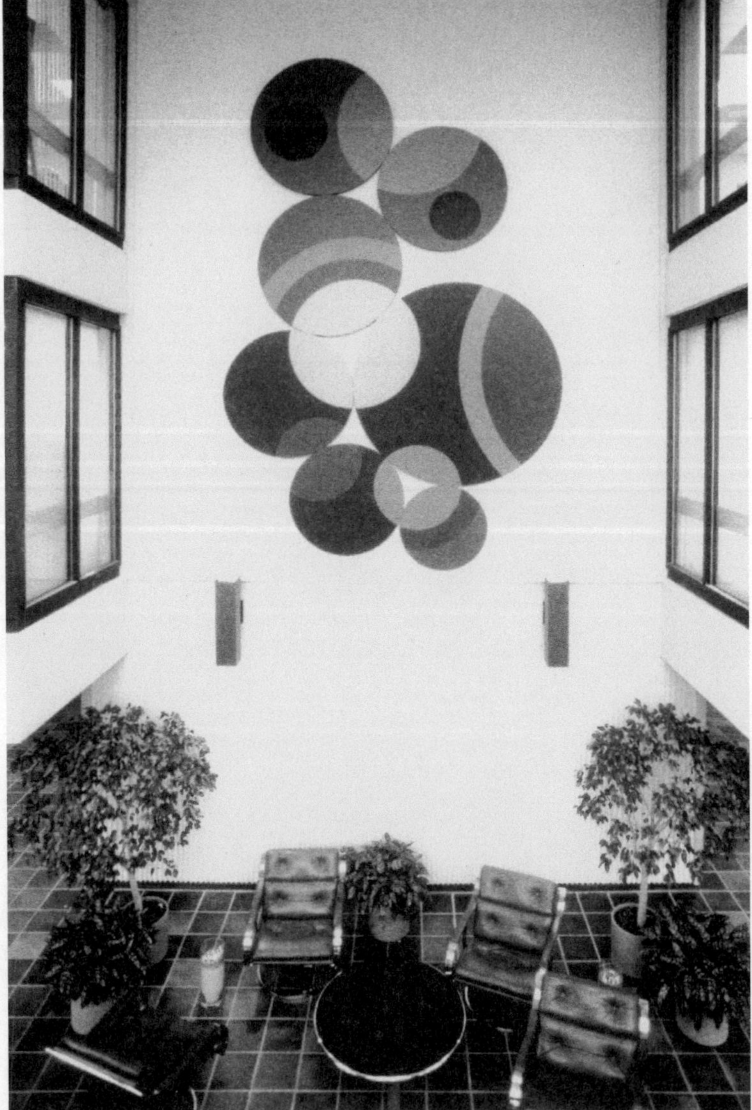

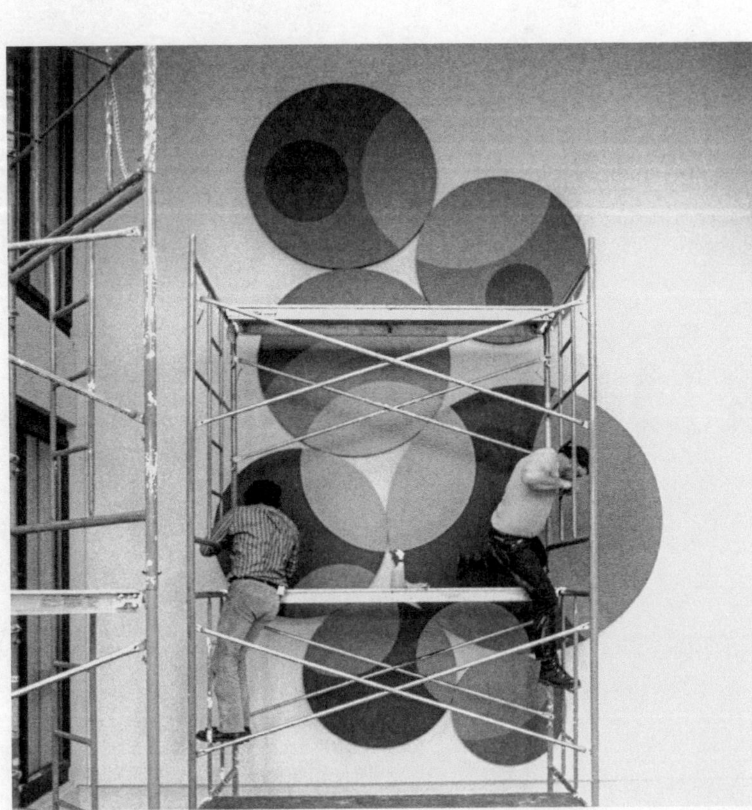

19 Installationsansicht | Installation view Pharmaceutical Development Building Ciba-Geigy (heute | now Novartis), Summit, New Jersey

20 Leon Polk Smith, *Twilight*, 1979, Acryl auf Leinwand | Acrylic on canvas, 77 × 229 × 3,5 cm, Privatsammlung | Private collection, Berlin, Foto | Photo: Eric Jobs, © 2023, ProLitteris, Zürich

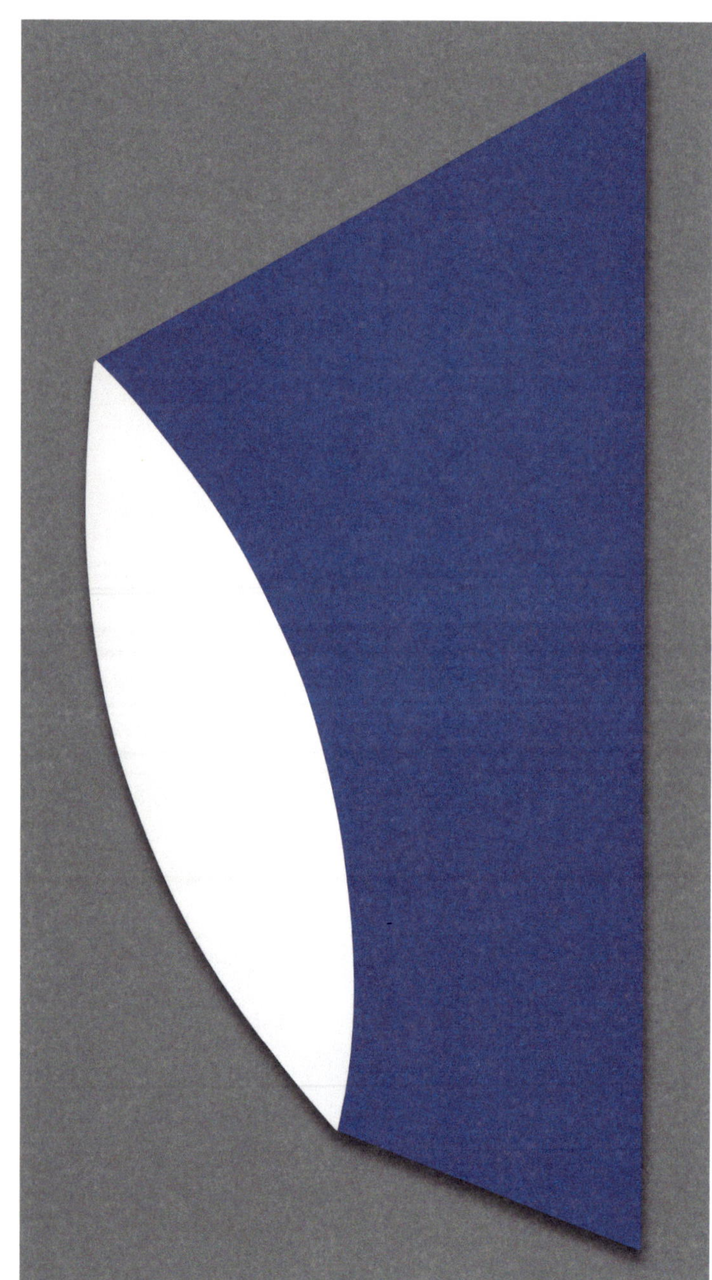

21 Leon Polk Smith, *New Moon for August*, 1983, Acryl auf Leinwand | Acrylic on canvas, 304,8 × 152,4 cm, Crystal Bridges Museum of American Art, Bentonville, Schenkung von der | Gift of the Leon Polk Smith Foundation, anlässlich der Einweihung des Museums | on the occasion of the Museum's inauguration 2011.41, Foto | Photo: Edward C. Robison III, © 2023, ProLitteris, Zürich

One of the most outstanding examples from the *Constellation* series is *Constellation Twelve Circles* (1969) **18** in which seven differently sized circular canvases form an ensemble of complete and implied circles that extend across multiple panels and incorporate the wall as part of the composition. “The activation of the whole surface—the internal space of the work with the interstices of wall space and the invitation to multiply the forms in all directions—is the objective attained,” writes art historian Claudine Humblet, describing the effect of the visual structure.[12] The special significance of *Constellation Twelve Circles* is also shown by the fact that this work was produced a second time in 1988, directly commissioned by the Swiss pharmaceutical company Ciba-Geigy[13] (now Novartis) for the lobby of its development building in Summit, New Jersey—this time on a larger scale on aluminum panels and differently aligned on the wall. As documented by installation drawings, Smith experimented with different ways of hanging *Constellation Twelve Circles*.[14] While the original 1969 work in acrylic on canvas was arranged horizontally, the drawings for Ciba-Geigy show not only a horizontal arrangement, but also an adjusted 45° rotation (fig. p. 47). Then there is the implemented hanging with its astonishing, vertical orientation **19**. The artist was thus capable of presenting one and the same work in three possible variations. Markings on the panels of other *Constellations* concerning their orientation and/or arrangement show that Smith also intended alternative ways to install other works from this series.[15]

Spatial interaction between the elements in Smith’s works peaked in the *Constellations*. In the later years of his life, Smith himself linked his spatial conceptions to his experience of space on the plains of Oklahoma, where he grew up:

> One of my main interests in art as a student was space—and that has continued to be one of the most interesting elements of art to me. [...] Certainly I found a new way of using it from Mondrian’s work and that gave me a basis for the depth of feeling that I had for space—having grown up on the plains of Oklahoma.[16]

This feeling for space, derived from his experience of nature in his home state, is particularly resonant in works such as *Twilight* (1979) **20**, *New Moon for August* (1983) **21**, and *Sunset Caribe* (1983) **22**. Like the *Correspondences*, these are based on an interplay between two colored forms. Unlike the *Correspondences*, however, with the exception of *Twilight*, they are shaped canvases and in a large format. Some of the lines within each picture are designed to reflect the image’s shape. The size of the picture formats gives the encounter between the colored forms a stronger spatial effect, which the beholder can almost physically experience. In contrast to other Hard-edge artists, Smith saw his works as being closely linked to his experience of nature. *Twilight*, *New Moon for August*, and *Sunset Caribe* come across like extracts from a cosmic or metaphysical space. He summed this up himself as follows: “If I hadn’t been born and raised on the plains, I don’t know how my work would have come about. It’s full of that open space and the big sky feeling, which is a missing element in the work of some artists who were influenced by my paintings.”[17] When asked about the coloring of his paintings, which after the classic red, blue, yellow, white, and black of his early years soon changed to intense orange, violet, and green hues, he once said, “You should get away from the colors you find on earth; they’re limiting. Anyway, I never thought of nature as if it stopped at our sky. I’ve always thought of my paintings as going beyond earth.”[18] Going beyond the Earth, going beyond the visible, feeling overwhelmed in front of the vastness of the landscape and sky: Leon Polk Smith’s works lead us from pictorial spaces made of forms and colors into a visual world of the sublime, letting us travel beyond space.

22 Leon Polk Smith, *Sunset Caribe*, 1983, Acryl auf Leinwand | Acrylic on canvas, 152 × 284 cm, Leon Polk Smith Foundation, Courtesy of Lisson Gallery, © 2023, ProLitteris, Zürich

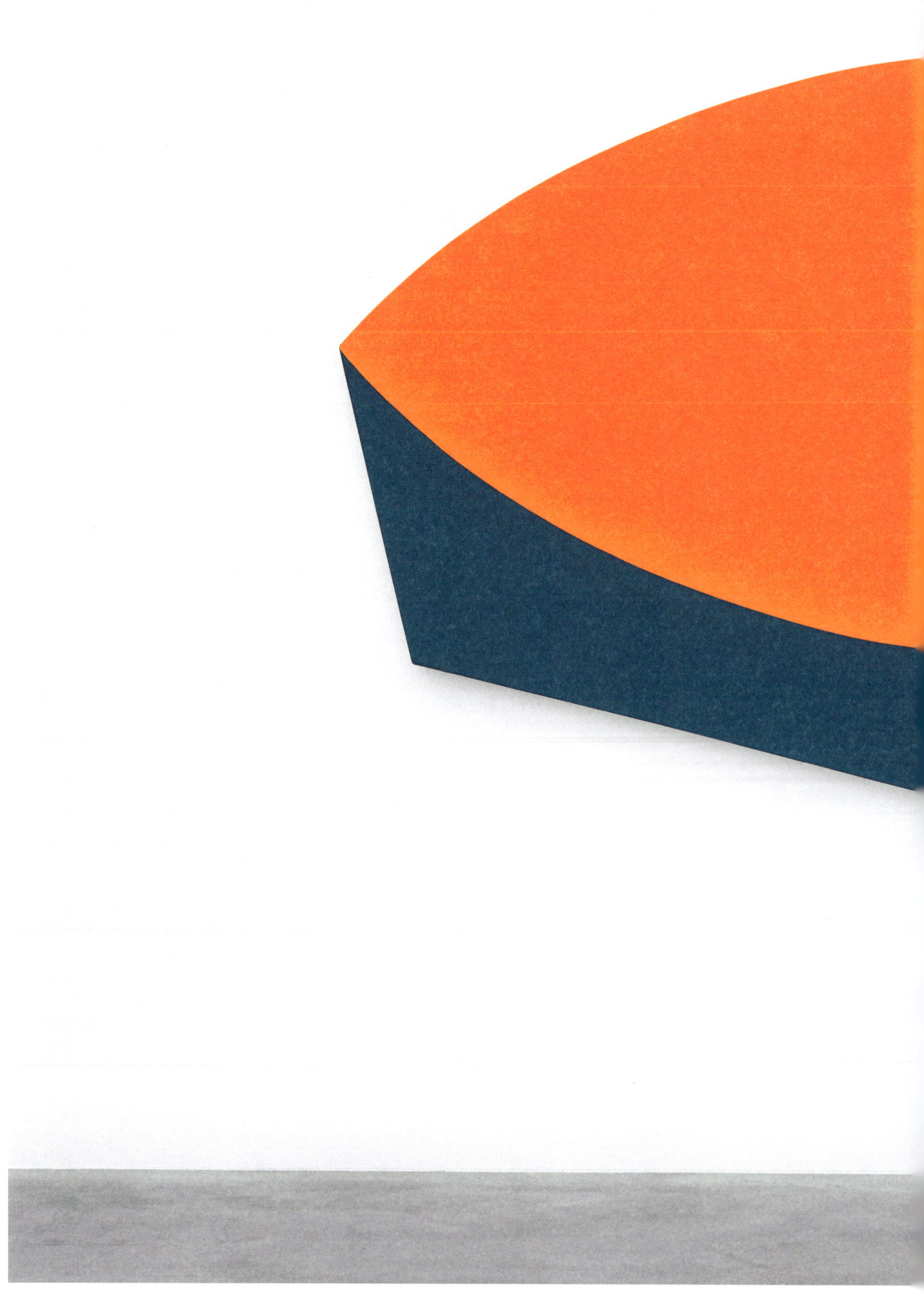

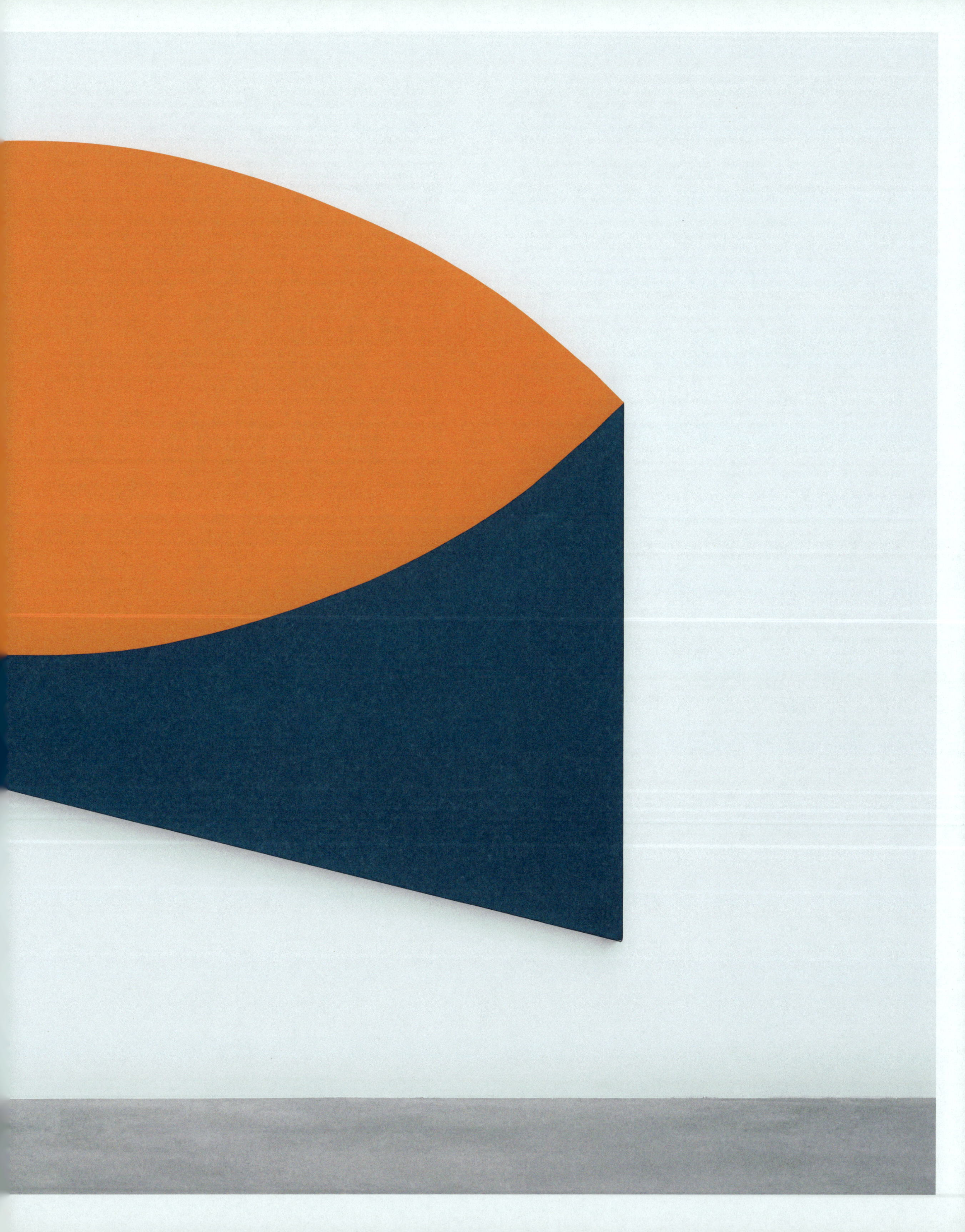

D

1 Nelson Aldrich Rockefeller, Gouverneur des Bundesstaates New York (1959–1973) und 41. Vizepräsident der USA (1974–1977), beauftragte Fritz Glarner 1963 mit der künstlerischen Gestaltung des Esszimmers seiner New Yorker Stadtwohnung im 30 Rockefeller Plaza. Der *Rockefeller Dining Room* wurde 1965 fertiggestellt und ist seit 1994 Teil der Sammlung des Museum Haus Konstruktiv. Die flächendeckenden Leinwandmalereien von Fritz Glarner werden in einem extra dafür rekonstruierten Raum als Dauerinstallation präsentiert.

2 Leon Polk Smith im Gespräch mit Brooke Kamin Rapaport, Transkript unter: https://leonpolksmithfoundation.org/wp-content/uploads/2019/05/Rapaport_Interview_LPS_transcript.pdf (zuletzt abgerufen: 1.9.2022).

3 Im genannten Transkript ist Charmion von Wiegand fälschlicherweise als «VonWiegen» festgehalten.

4 Siehe hierzu: Claudine Humblet, *The New American Abstraction 1950–1970*, Mailand 2007, S. 259. Die Autorin verweist auf Lawrence Alloways Nennung dieser Ausstellung wie folgt: «Post Mondrian Painters in America, May–June 1949, Sidney Janis Gallery («For Release»: typescript document, Sidney Janis Gallery Archives). List of participants: Albers, Bolotovsky, Diller, Glarner, Holtzman, Model, Pereira, Salemme, Smith». Siehe: https://leonpolksmithfoundation.org/wp-content/uploads/2015/04/the-new-american-abstraction.pdf (zuletzt abgerufen: 1.9.2022). Das Smithsonian Archives of American Art listet einen Brief der Sidney Janis Gallery, der den Rückzug Glarners von der genannten Ausstellung bestätigt. Von Wiegand wird nicht erwähnt. Vgl. https://edan.si.edu/slideshow/viewer/?damspath=/CollectionsOnline/smitleon/Box_0003/Folder_040 (zuletzt abgerufen: 1.9.2022).

5 Leon Polk Smith im Gespräch mit Brooke Kamin Rapaport (wie Anm. 2), S. 2.

6 Im 1936 erstmals publizierten Katalog *Museum of Living Art – A.E. Gallatin Collection* sind beide Gemälde abgebildet, siehe: https://archive.org/details/musliv00gall (zuletzt abgerufen: 1.9.2022).

7 Lucius Grisebach, «Raum in der Fläche modellieren», in: *Leon Polk Smith. Collagen 1981–1983*, Ausst.-Kat. Nationalgalerie Berlin, 1984, S. 9.

8 Leon Polk Smith in einem Interview mit Konstanze Crüwell-Doertenbach, 1987, siehe: https://leonpolksmithfoundation.org/research-resources/interviews/chruwell-doertenbach/ (zuletzt abgerufen: 1.9.2022), S. 3. (Die Interviewerin ist dort als Chruwell-Doertenbach angegeben.) Ein Wiederabdruck des Interviews findet sich in: *Leon Polk Smith*, Ausst.-Kat. Wilhelm-Hack-Museum, Ludwigshafen am Rhein 1989, S. 103–109, hier S. 105.

9 Angela Thomas, *crossover culture – max bill und georges vantongerloos beziehungen zu den U.S.A.*, publiziert im November 2021 unter: https://maxbill.ch/downloads/at_crossover-culture_de_web.pdf (zuletzt abgerufen: 1.9.2022), S. 30.

10 Leon Polk Smith im Gespräch mit d'Arcy Hayman, abgedruckt in: Ina Prinz (Hrsg.), *Leon Polk Smith im Arithmeum*, Ausst.-Kat. Arithmeum Bonn, Bonn 2001, S. 6–17, hier S. 8.

11 Mein Dank gebührt Hans Jörg Glattfelder für das freundliche und aufschlussreiche persönliche Gespräch am 4. Juli 2022 in Basel. Der Briefwechsel zwischen Leon Polk Smith und Hans Jörg Glattfelder ist im Smithsonian Archives of American Art gelistet unter: https://edan.si.edu/slideshow/viewer/?damspath=/CollectionsOnline/smitleon/Box_0004/Folder_033 (zuletzt abgerufen: 1.9.2022).

12 Claudine Humblet (wie Anm. 4), S. 243.

13 Der Briefwechsel und Vertrag zwischen Leon Polk Smith und Ciba-Geigy ist zugänglich im Smithsonian Archives of American Art, siehe: https://edan.si.edu/slideshow/viewer/?damspath=/CollectionsOnline/smitleon/Box_0001/Folder_030 (zuletzt abgerufen: 1.9.2022).

14 Mein herzlicher Dank geht an Martin Furler Bassand, Global Art Curator Novartis, für die Zurverfügungstellung der Installationszeichnungen.

15 Für diese wichtige Beobachtung möchte ich mich herzlich bei Patterson Sims, Präsident der Leon Polk Smith Foundation, bedanken.

16 Leon Polk Smith in einem Interview mit William F. Jeffett, 22. März 1985, siehe: https://leonpolksmithfoundation.org/wp-content/uploads/2018/12/lps-letter_william-jeffett.pdf (zuletzt abgerufen: 1.9.2022), S. 2.

17 Ebd., S. 3.

18 Robert Hughes, «Leon Polk Smith», in: *Time Magazine*, 21. Dezember 1973, siehe: https://leonpolksmithfoundation.org/research-resources/selected-essays-reviews/hughes-1973/ (zuletzt abgerufen: 1.9.2022), S. 3.

E

1 Nelson Aldrich Rockefeller, Governor of New York (1959–1973) and 41st Vice President of the US (1974–1977), commissioned Fritz Glarner in 1963 to provide an artistic design for the dining room in his New York City apartment at 30 Rockefeller Plaza. The *Rockefeller Dining Room* was completed in 1965 and has been part of Museum Haus Konstruktiv's collection since 1994. Glarner's paintings on canvas, which cover entire surfaces, are presented as a permanent installation in a specially reconstructed room.

2 Leon Polk Smith in an interview with Brooke Kamin Rapaport, "An Interview with Leon Polk Smith," in *Leon Polk Smith: American Painter* (Brooklyn: Brooklyn Museum, 1996), https://leonpolksmithfoundation.org/wp-content/uploads/2019/05/Rapaport_Interview_LPS_transcript.pdf.

3 In the corresponding transcript, Charmion von Wiegand's name is incorrectly written as "VonWiegen."

4 Claudine Humblet, *The New American Abstraction 1950–1970* (Milan: Skira, 2007), 259, https://leonpolksmithfoundation.org/wp-content/uploads/2015/04/the-new-american-abstraction.pdf. The author refers to this exhibition using Lawrence Alloway's naming, as in the following: "Post Mondrian Painters in America, May–June 1949, Sidney Janis Gallery ('For Release': typescript document, Sidney Janis Gallery Archives). List of participants: Albers, Bolotovsky, Diller, Glarner, Holtzman, Model, Pereira, Salemme, Smith." A letter from the Sidney Janis Gallery confirming Glarner's withdrawal from the exhibition is listed in the Smithsonian's Archives of American Art. It makes no mention of von Wiegand: https://edan.si.edu/slideshow/viewer/?damspath=/CollectionsOnline/smitleon/Box_0003/Folder_040.

5 Smith in interview with Rapaport, 2.

6 These two paintings are pictured in the catalogue *Museum of Living Art: A.E. Gallatin Collection*, first published in 1936 in New York, https://archive.org/details/musliv00gall.

7 Lucius Grisebach, "Raum in der Fläche modellieren" (Modeling Space in the Plane), in *Leon Polk Smith: Collagen 1981–1983* (Leon Polk Smith: Collages 1981–1983), exh. cat. Nationalgalerie Berlin (Berlin: Nationalgalerie, 1984), 9.

8 Leon Polk Smith in an interview with Konstanze Crüwell-Doertenbach, "A Conversation between Konstanze Chruwell-Doertenbach and Leon Polk Smith," *Nike (Munich)* 19 (July/August/September 1987), reprinted in *Leon Polk Smith*, exh. cat. Wilhelm-Hack-Museum Ludwigshafen (Ludwigshafen: Wilhelm-Hack-Museum, 1989), 103–109, https://leonpolksmithfoundation.org/research-resources/interviews/chruwell-doertenbach, 3. (The interviewer is referred to as Chruwell-Doertenbach).

9 Angela Thomas, *Crossover Culture: Max Bill's and Georges Vantongerloo's Ties with the United States*, published in November 2021, https://maxbill.ch/downloads/at_crossover-culture_de_web.pdf, 30.

10 Leon Polk Smith in an interview with d'Arcy Hayman, Leon Polk Smith and D'Arcy Hayman, "The Paintings of Leon Polk Smith," *Art and Literature: An International Review* 3 (Autumn–Winter 1964): 2, https://leonpolksmithfoundation.org/research-resources/interviews/darcy-hayman.

11 I am very grateful to Hans Jörg Glattfelder for the friendly and informative face-to-face conversation on July 4, 2022, in Basel. The correspondence between Smith and Glattfelder is listed in the Smithsonian's Archives of American Art, https://edan.si.edu/slideshow/viewer/?damspath=/CollectionsOnline/smitleon/Box_0004/Folder_033.

12 Humblet, *New American Abstraction*, 243.

13 The correspondence and contract between Leon Polk Smith and Ciba-Geigy can be accessed in the Smithsonian's Archives of American Art, https://edan.si.edu/slideshow/viewer/?damspath=/CollectionsOnline/smitleon/Box_0001/Folder_030.

14 My sincere thanks to Martin Furler Bassand, Global Art Curator at Novartis, for providing the installation drawings.

15 My heartfelt thanks to Patterson Sims, President of the Leon Polk Smith Foundation, for this observation.

16 Leon Polk Smith in an interview with William F. Jeffett, March 22, 1985, https://leonpolksmithfoundation.org/wp-content/uploads/2018/12/lps-letter_william-jeffett.pdf, 2.

17 Ibid., 3.

18 Robert Hughes, "Leon Polk Smith," *Time* (21 December 1973): 3, https://leonpolksmithfoundation.org/research-resources/selected-essays-reviews/hughes-1973.

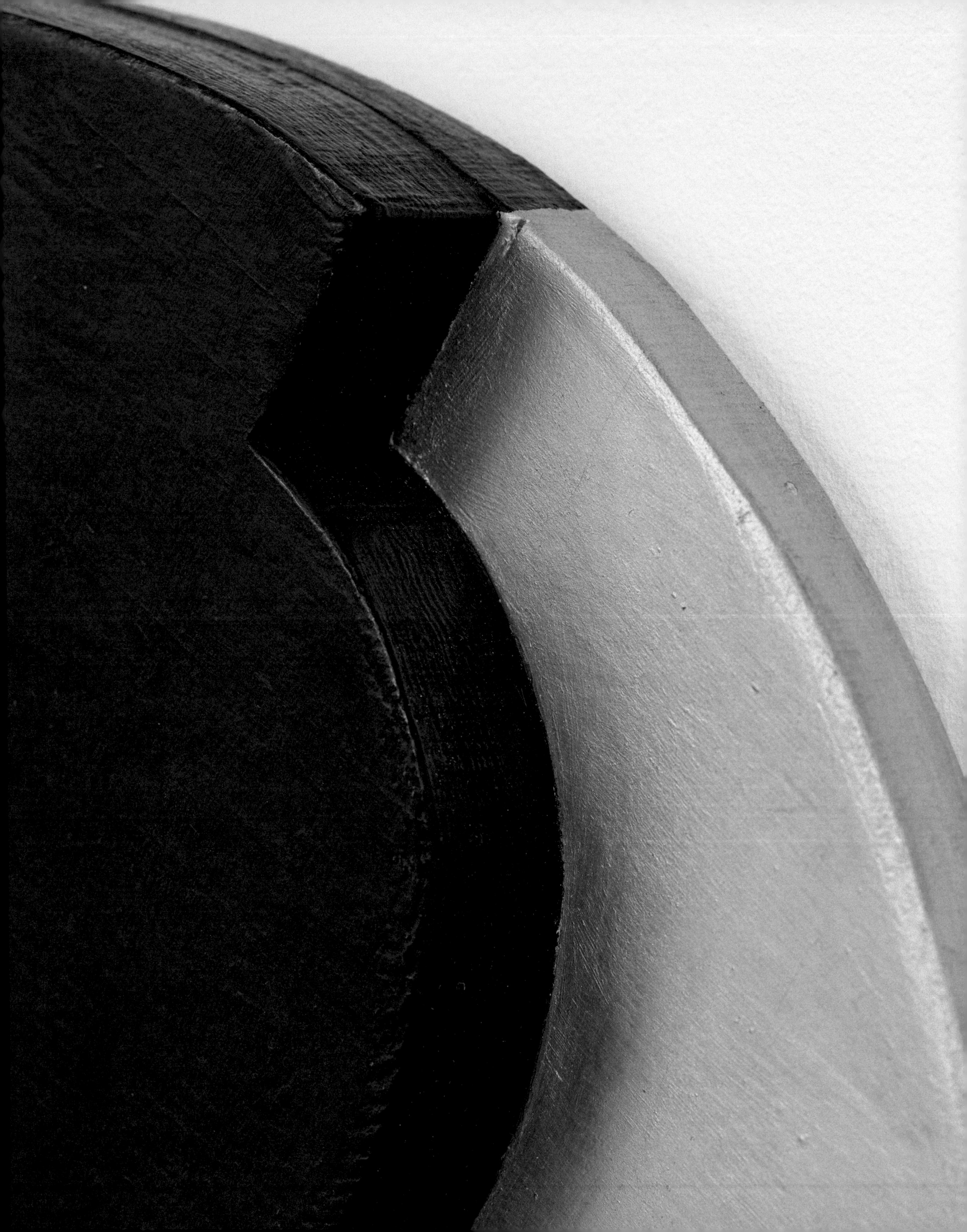

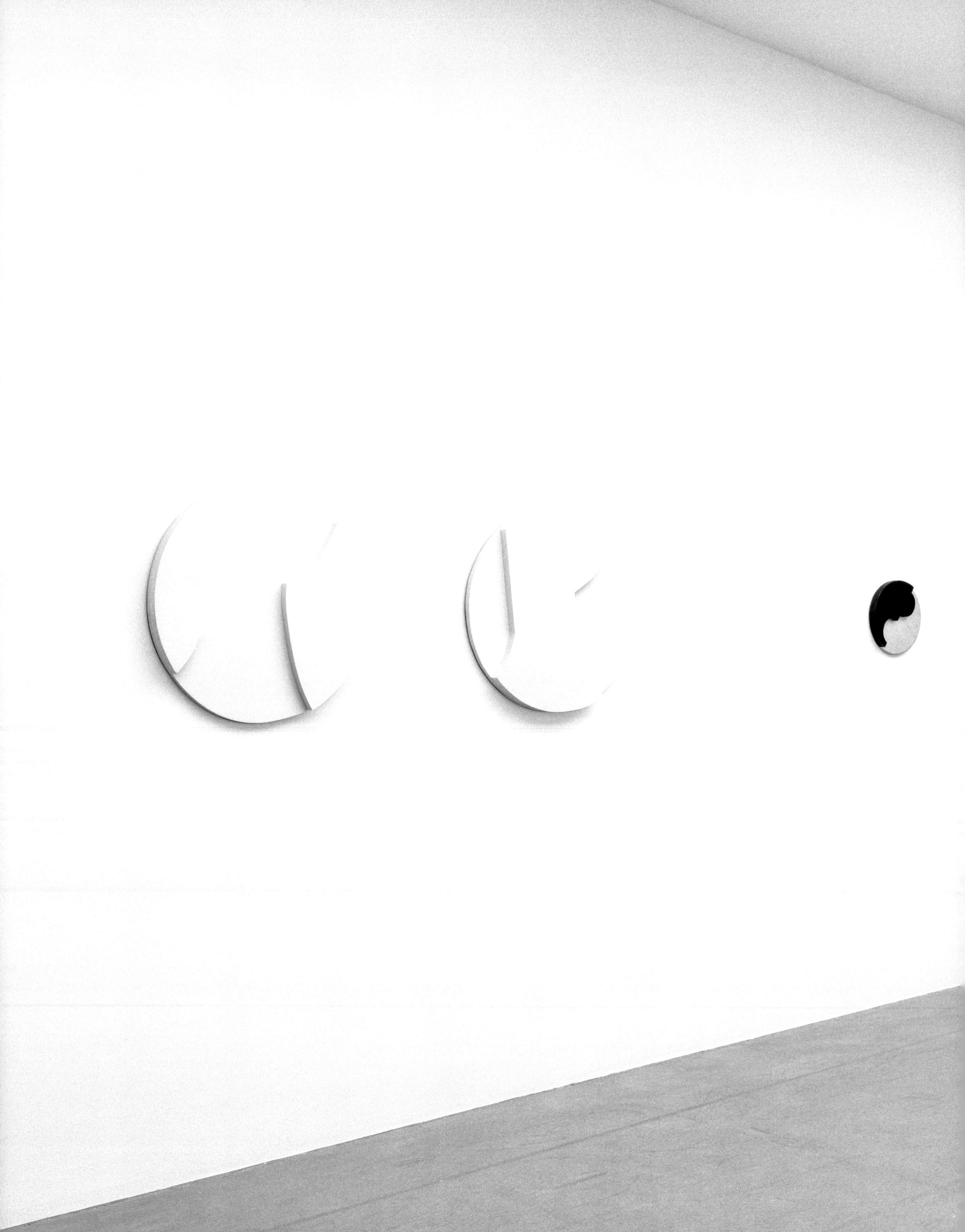

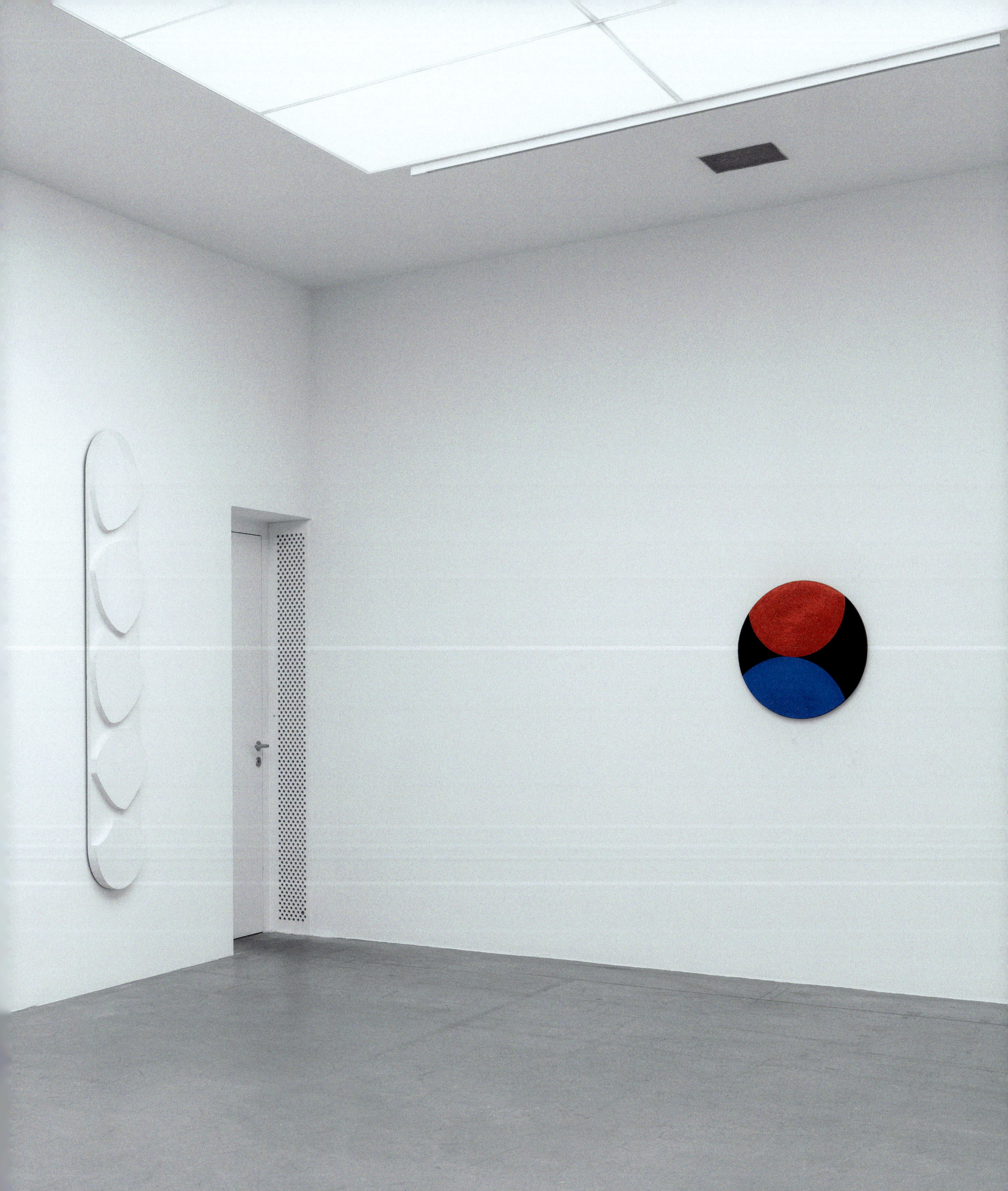

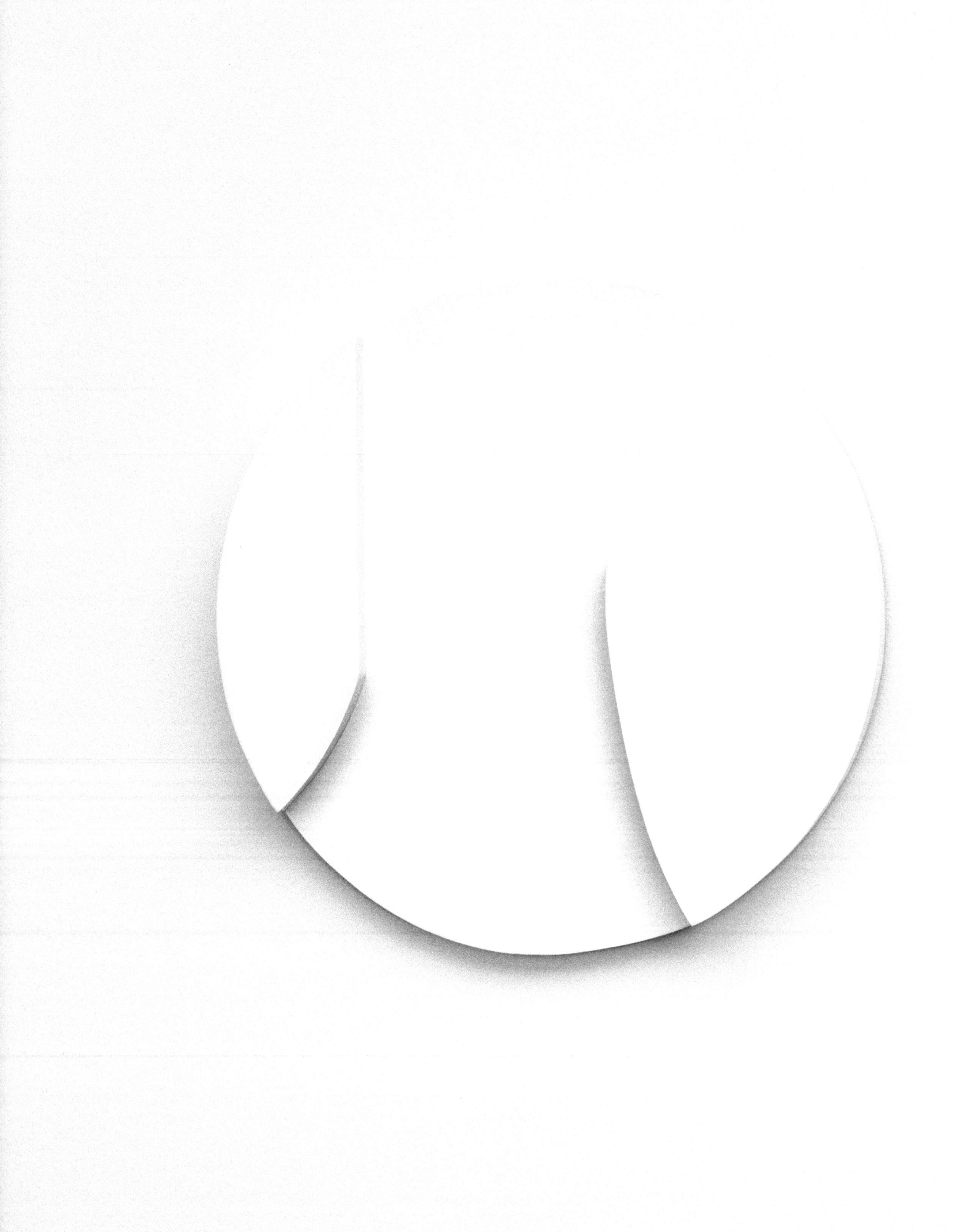

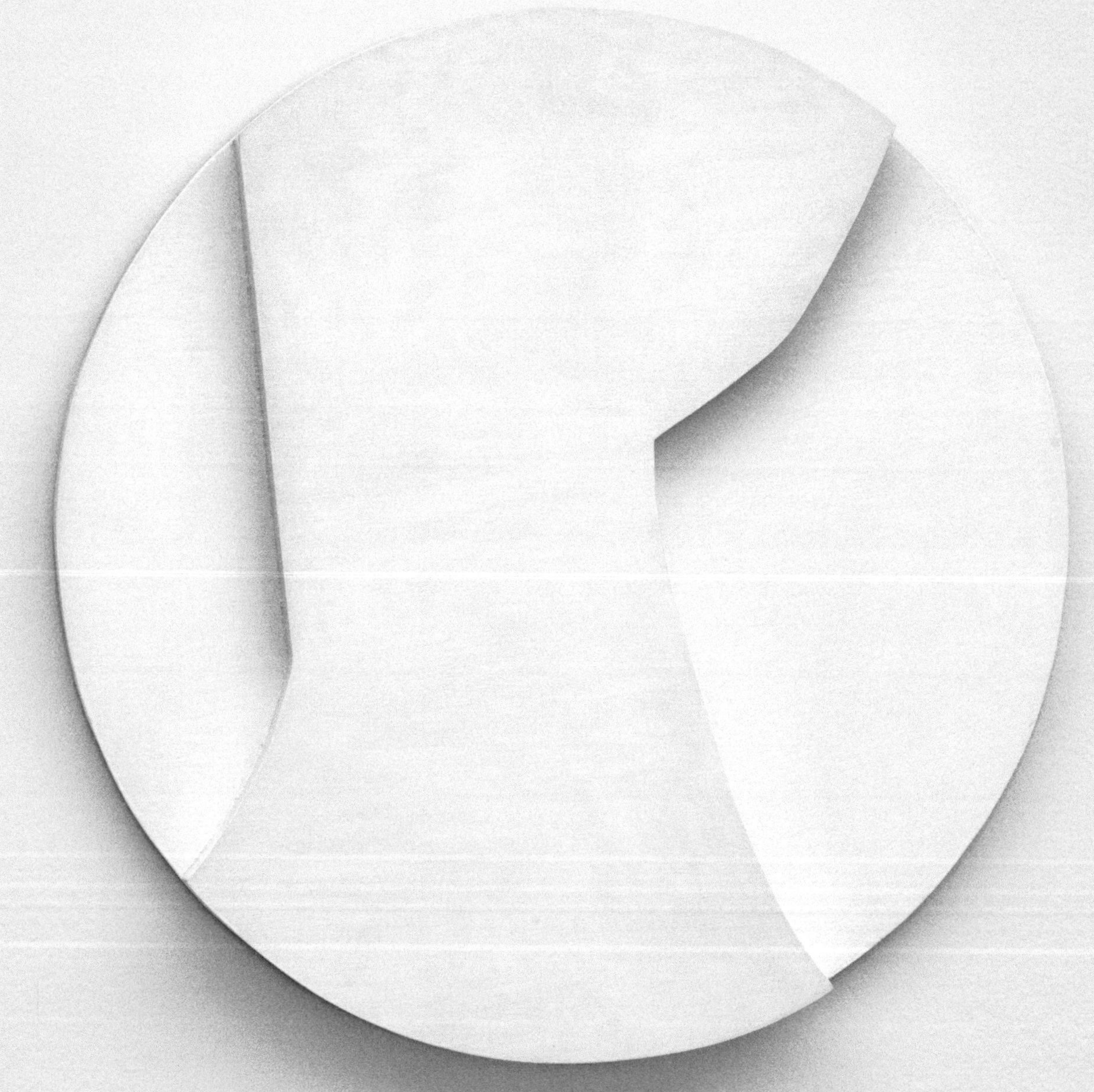

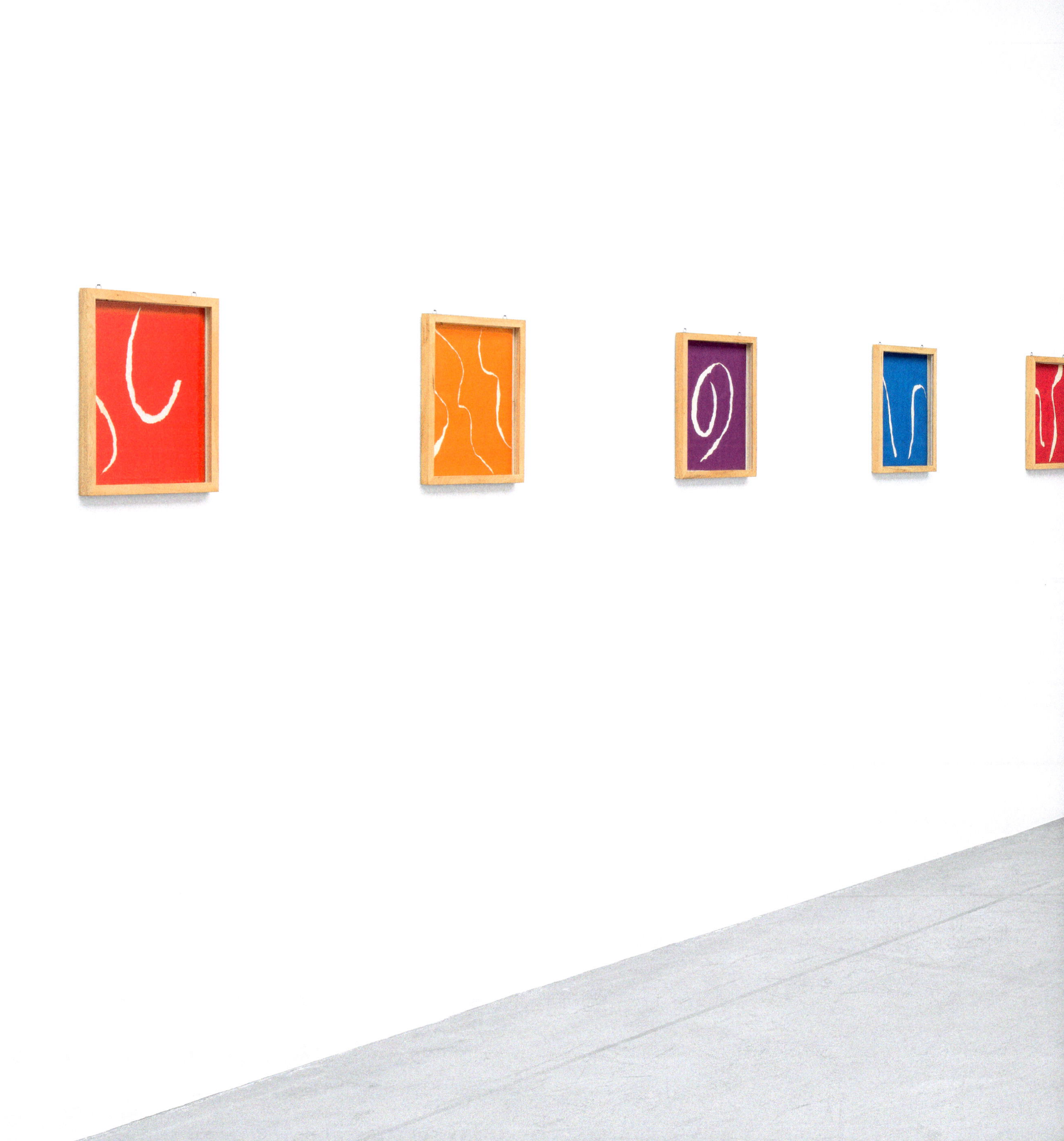

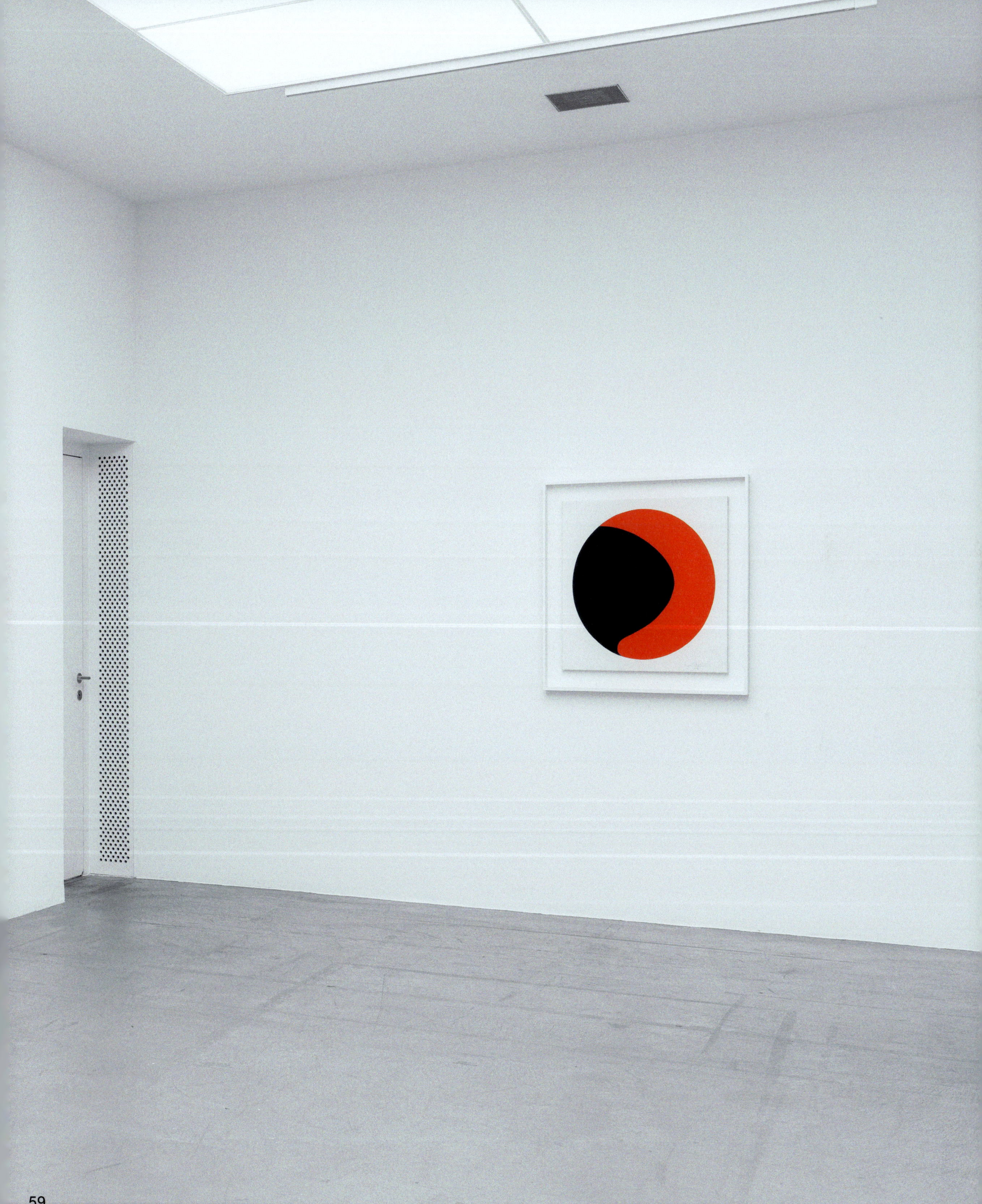

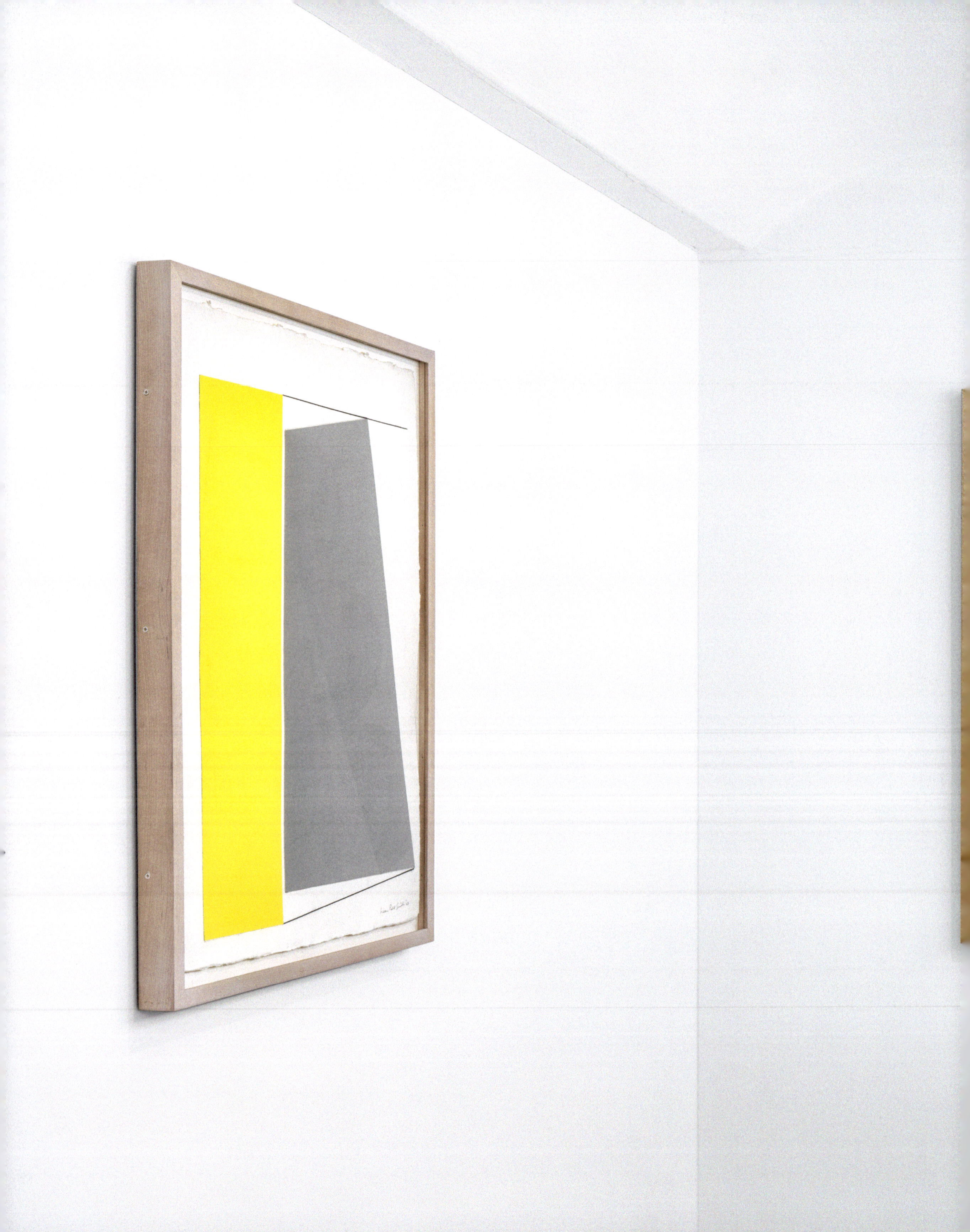

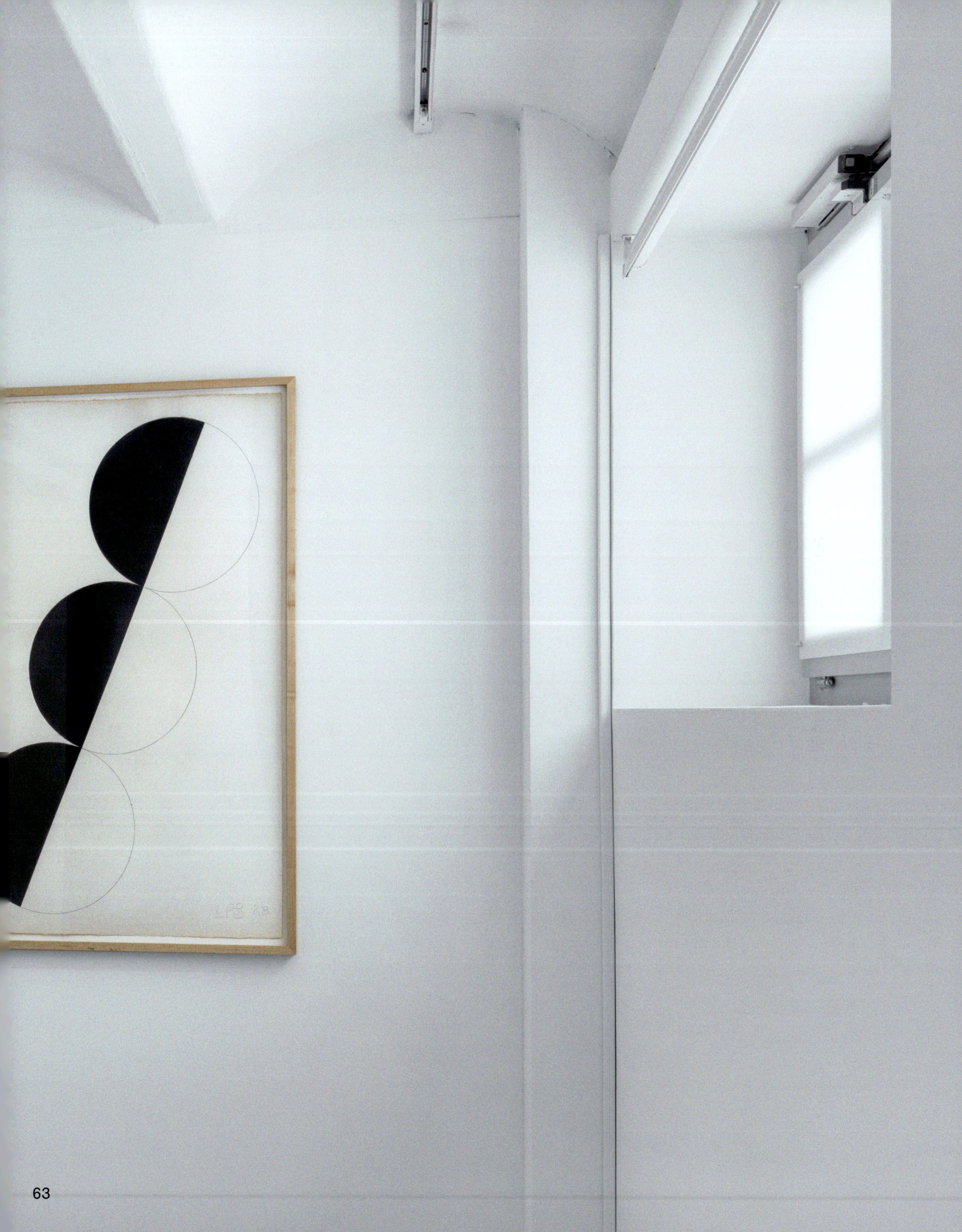

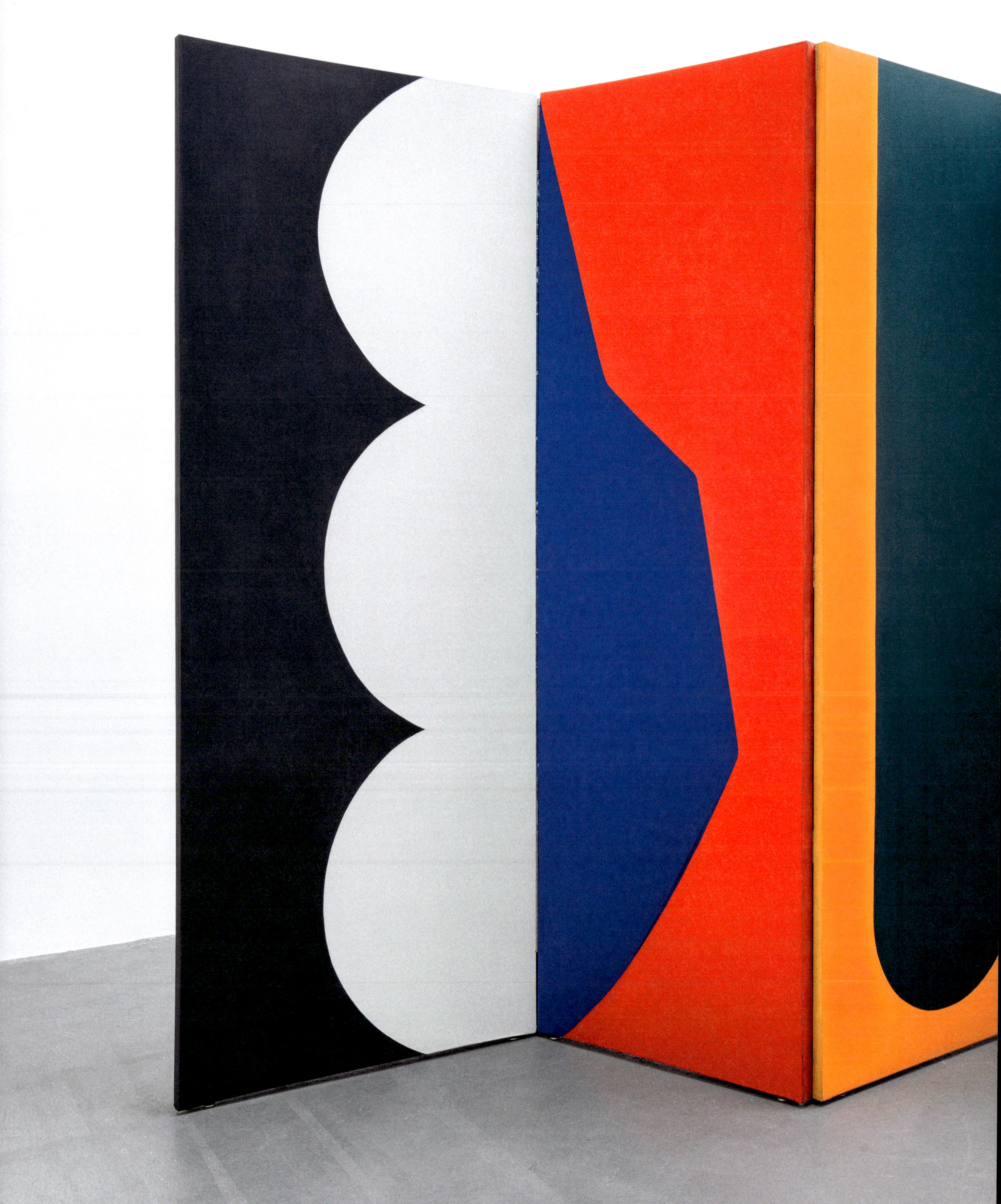

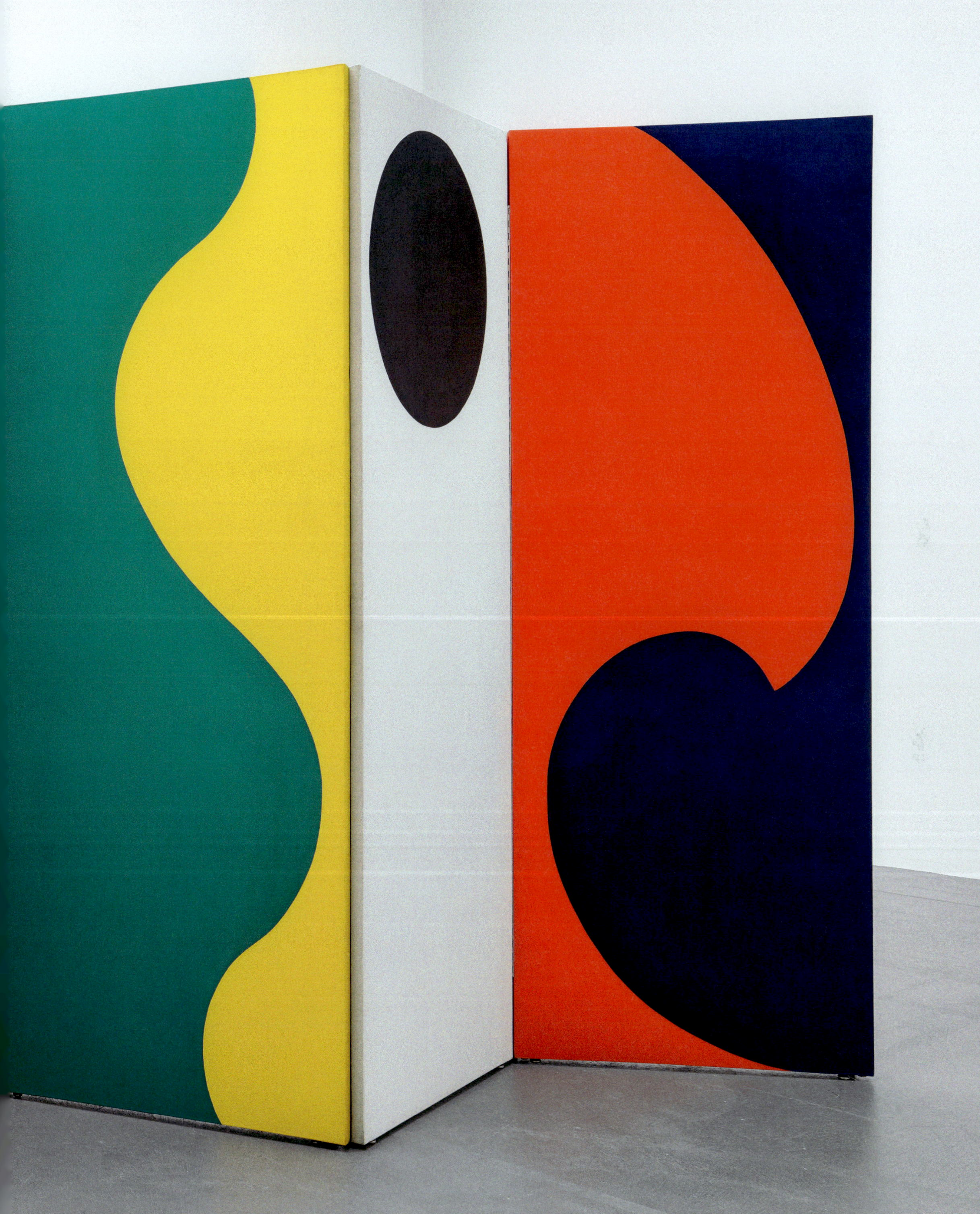

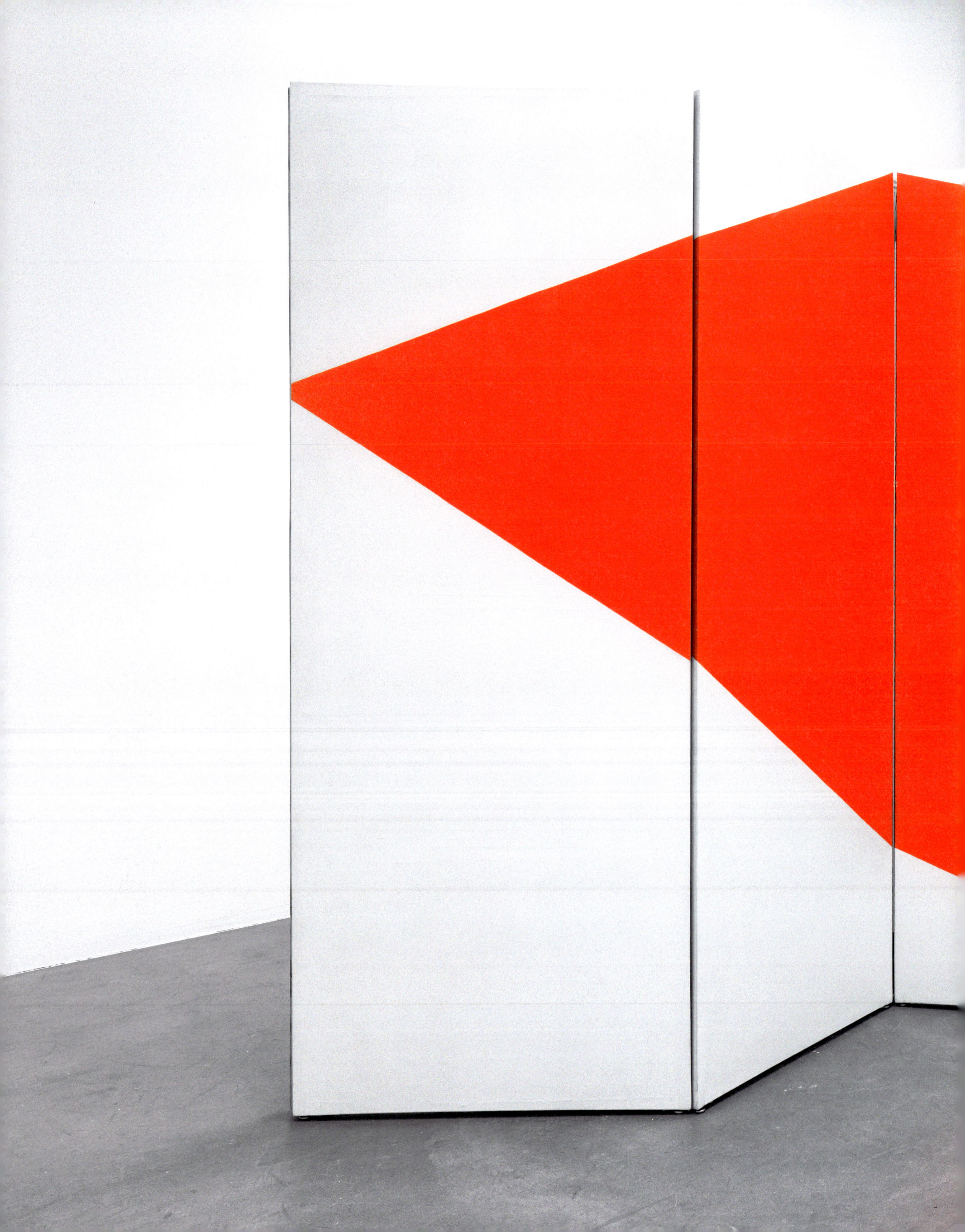

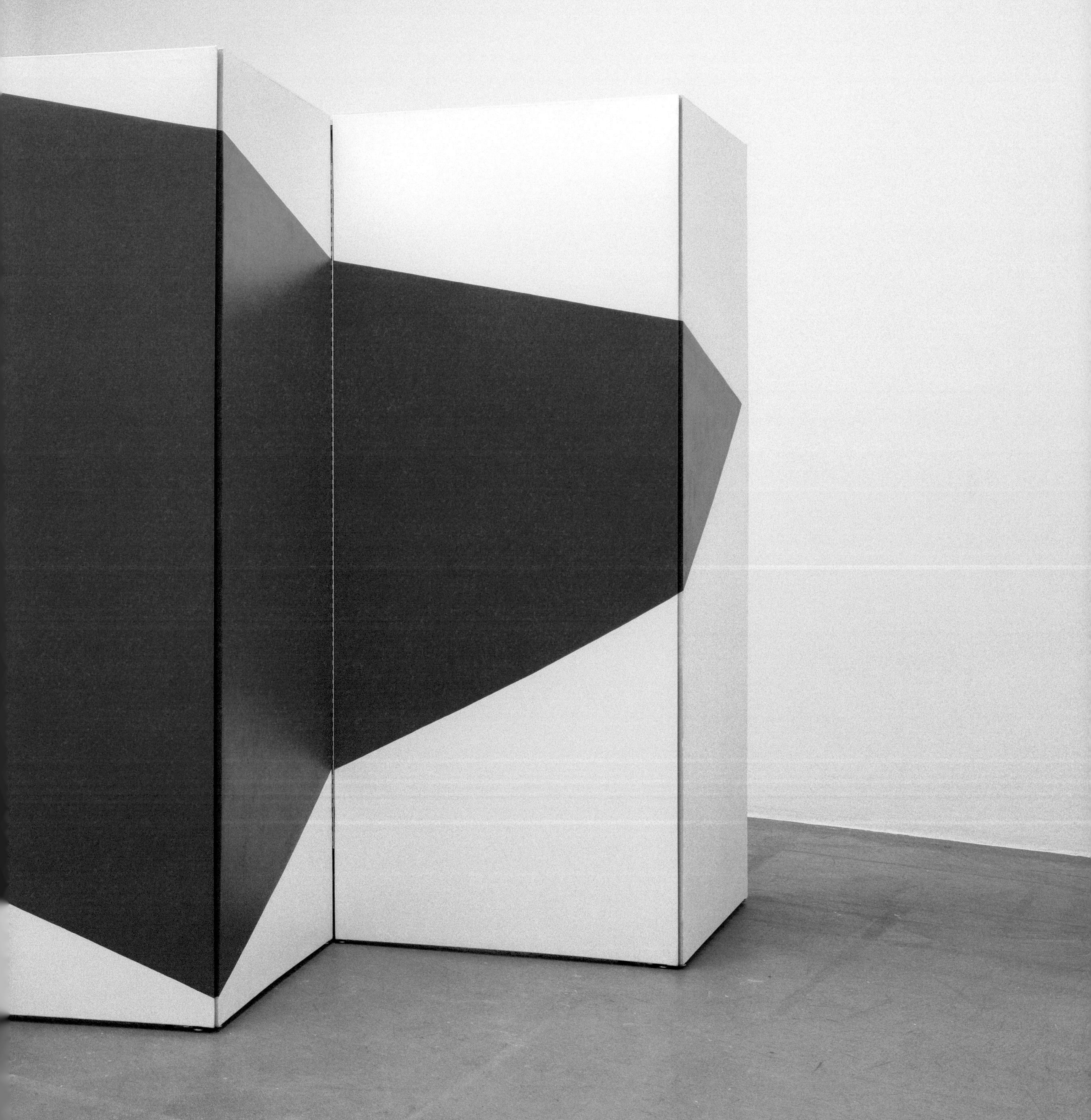

Leon Polk Smith und Europa

Leon Polk Smith and Europe

69

Brandon Taylor

D

Die Ausstellung im Museum Haus Konstruktiv richtet den Fokus auf die Beziehung zwischen der Kunst von Leon Polk Smith und jener der europäischen Moderne. Doch welche europäische Moderne meinen wir? Und wie kam ein in Oklahoma geborener Amerikaner, der als Künstler ausschliesslich in New York lebte und arbeitete, überhaupt zu einer solchen Beziehung? Diese Fragen sind spannend, und ihre Antworten legen nahe, dass es die gängige Gleichsetzung Smiths mit Hard Edge oder dem geometrischen Stil zu erweitern gilt.

Bei Smiths ersten Aufenthalten in New York 1936/37 gab es bereits eine Fülle an europäischer Kunst zu sehen. 1936 richtete der junge Kurator Alfred Barr im Museum of Modern Art seine epochale Ausstellung *Cubism and Abstract Art* aus, in der die moderne Kunst insgesamt als ein rein europäisches Unterfangen vorgestellt wurde. Die kurz zuvor am Union Square in Manhattan eröffnete, kleine, aber feine Sammlung von Albert Gallatin, der Europa selbst ausgiebig bereist hatte, umfasste hochkarätige Werke von Pablo Picasso, Jean Arp, Joan Miro, Piet Mondrian, Constantin Brancusi und anderen. Ab 1939 konnte man in dem von der europäischen Adeligen Hilla von Rebay geführten Museum of Non-Objective Painting, das zunächst in der East 54th Street untergebracht war, bevor es den Grundstein für das heutige Guggenheim Museum in der Fifth Avenue bildete, eine exquisite Sammlung europäischer abstrakter Kunst sehen. Dann, mit dem Kriegseintritt der USA im Januar 1941 und der Ankunft europäischer Dadaist:innen, Konstruktivist:innen, Surrealist:innen, Bauhaus- und De-Stijl-Künstler:innen an der Ostküste – die meisten von ihnen hatten die gefährliche Reise über den Atlantik auf sich genommen, um sich in Sicherheit zu bringen –, wurde die Stadt zu jenem Schmelztiegel der Nationalitäten und künstlerischen Verbindungen, der sie bis heute ist.

Als Smith 1944 ganz in die Stadt zog, rückte die Sache der europäischen Kunst vollends in den Fokus. Nach einer kurzen Phase des Experimentierens mit dem Surrealismus 1941 und 1942 schlug ihn das Schaffen Mondrians in Bann, der nach ein paar unproduktiven Jahren in England 1940 in New York eingetroffen war. Smith war beeindruckt vom Dialog zwischen «Form» und «Raum» in Mondrians geradlinigen Gemälden und wusste sofort, dass diese beiden Begriffe auch in seiner Kunst eine grosse Rolle spielen würden. Ein Platz in Mondrians Gravitationsfeld aber war letztendlich nicht das, was ihm vorschwebte. Zudem gewährte ihm die Gruppe um Mondrian, der Fritz Glarner, Charmion von Wiegand, Burgoyne Diller, Harry Holtzman und Ilya Bolotowsky angehörten, nicht die Flexibilität und Unabhängigkeit, die er brauchte. Diese Künstler waren Mitglieder in der Vereinigung AAA – American Abstract Artists, die von Glarner (einem gebürtigen Schweizer) und anderen 1936 gegründet worden war. Deren selbsterklärtes Ziel war es, aus ausgesuchten Praktiken der europäischen Moderne eine genuin amerikanische Avantgarde zu formen, wobei insbesondere De Stijl strikte Geradlinigkeit vorschrieb. Stand für Smith zunächst die Aushandlung der eigenen Position innerhalb des De-Stijl-Orbits im Vordergrund, erforderte bald auch die Auseinandersetzung mit seiner Abstammung aus Oklahoma seine Aufmerksamkeit: zum einen die rohe Körperlichkeit des Farmerlebens, zum anderen die Weite des Himmels und der Ebene – ganz zu schweigen von den Mythen der Chickasaw-Kultur, in der er aufgewachsen ist. Über Smiths kleines Gemälde *OK Territory* von 1943 heisst es in einem unlängst erschienenen biografischen Überblick, es sei ebenso «inspiriert von den mit Mondrian verbundenen De-Stijl-Malern» wie von «Rindern, Viehzucht und der Tradition der Native Americans» ❶.[1]

Diese Zweiheit aus Körperlichkeit und abstrakter Form sollte das Schaffen Leon Polk Smiths fortan prägen. Die Zeit seiner langsamen Loslösung von Mondrians Vorbild in den späten 1940er- und frühen 1950er-Jahren war zugleich die Zeit, in der der Expressionismus der New York School – man denke an Jackson Pollock, Willem de Kooning, Franz Kline und andere Talente des geschnippten, gekratzten und gespritzten Zeichens – erst seinen Aufstieg und dann eine allmähliche Erschöpfung erlebte. Unterdessen blieb die Anerkennung derjenigen, die einer flächigen, antisubjektiven Arbeitsweise den Vorzug gaben – Ellsworth Kelly und Irene Rice Pereira in den USA oder Robyn Denny und Victor Vasarely in Europa – dürftig und unstet. Erst 1954 stiess Smith auf das Format, das ihn von nun an beschäftigen sollte. Wie er später in einem Interview mit der Dichterin, Künstlerin und UNESCO-Beauftragten d'Arcy Hayman sagte, entdeckte er in jenem Jahr «ein besonderes Raumkonzept», als er einen Sportkatalog durchblätterte und ihm Linienzeichnungen von Baseball- und Basketball-Bällen ins Auge fielen. Diese Zeichnungen gewannen für ihn eine eigentümliche Bedeutsamkeit – wohlgemerkt nicht

E The present exhibition at Museum Haus Konstruktiv brings into focus the relation of Leon Polk Smith's art to European modernism. But which European modernism do we mean? And how could an Oklahoma-born American who lived and worked as an artist entirely in New York have such a relationship at all? The questions are intriguing, and the answers suggest a broadening of Smith's usual identifications with Hard-edge or geometric style.

At the time Smith made his first visits to New York in 1936–37, there was already plenty of European art to see. In 1936, the young curator Alfred Barr staged his epochal *Cubism and Abstract Art* show at the Museum of Modern Art, which proposed that modern art as a whole was an entirely European affair. There were high-quality works by Pablo Picasso, Jean Arp, Joan Miro, Piet Mondrian, Constantin Brancusi, and others in the small but select collection of Albert Gallatin, himself well-travelled in Europe, which had recently opened to visitors in Manhattan's Union Square. By 1939, a superb haul of European abstract art amassed by the European aristocrat Hilla von Rebay could be seen at the Museum of Non-Objective Painting, housed for the time being on East 54th Street before forming the basis of the current Guggenheim Museum on Fifth Avenue. Then, with the entry of the US into the war in January 1941 and the arrival on the East Coast of European Dadaists, Constructivists, Surrealists, and Bauhaus and De Stijl artists—the majority having made the dangerous journey across the Atlantic in a bid for safety—the city became the melting pot of nationalities and artistic affiliations that it remains today.

It was with Smith's full-time move to the city in 1944 that the question of European art came fully into focus. After a brief spell experimenting with Surrealism in 1941 and 1942, he became absorbed by the work of Mondrian, who had arrived in New York in 1940 after an unproductive couple of years in England. Smith was impressed by

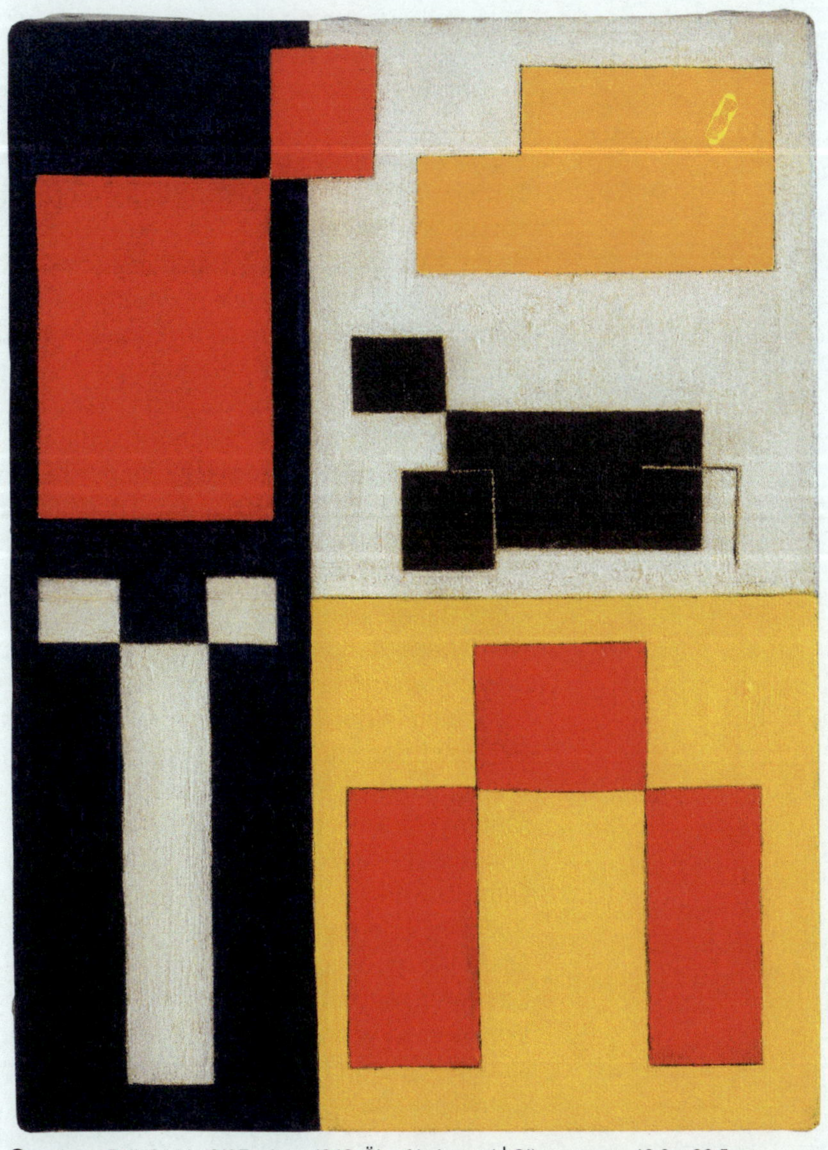

❶ Leon Polk Smith, *OK Territory*, 1943, Öl auf Leinwand | Oil on canvas, 40,6 × 30,5 cm, Brooklyn Museum New York, © 2023, ProLitteris, Zürich

wegen ihres Bezugs zu amerikanischen Nationalsportarten, sondern wegen der fliessenden, geschwungenen Räume, die der Kreisform innewohnen und sie beleben. Das Format barg offenbar Möglichkeiten, die er nie ganz definieren konnte. Gegenüber Hayman sagte er (ihr Gespräch fand 1964 statt): «Und ich weiß bis heute nicht, welche Bildräume auf diese Weise entstehen. Es sind gewiß nicht nur die erdbezogenen Räume, mit denen wir seit Jahrhunderten vertraut sind. In meinen Augen handelt es sich dabei um andere Räume, die sich der gesamten Welt erst im letzten Jahrzehnt erschlossen haben.»[2] Es war, als sei etwas Globales, Atmosphärisches bildhaft geworden. Die ersten Werke der Serie erinnern an die frühen Aufnahmen der Erde von oben ❷. Wobei anzumerken ist, dass die «anderen Räume» von Smiths frühen Tondi realiter durch die russischen Sputniks erreicht wurden, die 1957 die Erde umkreisten und überall auf der Welt für Staunen sorgten.

Smiths Überlegungen zu seiner Kunst können, das muss man dazu sagen, tastend und unsicher klingen. Er war nie ein Theoretiker seiner eigenen Kunst, sondern begriff seine Arbeitsweise intuitiv und äusserte sich oft verwundert über das, was er machte und warum er es machte. «Es kommt mir so vor, als ob ich das, was ich darüber weiß, bereits verinnerlicht hatte, bevor ich es gelernt habe», sagt er wunderbar paradox im Interview mit d'Arcy Hayman.[3] Sie hatte sich nach seinem Interesse für Zen und das alte vedische Denken erkundigt, in dem die Zeit nicht linear verläuft und Gegensätze stets zusammentreffen. Diese Frage interessierte ihn, wiewohl er keine Antwort darauf hatte. Jahre später erwiderte er die Frage einer anderen Journalistin, welchen Stellenwert Politik, Psychologie und «Soziales» in seiner Kunst hätten, indem er darauf pochte, dass diese Themen in seinem Werk überhaupt keinen Stellenwert hätten.[4] Es scheint eindeutig, dass Entscheidungen von Anfang an – oder zumindest ab 1954 – nicht auf der Grundlage von Geschmack oder Theorie, sondern aus einer Verbindung mit dem Bildobjekt selbst getroffen wurden. Ich möchte hier darlegen, dass das Zusammenfliessen von kosmischem Bewusstsein und erdgebundenen Realitäten in Smiths Werk bald Anknüpfungspunkte finden sollte, und zwar nicht in der amerikanischen Malerei, sondern in dem, was in Europa als konkrete Kunst bezeichnet wurde.

Den Begriff des Konkreten in der modernen Kunst hatte Theo van Doesburg kurz vor seinem Tod im Jahr 1931 aufgebracht. Aufgegriffen wurde er von Jean Arp und Wassily Kandinsky, die beide in den späten 1930er-Jahren in Paris lebten und die Terminologie der Abstraktion aus unterschiedlichen Gründen als obsolet erachteten. Für sie wie auch für Max Bill, Leo Leuppi und Richard Paul Lohse in der Schweiz bedeutete Konkretion eine Bejahung sowohl der essenziellen Materialität als auch der ideellen, wenn nicht gar metaphysischen Funktion von Kunst. Im Sinne der Konkretion war es nicht nur richtig, sondern vielmehr geboten, dass die Arbeit des Künstlers oder der Künstlerin am Material kein Akt des subjektiven Ausdrucks ist, sondern eine Konstruktion von Beziehungen zwischen Linien, Flächen, Reihen, Massstab, Intervallen sowie grafischen und tonalen Setzungen, die mit Aspekten der Natur verbunden, aber auch, wie in Lohses Fall, weltanschaulicher Art sein konnten.[5]

Vor diesem Hintergrund wurde 1960 in Zürich die grosse und umfassende Ausstellung *konkrete kunst – 50 jahre entwicklung* eröffnet, kuratiert von Max Bill mit Unterstützung der Pariser Galeristin Denise René und der New Yorker Galeristin Madeleine Chalette, die beide sehr für das Werk von Leon Polk Smith schwärmten. Zürich, einst gleichbedeutend mit den Ursprüngen von Dada, hatte mit der konkreten Kunst bis zu den 1940er-Jahren die in der westlichen Welt wohl produktivste antisurrealistische Strömung in der Tradition von Konstruktivismus, De Stijl und Bauhaus hervorgebracht; Bill beschrieb sie 1949 als eine künstlerische Arbeitsweise, die «unnaturalistisch und dennoch naturnah» sei.[6] Eine Arbeitsweise, die jener von Smith sehr nahekam. Während die überwiegende Mehrheit der in der Zürcher Schau vorgestellten Künstlerinnen und Künstler aus der Schweiz und anderen Ländern Europas kam (unter ihnen Lohse, Camille Graeser, Verena Loewensberg, Vera Molnar, Georges Vantongerloo), fiel die Auswahl amerikanischer Kunst relativ vorsichtig aus. So wurden Arbeiten von Diller, Glarner, von Wiegand, Mark Rothko, Mark Tobey und Leon Polk Smith gezeigt – Letzterer war mit dem Tondo *Pontotoc* aus dem Jahr 1958 vertreten –, nicht aber Werke von Pollock, Robert Motherwell oder de Kooning ❸. Aus Paris waren Jean Dubuffet, Serge Poliakoff und Georges Mathieu mit Werken zugegen, nicht aber Camille Bryen, Jean-Michel Atlan oder Jean-Paul Riopelle.

In den USA wiederum, wo der Expressionismus der New York School allmählich verblasste, zeichnete sich nun eine allgemeine Tendenz zu einfachen, akkurat

Mondrian's dialogue of "form" and "space" in his rectilinear paintings and knew immediately that the two terms would loom large in significance in his own art. Yet a place within Mondrian's gravitational field was not ultimately what he wanted. Nor did the group around Mondrian comprising Fritz Glarner, Charmion von Wiegand, Burgoyne Diller, Harry Holtzman, and Ilya Bolotowsky allow him the flexibility and independence that he would come to need. Those artists were members of the AAA (American Abstract Artists) group, founded by Glarner (himself born in Switzerland) and others in 1936. Its self-appointed mission was to fashion a genuinely American avant-garde from selected practices of European modern art, of which De Stijl in particular mandated strict rectilinearity. Yet for Smith, while negotiating a position within the De Stijl orbit was initially a priority, reckoning with the qualities of his Oklahoma background called for recognition too: the brute physicality of farming life on the one hand, the largeness of the sky and plain on the other—not to mention the mythologies of his family's Chickasaw culture he grew up in. Smith's small painting *OK Territory* of 1943 is described in a recent biographical chronology as just as much "inspired by the De Stijl painters associated with Mondrian" as by "cattle, ranching and the Native American tradition" ❶.[1]

Such a duality of physicality and abstract form was to mark Leon Polk Smith's work from that moment on. Yet the period of his slow release from Mondrian's precedent throughout the later 1940s and early 1950s was the time of the ascent, then the gradual exhaustion, of New York School Expressionism: that of Jackson Pollock, Willem de Kooning, Franz Kline, and other talents of the flicked, scraped, and spattered mark. For those drawn to a flat, anti-subjective technique meanwhile—Ellsworth Kelly and Irene Rice Pereira in the US, or Robyn Denny and Victor Vasarely in Europe—recognition remained provisional and uncertain. It was not until 1954 that Smith discovered the format that would preoccupy him henceforward. As he remarked in a later interview with the poet, artist, and UNESCO administrator d'Arcy Hayman, it was in that year that he discovered "a particular space concept" while glancing through a sports catalogue and seeing there line drawings of baseballs and basketballs. These drawings became strangely meaningful for him—not, quite evidently, for their reference to American national pastimes but for the flowing, curving spaces that live within, and animate, the circular form itself. The format seemed to contain possibilities that he could never quite define. He would say to Hayman (the date of the interview is 1964), "I still don't know what this space is. It isn't just the earthly space that we have been familiar with for centuries, [...] it has something to do with the other spaces that the whole world has really been interested in for the past decade."[2] It was as if something global, something atmospheric, was being figured. The earliest works in the series evoke the early photographic record of the Earth as seen from above ❷. It is to be noted that the "other spaces" of Smith's early tondos would be achieved in practice by the orbiting Russian Sputnik in 1957, which was looked upon with fascination around the globe.

It should be said that Smith's own reflections on his art can sound groping and insecure. Never a theorist of his own art, he understood his working attitudes intuitively and often expressed puzzlement as to what he found himself doing and why. "What I do know seems that I always knew it before learning of it," he says with magnificent paradox in the interview with d'Arcy Hayman.[3] She had asked him about his interest in Zen and ancient Vedic thought in which time is not linear and where contraries always meet. It was a question that interested him, even though he did not know the answer. Years later he would deflect another journalist who asked him about the place of politics, psychology, and "the social" in his art by insisting that those matters did not have a place in his work at all.[4] It seems clear that, from the outset, or at least from 1954 on, decisions were taken not on the basis of taste or theory, but from within a relationship with the picture-object itself. It will be my argument here that the meeting of cosmic awareness and earthbound realities in Smith's work would soon find affinities not in American painting, but in what in Europe was known as Concrete Art.

The concept of the "concrete" in modern art had originated with Theo van Doesburg shortly before his death in 1931 but had been picked up by Jean Arp and Wassily Kandinsky, both in Paris in the later 1930s, for whom, for different reasons, the terminologies of abstraction had become meaningless. For them, and for Max Bill, Leo Leuppi, and Richard Paul Lohse in Switzerland, Concretism affirmed both the essential materiality of art as well as its ideal or even metaphysical role. Concretism legitimated—even made imperative—the artist's work upon material not as the site of subjective expression but

❷ Leon Polk Smith, *First-One*, 1954, Öl auf Baumwolle | Oil on cotton duck, Ø 100,3 cm, Collection Buffalo AKG Art Museum, Buffalo, Schenkung von | Gift of Natalie & Irving Forman, 2004, © 2023, ProLitteris, Zürich

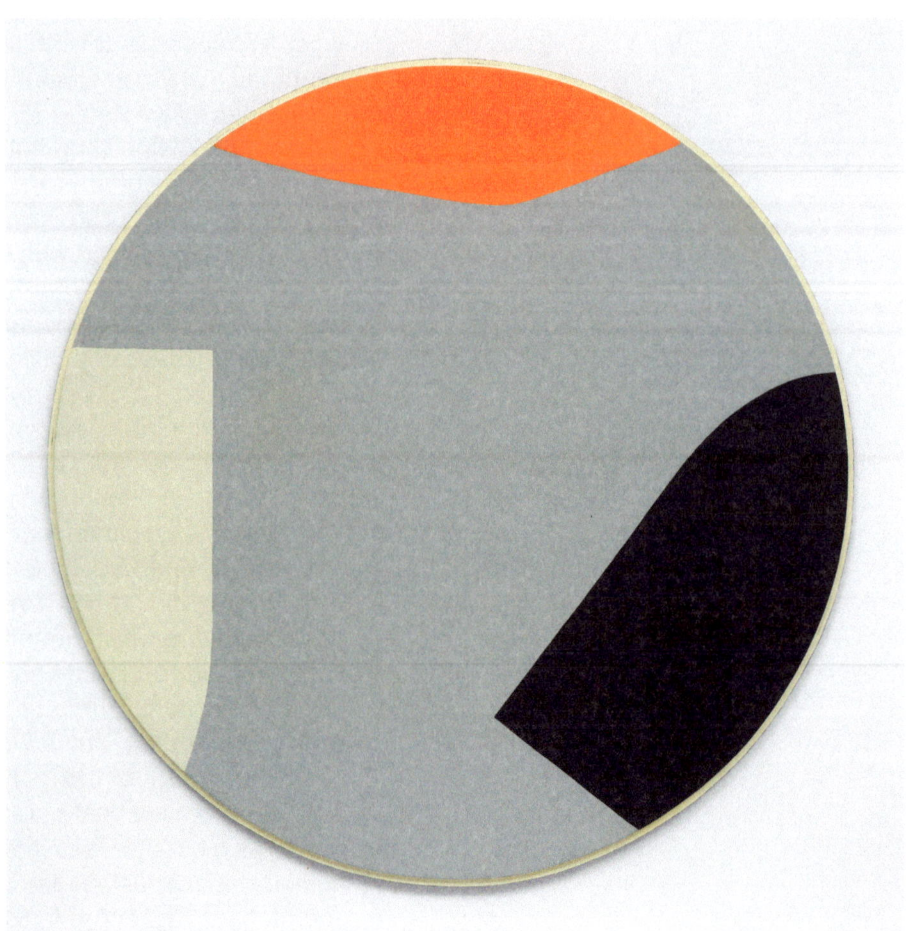

❸ Leon Polk Smith, *Pontotoc*, 1958, Öl auf Leinwand | Oil on canvas, Ø 122,5 cm, Leon Polk Smith Foundation, Courtesy of Lisson Gallery, © 2023, ProLitteris, Zürich

as the construction of relations of line, area, sequence, scale, interval, as well as graphic and tonal vocabulary, which were related to aspects of nature but could become, for example, in Lohse's case, ideological.[5]

This is the larger background against which there opened in Zurich in 1960 a vast and capacious exhibition *konkrete kunst – 50 jahre entwicklung* (concrete art: 50 years of development), curated by Max Bill with support from the Paris gallerist Denise René and New York gallerist Madeleine Chalette, both enthusiasts of Leon Polk Smith's work. Zurich, once identified with the origins of Dada, had by the 1940s nurtured Concretism as the most fertile anti-Surrealist phenomenon in Western art in the tradition of Constructivism, De Stijl, and the Bauhaus and was, in Bill's words, a method of art that was "close to nature while being a-naturalistic."[6] It was a methodology close to Smith's own. And although, for the Zurich show, Swiss and other Europeans (Lohse, Camille Graeser, Verena Loewensberg, Vera Molnar, Georges Vantongerloo, and others) were numerically prominent, in relation to American art it trod carefully, thus Diller, Glarner, von Wiegand, Mark Rothko, Mark Tobey, and Leon Polk Smith, represented by the tondo *Pontotoc* of 1958, were shown, but not Pollock, Robert Motherwell, or de Kooning ❸. From Paris there was room for Jean Dubuffet, Serge Poliakoff, and Georges Mathieu, but not for Camille Bryen, Jean-Michel Atlan, or Jean-Paul Riopelle.

In the US itself, with New York School Expressionism on the wane, it was by now a generic tendency toward simple, cleanly defined, and evenly colored shapes that came to represent a direction whose identity was not, for the time being, particularly clear. It fell to the Los Angeles critic and curator Jules Langsner to group the West Coast painters Karl Benjamin, Lorser Feitelson, Frederick Hammersley, and John McLaughlin together for a 1959 show in Los Angeles in which the term "hard-edge" began to be used.[7] Whatever the merits of the term—others tried were "slide-rule school" and "abstract classicism"—the question of the relation of Hard-edge to a much wider international spectrum of generically abstract art practices came under immediate review. Critics and historians working for the major art museums on both sides of the Atlantic now began to compete in the recognition, identification, and description of new, post-Expressionist tendencies in art.

The process was one in which Leon Polk Smith was inevitably caught up. On one level, in the smaller New York galleries outside the limelight but still influential to those in the know, a reassessment of previous European abstract art was already underway. Madeleine Chalette and her husband Arthur Lejwa, having escaped the Nazi invasions of Poland and France, had opened their Galerie Chalette on West 57th Street in 1953 and initially specialized in prints and paintings from those countries, until 1960 when, with the help of Denise René from Paris and the Bauhaus artist Josef Albers, now teaching at Yale after a stellar career at Black Mountain College, they mounted *Construction and Geometry in Painting: From Malevich to "Tomorrow."* It was a show that brought together works not only by Russian Suprematists and Constructivists, but also by major Concrete artists from Switzerland, Holland, and France, including Bill, César Domela, and the young Victor Vasarely, in addition to some Americans, including Smith himself. Unfazed by American scares about Russia and communism at the height of the Cold War, the Galerie Chalette would become one of Smith's most consistent supporters during the critical debates around Hard-edge painting and sculpture that were to follow. He would be accorded personal shows at Chalette every year bar one between 1965 and 1970.[8]

It was soon the turn of major New York art museums to define how much (or how little) Hard-edge painting and sculpture owed to the European past. *Geometric Abstraction in America*, curated at the Whitney Museum in 1962, placed Smith within a grouping that paid lip service to European Constructivism and Concrete Art while presenting the deployment of geometry as a diverse and independent American trend. Yet Smith's identity as Hard-edge or geometric was problematic. When William Seitz selected works for his celebrated *The Responsive Eye* exhibition at the Museum of Modern Art in 1964, his thesis was that "ophthalmic" or "optical" values had not only supplanted Hard-edge as a category but mirrored preoccupations belonging to a popular, if not populist, cultural agenda. In Seitz's framing, the term optical—later Op—referred not to the physiology of sight but to a rise of interest in "what the eye does" in its active discriminations, its intentional dealings with the data of sight. Thresholds of perception, the limits of coherence of particular *gestalts* in conditions of low illumination, *moiré* pulsations, two-color conjunctions in patterned or rhyming orders, optical bulging, rhythms, and

definierten Farbformen ab, die für eine vorläufig noch nicht klar benennbare Richtung standen. Dem Kritiker und Kurator Jules Langsner aus Los Angeles fiel es zu, vier an der Westküste ansässige Maler – Karl Benjamin, Lorser Feitelson, Frederick Hammersley und John McLaughlin – 1959 zu einer Ausstellung in Los Angeles zusammenzubringen, in der der Begriff «Hard Edge» erstmals verwendet wurde.[7] Unabhängig von den Vorzügen dieses Begriffs – man hatte es auch mit «Rechenschieber-Schule» und «abstrakter Klassizismus» versucht – wurde die Frage nach dem Verhältnis von Hard Edge zu einem deutlich breiteren internationalen Spektrum generisch abstrakter Kunstpraktiken einer unmittelbaren Prüfung unterzogen. Kritiker:innen und Historiker:innen, die für die grossen Kunstmuseen beidseits des Atlantiks arbeiteten, begannen nun, um die Ermittlung, Identifizierung und Beschreibung neuer postexpressionistischer Tendenzen in der Kunst zu wetteifern.

In diesen Prozess wurde Leon Polk Smith unweigerlich miteinbezogen. Auf einer Ebene, in den kleineren New Yorker Galerien, die nicht im Rampenlicht standen, für Eingeweihte aber durchaus einflussreich waren, hatte bereits eine Neubewertung der bisherigen abstrakten Kunst aus Europa eingesetzt. Madeleine Chalette und ihr Mann Arthur Lejwa, die dem Nazi-Einmarsch in Polen und Frankreich entkommen waren, hatten 1953 ihre Galerie Chalette in der West 57th Street eröffnet. Zunächst hatten sie sich auf polnische und französische Drucke und Gemälde spezialisiert, bis sie 1960 – mit Unterstützung von Denise René aus Paris und dem Bauhaus-Künstler Josef Albers, der nach einer bemerkenswerten Karriere am Black Mountain College nun in Yale lehrte – die Ausstellung *Construction and Geometry in Painting: From Malevich to «Tomorrow»* organisierten. Diese Ausstellung vereinte nicht nur Werke der russischen Suprematisten und Konstruktivisten, sondern auch solche bedeutender konkreter Künstler:innen aus der Schweiz, den Niederlanden und Frankreich, darunter Bill, César Domela und der junge Victor Vasarely, sowie einige Amerikaner:innen, unter ihnen Smith. Unbeirrt von den amerikanischen Ängsten vor Russland und dem Kommunismus in dieser Hochphase des Kalten Krieges sollte sich die Galerie Chalette im Zuge der kritischen Debatten, die noch um die Hard-Edge-Malerei und -Skulptur entbrannten, als eine der beständigsten Unterstützerinnen Smiths erweisen. Zwischen 1965 und 1970 wurde ihm, mit einer Ausnahme, jedes Jahr eine Einzelausstellung in der Galerie ermöglicht.[8]

Bald war es an den grossen New Yorker Kunstmuseen, festzulegen, wie viel (oder wie wenig) die Hard-Edge-Malerei und -Skulptur der europäischen Vergangenheit zu verdanken hatte. Die 1962 im Whitney Museum kuratierte Ausstellung *Geometric Abstraction in America* ordnete Smith einer Gruppe zu, die die konstruktive und konkrete Kunst aus Europa ausdrücklich würdigte, die Anwendung der Geometrie indes als einen eigenen und unabhängigen amerikanischen Trend präsentierte. Doch Smiths Zuschreibung zu Hard Edge oder zur geometrischen Kunst war problematisch. Als William Seitz im Jahr 1964 Werke für seine gefeierte Ausstellung *The Responsive Eye* im Museum of Modern Art auswählte, lautete seine These, dass «ophthalmische» oder «optische» Werte die Kategorie Hard Edge verdrängt hätten und zugleich die Anliegen einer populären, wenn nicht gar populistischen Kulturagenda widerspiegelten. In Seitz' Verständnis bezog sich der Begriff «optical» – später «Op» – nicht auf die Physiologie des Sehens, sondern auf ein zunehmendes Interesse an dem, «was das Auge macht», an seinen aktiven Unterscheidungen, an seiner intentionalen Verarbeitung visueller Daten. Grenzwerte der Wahrnehmung, die geringere Kohärenz bestimmter Gestalten bei schwacher Beleuchtung, das Pulsieren von Moiré, die Verknüpfung zweier Farben in gemusterten oder getakteten Ordnungen, optisches Hervortreten, Rhythmen und Reizüberflutung: All dies wurde wahlweise anhand der Werke von Ad Reinhardt, Bridget Riley und anderen sowie am Beispiel von Werken der amerikanischen Hard-Edge-Maler veranschaulicht, unter ihnen Feitelson, Kelly, Jules Olitski, Alexander Liberman und natürlich Smith.[9]

Seitz hatte richtig erkannt, dass die sogenannten Op-Phänomene in der damaligen Kultur allgegenwärtig waren. Optische Kippfiguren wie die Schröder-Treppe, der Necker-Würfel oder Joseph Jastrows Ente-Kaninchen-Bild, die zwei verschiedene Bildwahrnehmungen anbieten, wenn die visuelle Aufmerksamkeit schwankt, wurden regelmässig im *Scientific American* oder in Zeitschriften wie *Popular Science Monthly* gezeigt. Einführungen in die Gestaltpsychologie, in denen schwarze und weisse Liniendiagramme illustrierten, wie das Auge zwischen widersprüchlichen «Ganzheiten» entschied, waren allgemein verfügbar und wurden viel gelesen.[10] Die Gestalttheorie, die rund drei Generationen vorher in Deutschland entstanden war, hatte sich leicht an die

sensory overload: These were all variously exemplified by Ad Reinhardt, Bridget Riley, and others alongside works by Hard-edge American painters, such as Feitelson, Kelly, Jules Olitski, Alexander Liberman, and of course Smith.[9]

Seitz was correct in having recognized that so-called Op phenomena were everywhere in the culture at the time. Visual puzzles, such as the Schroeder staircase, the Necker Cube, or Joseph Jastrow's Duck-Rabbit image, all prone to flipping from one image to another and back as visual attention wavered, featured routinely in *Scientific American* or such magazines as *Popular Science Monthly*. Introductory books on Gestalt psychology, where black and white line diagrams illustrated how the eye adjudicated between conflicting "wholes," were widely available and being read.[10] Gestalt theory, which originated in Germany some three generations earlier, had become easily adapted to the American scene. Rudolf Arnheim, born in Berlin and a student of Wolfgang Köhler (and both by now in the US), published his widely read *Art and Visual Perception: A Psychology of the Creative Eye* in 1954. His and Köhler's theories stood in stark contrast to—even formed the inverse of—more speculative European research into the exercise of vision, notably Maurice Merleau-Ponty's *Phénoménologie de la perception*, published in 1945 and first appeared in English in 1962.[11]

For all its preoccupation with popular optics, *The Responsive Eye* failed to address its paintings and other objects as either politics or art. About the impersonal fabrication techniques of groups such as Padua's Gruppo N and the Spanish Equipo 57, each motivated by teamwork rather than individualism and by common purpose rather than personal vision, Seitz remarked nervously that they aspired "almost to socialism." Artists from Nouvelle Tendance (international), ZERO (Germany), second-generation Constructivists (Henryk Berlewi), South American neo-Concretists (Jesús Rafael Soto, Hugo Demarco), and members of the French Groupe de Recherche d'Art Visuel (GRAV) (François Morellet, Yvaral, Francisco Sobrino), all motivated by radical social ideas, were "not revolutionaries [but] aspired to full cooperation with the modern world."[12] Within such a depoliticized agenda, Smith's painting *Correspondence White-Orange* of 1964 was presented shorn of any reference to the larger affects projected by the work ❹.[13]

For the latter, Smith's working circumstances can be consulted. After a move to a large studio apartment on East 19th Street, New York, in 1964, he resumed an earlier friendship with the Cuban-born artist Carmen Herrera, who now became a near neighbor and whose practice encouraged him in the transfer of the curved space effect of the tondo paintings to the series of rectangular canvases painted in two colors known as *Correspondences*. Herrera had traveled and exhibited extensively in South America and her native Cuba, knew well the Concrete Art movements there, and lived and worked between 1948 and 1954 in Paris, where she exhibited alongside pioneers of international modernism at the *Salon des Réalités Nouvelles*, the major European staging ground for Concretists and representatives of *art non-figuratif* at the time, including Sonia Delaunay, Alberto Magnelli, Arp, Domela, Jean Gorin, and Auguste Herbin, before returning to New York ❺.[14] These information networks mattered. Through Herrera as well as the experience of the Zurich show, Smith was soon well acquainted with major practices and directions in mid-century European and Latin American art.

Secondly, and with the *Correspondence* series by now under way, Smith's interview with d'Arcy Hayman had broadened his international presence still further. *Art and Literature* was becoming, and by 1964 had become, a touchstone for English-language reflections on and by the European and American avant-gardes. Published in Switzerland (with editorial offices in Paris) by the American poet John Ashbery, the English artist couple Ann Dunn and Rodrigo Moynihan, and the writer Sonia Orwell, its reach and significance was considerable. Smith's interview appeared alongside writings by John Cage, André Masson, Georges Bataille, Robert Rauschenberg, and Roland Barthes, all of them on the leading edge of a post-national contemporaneity in art.[15] His presence in such company was not likely to be misunderstood.

Indeed, a second prestigious New York show, curated for the Guggenheim Museum in 1966 by the young English critic Lawrence Alloway, would now internationalize Smith's work still further. Alloway had worked in London at the Institute of Contemporary Arts in the 1950s and had a keen sense of Europe's modernist past as well as of painting's complex manoeuvers and techniques. He had already noticed a small American group show at Arthur Tooth's gallery in London in 1961 and had written appreciatively about Smith's contribution.[16] Once installed at the Guggenheim, Alloway's mission now

amerikanische Szene anpassen lassen. Der gebürtige Berliner Rudolf Arnheim, ein Schüler von Wolfgang Köhler (beide lebten mittlerweile in den USA), veröffentlichte 1954 sein vielbeachtetes Werk *Art and Visual Perception: A Psychology of the Creative Eye* (1978 als Neufassung auf Deutsch erschienen unter dem Titel *Kunst und Sehen. Eine Psychologie des schöpferischen Auges).* Seine und Köhlers Theorien unterschieden sich deutlich von den spekulativeren europäischen Forschungen über den Akt des Sehens, ja standen sogar im Gegensatz zu ihnen, insbesondere zu Maurice Merleau-Pontys *Phénoménologie de la perception,* die 1945 publiziert wurde und 1962 erstmals auf Englisch erschien.[11]

Bei aller Auseinandersetzung mit populären optischen Erscheinungen versäumte es *The Responsive Eye,* die ausgestellten Gemälde und übrigen Objekte als Politik oder als Kunst einzuordnen. Zu den anonymisierten Produktionstechniken von Gruppierungen wie Gruppo N aus Padua und Equipo 57 aus Spanien, die eher durch Teamarbeit als durch Individualismus und vielmehr durch ein gemeinsames Ziel als durch persönliche Visionen motiviert waren, bemerkte Seitz nervös, sie würden «beinahe den Sozialismus» anstreben. Künstler:innen der Nouvelle Tendance (international), von ZERO (Deutschland), Konstruktivist:innen der zweiten Generation (Henryk Berlewi), südamerikanische Neokonkrete (Jesús Rafael Soto, Hugo Demarco) und Mitglieder der französischen GRAV – Groupe de Recherche d'Art Visuel (François Morellet, Yvaral, Francisco Sobrino), alle angespornt von radikalen sozialen Ideen, waren «keine Revolutionäre, sondern strebten eine uneingeschränkte Zusammenarbeit mit der modernen Welt an».[12] Im Rahmen eines derart entpolitisierten Programms wurde Smiths Gemälde *Correspondence White-Orange* von 1964 ohne jeglichen Bezug zu den grösseren Affekten präsentiert, die es abbildet ❹.[13]

In diesem Zusammenhang lohnt sich ein Blick auf Smiths damalige Arbeitssituation. Nach seinem Umzug in eine grosse Atelierwohnung in der East 19th Street in New York 1964 nahm er seine frühere Freundschaft mit der in Kuba geborenen Künstlerin Carmen Herrera wieder auf, die nun eine unmittelbare Nachbarin wurde und deren Arbeit ihn darin bestärkte, den Effekt des scheinbar gekrümmten Raums in den Tondo-Gemälden auf die Serie der rechteckigen, zweifarbig bemalten Leinwände zu übertragen, die als *Correspondences* bekannt sind. Herrera hatte Südamerika und ihr Heimatland Kuba ausgiebig bereist und häufig dort ausgestellt. Sie kannte die dortigen Strömungen der konkreten Kunst gut und hatte, bevor sie nach New York zurückkehrte, zwischen 1948 und 1954 in Paris gelebt und gearbeitet. Hier hatte sie gemeinsam mit Pionier:innen der internationalen Moderne im Salon des Réalités Nouvelles ausgestellt, der damals wichtigsten europäischen Bühne für konkret und ungegenständlich arbeitende Künstler:innen wie Sonia Delaunay, Alberto Magnelli, Arp, Domela, Jean Gorin und Auguste Herbin ❺.[14] Diese Informationsnetzwerke waren wichtig. Durch Herrera und durch die Erfahrung mit der Zürcher Ausstellung war Smith bald mit den um die Jahrhundertmitte wichtigsten Praktiken und Richtungen der europäischen und lateinamerikanischen Kunst vertraut.

Ausserdem hatten Smiths Interview mit d'Arcy Hayman und die mittlerweile begonnene *Correspondence*-Reihe seine internationale Präsenz noch vergrössert. *Art and Literature* hatte sich bis 1964 zu einem echten Prüfstein für englischsprachige Reflexionen über die und von den europäischen wie amerikanischen Avantgarden entwickelt. Die von dem amerikanischen Dichter John Ashbery, dem englischen Künstlerpaar Ann Dunn und Rodrigo Moynihan sowie der Schriftstellerin Sonia Orwell in der Schweiz publizierte Zeitschrift (mit Redaktionssitz in Paris) besass eine beträchtliche Reichweite und Relevanz. Smiths Interview erschien neben Texten von John Cage, André Masson, Georges Bataille, Robert Rauschenberg und Roland Barthes, die allesamt an der Spitze einer postnationalen Kontemporanität in der Kunst standen.[15] Dass er sich in dieser Gesellschaft befand, war vermutlich kaum misszuverstehen.

Tatsächlich sollte eine zweite prestigeträchtige Ausstellung in New York, die 1966 von dem jungen englischen Kritiker Lawrence Alloway für das Guggenheim Museum kuratiert wurde, Smiths Werk noch weiter internationalisieren. Alloway hatte in den 1950er-Jahren in London am Institute of Contemporary Arts gearbeitet und verfügte über ein ausgeprägtes Gespür für die modernistische Vergangenheit Europas sowie für die komplexen Manöver und Techniken der Malerei. Er hatte 1961 bereits eine kleine amerikanische Gruppenausstellung in der Galerie von Arthur Tooth in London gesehen und sich anerkennend über Smiths Beitrag geäussert.[16] Sobald er sich im Guggenheim

4 Leon Polk Smith, *Correspondence White-Orange*, 1964, Öl auf Leinwand | Oil on canvas, 91 × 173 cm, JP Morgan Chase Art Collection, New York, © 2023, ProLitteris, Zürich

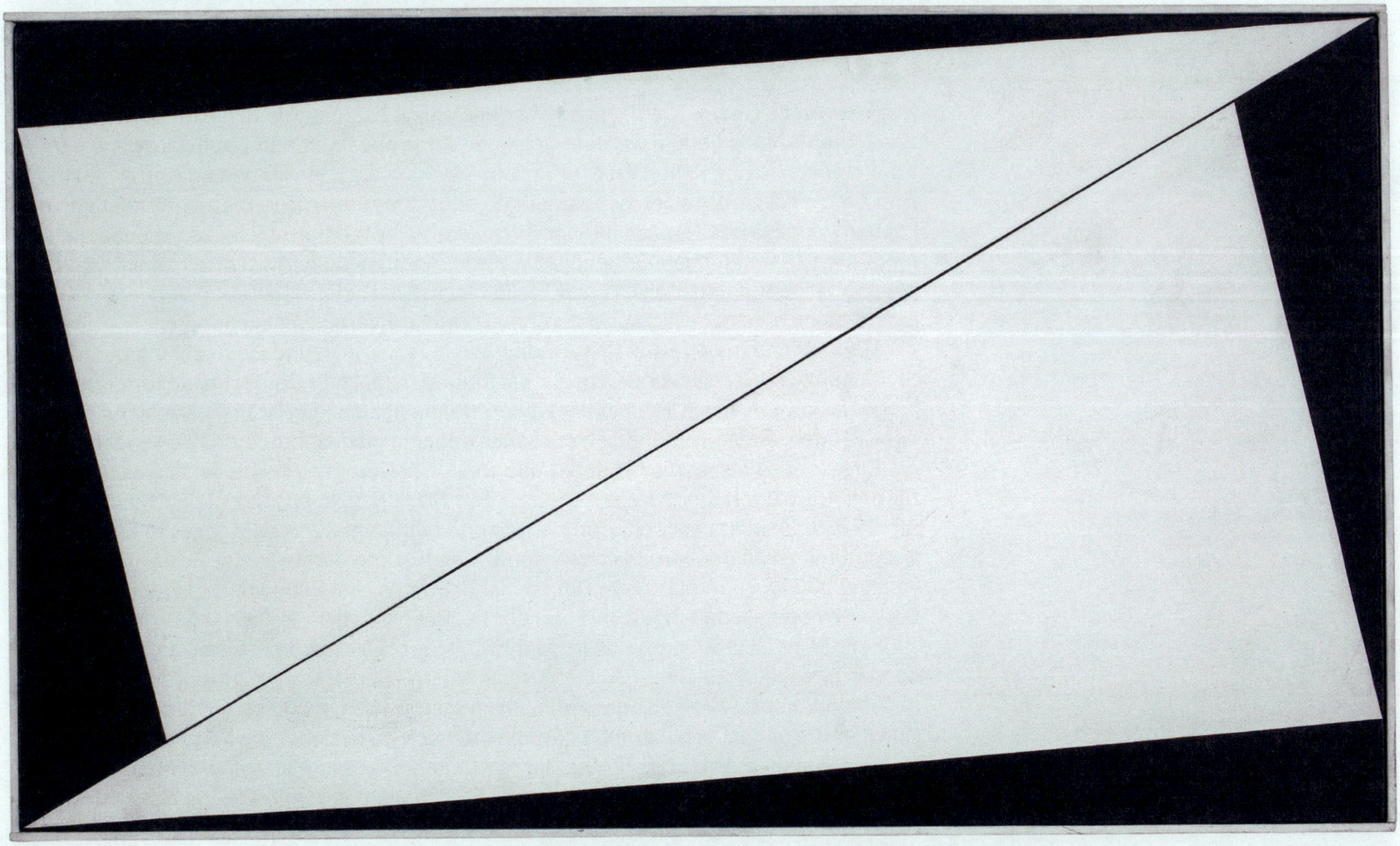

5 Carmen Herrera, *Equation*, 1958, Acryl auf Leinwand | Acrylic on canvas, 61 × 106,7 cm, Courtesy of Lisson Gallery, © 2023, ProLitteris, Zürich

installiert hatte, machte sich Alloway daran, Clement Greenbergs Kunstkritik unter die Lupe zu nehmen, derzufolge die USA Europa in der geschichtlichen Logik der Kunst immer weiter verdrängten, und Seitz' These von der Op-Art in ihrer jüngsten und popularisierenden Form zu widerlegen.

Das Verdienst von Alloways Ausführungen bestand darin, Smiths Werk (sowie das von Ellsworth Kelly, Ad Reinhardt und anderen) von Piet Mondrian, De Stijl und dem Konstruktivismus zu lösen und es irgendwo *zwischen* der strukturellen Präzision der früheren europäischen Moderne und dem, was international als generische Explosion der Hard-Edge-Malerei daherkam, zu verorten. Aus Alloways Sicht mobilisierte die systemische Malerei *sowohl* die hierarchischen Kompositionen, die einst in der konstruktivistischen und konkreten Kunst (Europa) zu finden waren, *als auch* die ganzheitlichen Tendenzen der Malerei, die nun als ein untergliedertes und unmoduliertes Feld (USA) verstanden wurde. Alloway zufolge zeugten die klaren Kanten, die technische Sauberkeit und die Flächigkeit von Smiths neuen Arbeiten in erster Linie von deren materieller Natur und Objekthaftigkeit, die an einem ganzen Schwung an Shaped Canvases von Künstlern wie Frank Stella, Robert Mangold, Kenneth Noland und Smith selbst anschaulich gemacht wurde. Darüber hinaus waren Smiths Tondi und seine rechteckigen *Correspondences* ebenso wie andere systemische Werke nicht als Geometrie oder Klassizismus, auch nicht als platonischer oder pythagoreischer Fundamentalismus, sondern als «menschliche Angebote» zu sehen. Die eigentliche Idee des Systems selbst «ergibt sich aus der Präsenz des Kunstwerks», aus seiner Eigenschaft als motiviertes Projekt und als Ding. Ein System könne sich auch aus der Entscheidung des Künstlers oder der Künstlerin entwickeln, in Gruppen oder Serien zu arbeiten, oder aus der Ausarbeitung von Perioden. Wie Alloway es ausdrückte, «konstituiert der Gang des Bildes ein System». Wiederholung «gibt der Syntax wieder Sinn». Systemische Malerei «öffnet das Kunstobjekt für Emotion und moralisches Empfinden». Gleichwohl bleibt das Kunstwerk «ein faktisches Abbild».[17]

Alloways Zweiheiten hier sind fast dieselben wie die von Leon Polk Smith. Raum und Form – Smiths eigene Begriffe für den Kontrapunkt von Projekt und Ding – zeugen vom instinktiven Verständnis des Künstlers für ebendiese dialektische Spannung im Werk. Tatsächlich erreichte diese Spannung ihren Höhepunkt und ihre Vollendung in einer neuen Serie namens *Constellations,* die 1967 begann, sich bis in die 1970er-Jahre hinein erstreckte und in der Smith die expansive Verräumlichung des Kunstwerks auf der Grundlage harter materieller Fakten auf eine neue Ebene hob. Wir sehen in diesen Werken fast kosmische Geometrien – grosse bogenförmige Krümmungen, die im physischen Werk ihren Anfang finden, vor dem geistigen Auge aber weit darüber hinausgehen. Wie Kurator:innen festgestellt haben, erfordern Smiths reale Leinwände und Konstruktionen, sind sie einmal gemacht, keine festgelegte oder unveränderliche Betrachterrelation und können (gemäss den Notizen auf der Rückseite vieler Werke) in einer von drei oder vier möglichen Ausrichtungen aufgehängt werden. Antigravitation wird erreicht, während das physische Werk greifbar an Ort und Stelle bleibt. Etwas der Konkretion Verwandtes erlangte somit eine neuartige und durchaus originäre Veranschaulichung ❻.

Seither haben begeisterte Kurator:innen in Frankreich und Deutschland Leon Polk Smith ganz unterschiedliche Orte zur Verfügung gestellt. In Deutschland kuratierte der junge Lucius Grisebach 1984 in der Neuen Nationalgalerie in Berlin eine Ausstellung seiner Collagen, einem vornehmlich europäischen und insbesondere deutschen Medium. Als Direktor des Museums für Kunst und Design in Nürnberg sorgte er fünf Jahre später für den Ankauf von Smiths Werk *Green – Two Black Edges,* das beispielhaft die Experimente des Künstlers mit scharfen Kanten und bemalten Rahmen zeigt ❼. In Frankreich wurde Smith, von der bereits erwähnten Unterstützung durch Denise René abgesehen, weniger häufig gewürdigt als in Deutschland. Pontus Hultén bewunderte seine *Victory Boogie Woogie*-Herleitungen im Zuge der riesigen Ausstellung *Paris – New York 1908–1968* im Centre Pompidou im Mai 1977.[18] Erst 1989 wurde in Ludwigshafen und dann in Grenoble von Jean-Paul Monery und Serge Lemoine eine grosse Ausstellung mit einundneunzig Werken von Smith zusammengestellt. Zu diesem Zeitpunkt war der Künstler dreiundachtzig Jahre alt und dachte noch immer über die Eingebungen nach, die sein Werk seit Mitte der 1940er-Jahre prägten. Es ist an der Zeit und angemessen, dass eine Zusammenführung von Smiths Werdegang mit der im Europa der Jahrhundertmitte entstandenen, sich stetig weiterentwickelnden Dialektik des Materiellen und Metaphysischen – ja sogar Kosmischen –, heute erneut hier in Zürich stattfindet.

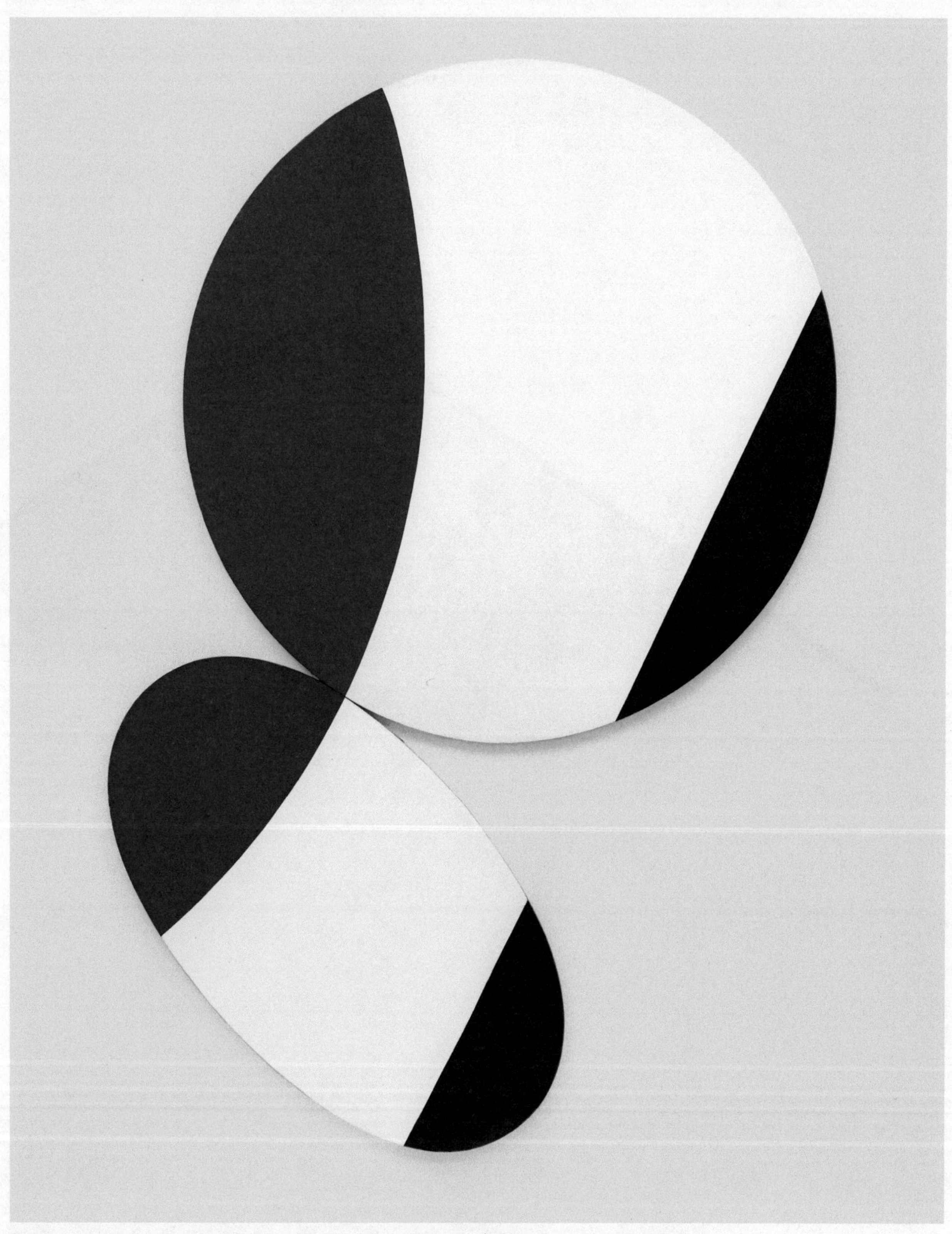

❻ Leon Polk Smith, *Constellation Milky Way*, 1970, Acryl auf Leinwand | Acrylic on canvas, 203 × 305 cm, National Gallery of Art, Washington, D.C., © 2023, ProLitteris, Zürich

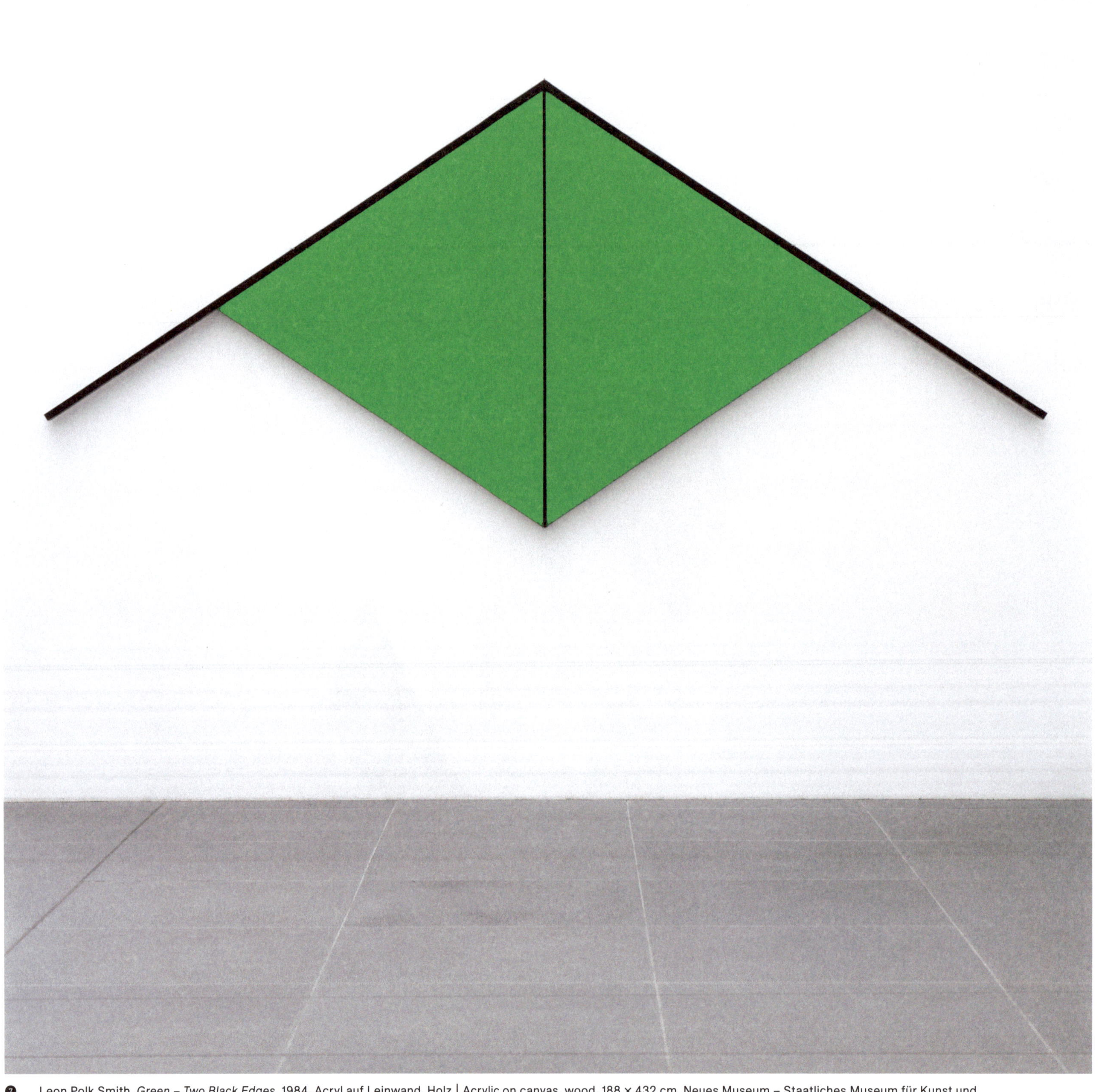

❼ Leon Polk Smith, *Green – Two Black Edges*, 1984, Acryl auf Leinwand, Holz | Acrylic on canvas, wood, 188 × 432 cm, Neues Museum – Staatliches Museum für Kunst und Design, Nürnberg, Foto | Photo: Neues Museum Nürnberg, © 2023, ProLitteris, Zürich

became to address Clement Greenberg's art criticism in which the US was steadily displacing Europe in the historical logic of art, as well as to refute Seitz's thesis of Op Art in its recent and popularizing form.

The merit of Alloway's argument was to detach Smith's work (and that of Ellsworth Kelly and Ad Reinhardt, among others) from Piet Mondrian, De Stijl, and Constructivism and to locate it somewhere *between* the structural precision of earlier European modernism and what appeared to be a generic explosion of Hard-edge painting internationally. Systemic painting for Alloway mobilized *both* the hierarchical form arrangements found in earlier Constructivist and Concrete Art (Europe) *and* the "wholistic" tendencies of painting now conceived of as a subdivided and uninflected field (the US). According to Alloway, the clean edges, technical neatness, and flat surfaces of Smith's new work testified first and foremost to its material nature and its identity as an object, exemplified by a spate of shaped canvases from the likes of Frank Stella, Robert Mangold, Kenneth Noland, and Smith himself. Further, Smith's tondo paintings as well as his rectangular *Correspondences* were to be seen, in common with other systemic works, not as geometry or classicism, nor as Platonic or Pythagorean fundamentalism, but "as human proposals." The very idea of a system then "follows from the presence of the work of art," from its identity as motivated project and as thing. A system could equally spring from the artist's decision to work in groups or runs of work, or in the elaboration of periods. As Alloway put it, "The run of the image constitutes a system." Repetition "returns meaning to the syntax." Systemic painting "opens the art object to emotion and the moral sense." Yet the work of art remains "a factual display."[17]

Alloway's dualities here are almost exactly Leon Polk Smith's own. Space and form—Smith's own terms for the counterpoint of project and thing—testify to the artist's instinctive grasp of just such a dialectical tension inside the work. Indeed, it was that tension that reached its climax and fulfilment in a new series called *Constellations*, begun in 1967 and extending through the 1970s, in which Smith took to a new level the expansive spatializing of the work of art from a basis of hard material fact. We see in those works almost cosmic geometries—large arcing curvatures that begin in the physical work yet extend in the mind's eye far beyond. As curators were coming to know, Smith's physical canvases and constructions, once made, require no fixed or absolute relation to the viewer and (according to notes made on the back of many works) can be hung in any one of three or four possible orientations. Antigravity is achieved, while the physical work remains palpably there. Something akin to Concretism thus acquired a novel—and surely original—exemplification ❻.

Since then, enthusiastic curators in France and Germany have accorded Leon Polk Smith various kinds of place. In Germany, the young Lucius Grisebach curated a show of his work in collage—a preeminently European and even German medium—at the Neue Nationalgalerie, Berlin, in 1984. As director of the Museum of Art and Design, Nuremberg, five years later he secured the purchase of the artist's *Green – Two Black Edges* in which Smith's experiments with sharp edges and painted frames can be seen ❼. In France, aside from the already mentioned support of Denise René, Smith has been less often acknowledged than in Germany. Pontus Hultén paid lip service to his *Victory Boogie Woogie* derivations for the Pompidou Centre's massive *Paris-New York 1908–1968* show in May 1977.[18] It was not until 1989, in Ludwigshafen and then Grenoble, that a major show of ninety-one of Smith's works was assembled by Jean-Paul Monery and Serge Lemoine. By then, the artist was eighty-three years old and still reflecting on the intuitions that since the mid-1940s had guided his work. It is timely and fitting that a meeting of Smith's career with the ever-evolving dialectic of the material and the metaphysical—even the cosmic—which evolved in Europe in mid-century, finds its articulation here in Zurich again today.

D

1 Leon Polk Smith Foundation, «Chronology», in: *Leon Polk Smith*, Lisson Gallery, New York 2017, S. 75.
2 Leon Polk Smith im Gespräch mit d'Arcy Hayman, abgedruckt in: Ina Prinz (Hrsg.), *Leon Polk Smith im Arithmeum*, Ausst.-Kat. Arithmeum Bonn, Bonn 2001, S. 6–17, hier S. 8.
3 Smith und Hayman, wie Anm. 2, S. 7.
4 Brief an Marianne Hoffmann, 20. Mai 1992, Archives of American Art.
5 Van Doesburgs Manifest zur konkreten Malerei wurde 1930 in Paris veröffentlicht. Zur Konkretion bei Arp and Kandinsky siehe: Brandon Taylor, *The Life of Forms in Art*, London / New York 2020, S. 98 ff. und S. 187 f.
6 Max Bill, «konkrete kunst» zur Ausstellung *zürcher konkrete kunst*, 1949; in: Margit Weinberg Staber (Hrsg.), *Konkrete Kunst: Manifeste und Künstlertexte*, Zürich 2001, S. 32.
7 Jules Langsner, *Four Abstract Classicists*, Ausst.-Kat. Los Angeles County Museum of Art, Los Angeles 1959.
8 Madeleine Chalette Lejwa schenkte Smiths Tondo *Anitou* (1958) später dem Museum of Modern Art.
9 Seitz weist darauf hin, dass die Art von Energie, die insbesondere durch Schwarz- und Weisswerte erzeugt werden, Gegenstand kontrollierter Experimente unter der Einnahme von Meskalin oder LSD wurden, und erwähnt in diesem Kontext Gerald Oster, den späteren Autor von *The Science of Moiré Patterns*, 1972. Siehe: William Seitz, *The Responsive Eye*, Ausst.-Kat. Museum of Modern Art, New York 1965, S. 31.
10 Wolfgang Köhler, *Gestalt Psychology: An Introduction to New Concepts in Modern Psychology*, New York 1947.
11 Maurice Merleau-Ponty, *Phénoménologie da la perception*, Paris 1945.
12 Seitz, *The Responsive Eye* (wie Anm. 9), S. 41.
13 Ein in dieser Hinsicht adäquates Gegenstück zu Seitz' Beschäftigung mit optischen Fragen war das 1967 veröffentlichte umfangreiche Forschungsprojekt des Bildhauers George Rickey: Darin verortete er seine Zeitgenoss:innen vor dem Hintergrund europäischer konstruktivistischer Konzepte, jedoch wiederum ungeachtet der verschiedenen Rollen, die nationale Kunstideologien in der Zeit seit 1917 spielten. Hier wurde Smith mit Künstler:innen wie Jean Arp (Elsass), Sophie Taeuber-Arp (Schweiz), Max Mahlmann (Deutschland), Richard Mortensen (Dänemark), Olle Baertling (Schweden), Arturo Bonfanti (Italien) sowie Anthony Hill und Victor Pasmore (Grossbritannien) zusammengeführt: als Exponent:innen von «Tangenten und Spannungen» – Kräften, die Farbformen anschwellen oder sich festklemmen liessen, quetschten oder eng an andere Formen anschmiegten, kopflastig erschienen oder tangential andere Formen oder den Rahmen touchierten; alles Werte, die eine gewisse «Instabilität» in der Gestaltung hervorrufen. Siehe: George Rickey, *Constructivism: Origins and Evolution*, New York 1967, S. 127–133.
14 Siehe: *Carmen Herrera: Lines of Sight*, Ausst.-Kat. Whitney Museum of American Art, New York 2016. Herrera war im Erscheinungsjahr 101 Jahre alt (sie starb 2022).
15 Im Frühjahr 1965 veröffentlichte Clement Greenberg seinen berühmten Aufsatz «Modernist Painting» in *Art and Literature*. Für ihn war der Anteil der europäischen abstrakten Kunst am amerikanischen Hard Edge eine Illusion. Ellsworth Kelly, Alexander Liberman, Jules Olitski, Paul Feeley und andere hätten ihre «hardness» nicht von Mondrian, dem Bauhaus, dem Suprematismus oder irgendetwas anderem geerbt, das vorher da war, so Greenberg, sondern von einer «softness» im Abstrakten Expressionismus, der seinerseits zwei höhere Tugenden an Hard Edge vererbt habe: «Offenheit und Klarheit». Greenbergs Aufsatz wurde 1960 zunächst in dem Radiosender Voice of America ausgestrahlt, bevor er in gedruckter Form erschien.
16 Lawrence Alloway, «London Letter», in: *Art International*, Bd. 2 (1961), S. 50 f.
17 Zitate von Alloway aus der Einführung zu: *Systemic Painting*, Ausst.-Kat. Guggenheim Museum, New York 1966, S. 11–21.
18 Siehe vor allem: Pontus Hultén, «Autour de Mondrian», in: *Paris – New York 1908–1968*, Ausst.-Kat. Centre Pompidou, Paris 1977, S. 570 ff.

E

1 Leon Polk Smith Foundation, "Chronology," *Leon Polk Smith*, Lisson Gallery (New York: Lisson Gallery, 2017), 75.
2 Leon Polk Smith and d'Arcy Hayman, "The Paintings of Leon Polk Smith," *Art and Literature: An International Review* 3 (Autumn–Winter 1964): 85.
3 Smith and Hayman, "Paintings of Leon Polk Smith," 83.
4 Letter to Marianne Hoffmann, 20 May 1992, Archives of American Art.
5 Van Doesburg's "Art Concret" manifestos were published in Paris in 1930. For "Concretion" in Arp and Kandinsky, see my *The Life of Forms in Art* (London and New York: Bloomsbury, 2020), 98ff and 187–8.
6 Max Bill, "konkrete kunst," for the exhibition *zürcher konkrete kunst*, 1949, in *Konkrete Kunst: Manifeste und Kunstlertexte*, ed. Margit Weinberg Staber (Zurich: Museum Haus Konstruktiv, 2001), 32.
7 Jules Langsner, *Four Abstract Classicists*, exh. cat. Los Angeles County Museum of Art (Los Angeles: Los Angeles County Museum of Art, 1959).
8 Madeleine Chalette Lejwa would later donate Smith's tondo *Anitou*, 1958, to the Museum of Modern Art.
9 Seitz points out that the kinds of energy generated by black and white tonal units in particular had become the subject of controlled experiments with the ingestion of mescaline or LSD, citing Gerald Oster, later the author of *The Science of Moiré Patterns*, 1972. See *The Responsive Eye*, exh. cat. Museum of Modern Art (New York: Museum of Modern Art, 1965), 31.
10 Wolfgang Köhler, *Gestalt Psychology: An Introduction to New Concepts in Modern Psychology* (New York: Liverlight Publishing, 1947).
11 Maurice Merleau-Ponty, *Phénoménologie da la perception* (Paris: Gallimard, 1945).
12 Seitz, *Responsive Eye*, 41.
13 A counterpart to Seitz's opticality on the plane was the extensive research project by the sculptor George Rickey, published in 1967, which placed contemporaries against the backdrop of European Constructivist concepts, yet shorn once more of the various parts played by national ideologies of art in the period since 1917. Here, Smith was grouped with artists such as Jean Arp (Alsace), Sophie Taeuber-Arp (Switzerland), Max Mahlmann (Germany), Richard Mortensen (Denmark), Olle Baertling (Sweden), Arturo Bonfanti (Italy), and Anthony Hill and Victor Pasmore (Great Britain) as exponents of "tangents and pressures"—forces that made color forms swell, wedge, squeeze, or tightly fit against other forms, appear top-heavy or graze tangentially against others or against the frame: all values productive of a certain "instability" in design. See George Rickey, *Constructivism: Origins and Evolution* (New York: George Braziller, 1967), 127–33.
14 See *Carmen Herrera: Lines of Sight*, exh. cat. Whitney Museum of American Art (New York: Whitney Museum of American Art, 2016), 2016 being the year in which she was 101 (she died in 2022).
15 Greenberg would publish his celebrated "Modernist Painting" essay in *Art and Literature* in the spring of 1965. For him, the debt of American Hard-edge to European abstract art was an illusion. Ellsworth Kelly, Alexander Liberman, Jules Olitski, Paul Feeley and others "have not inherited [their "hardness"] from Mondrian, the Bauhaus, Suprematism, or anything else that came before," suggested Greenberg, but from a "softness" in Abstract Expressionism that itself bequeathed to Hard-edge two higher virtues: "openness and clarity." Greenberg's article began as a radio broadcast for Voice of America in 1960 before its appearance in print.
16 Lawrence Alloway, "London Letter," *Art International*, vol. 2 (1961): 50–51.
17 Citations from Alloway, "Introduction," *Systemic Painting*, exh. cat. Guggenheim Museum (New York: Guggenheim Museum, 1966), 11–21.
18 See in particular Pontus Hultén, "Autour de Mondrian," *Paris-New York 1908–1968*, exh. cat. Centre Pompidou (Paris: Centre Pompidou, 1977), 570 ff.

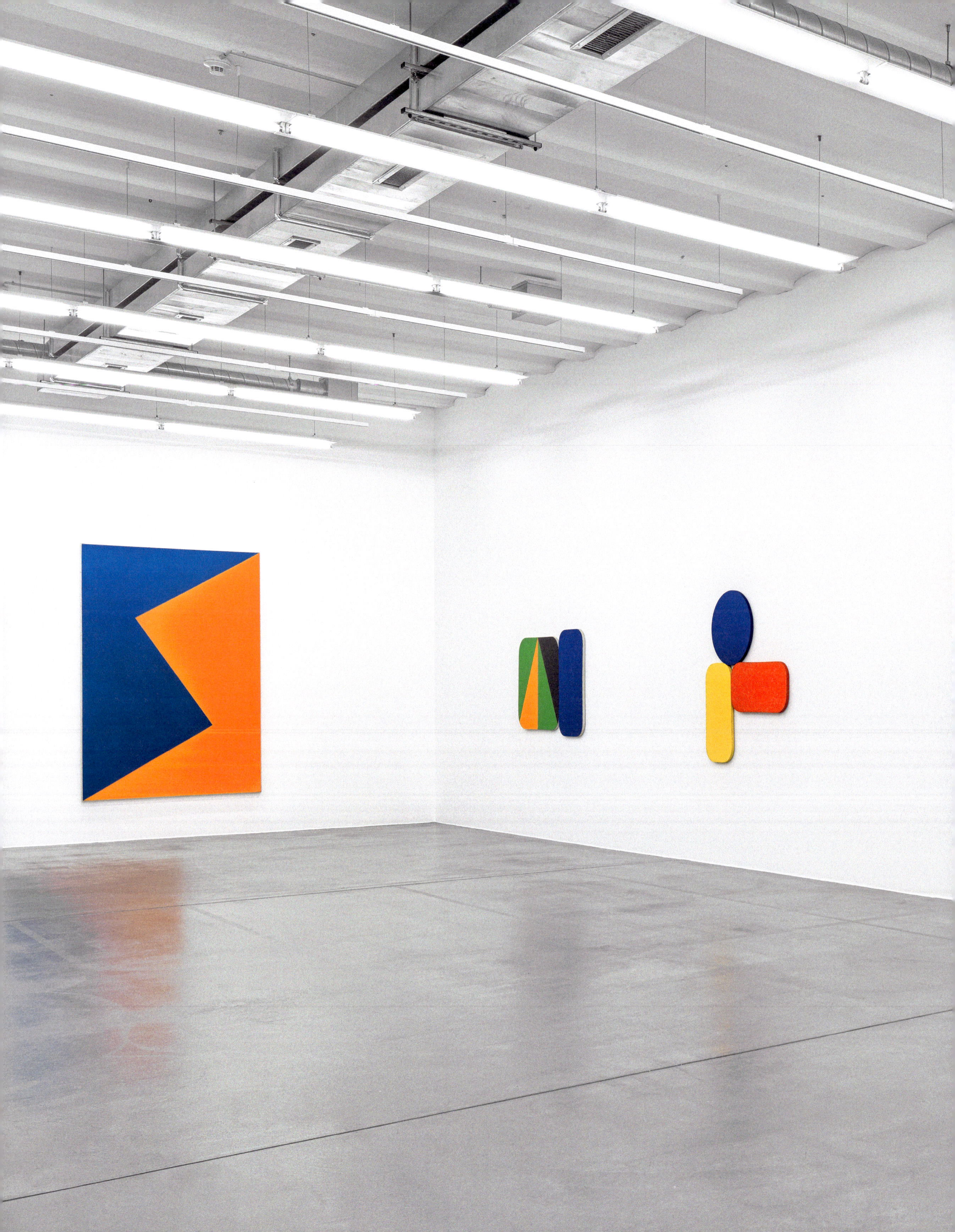

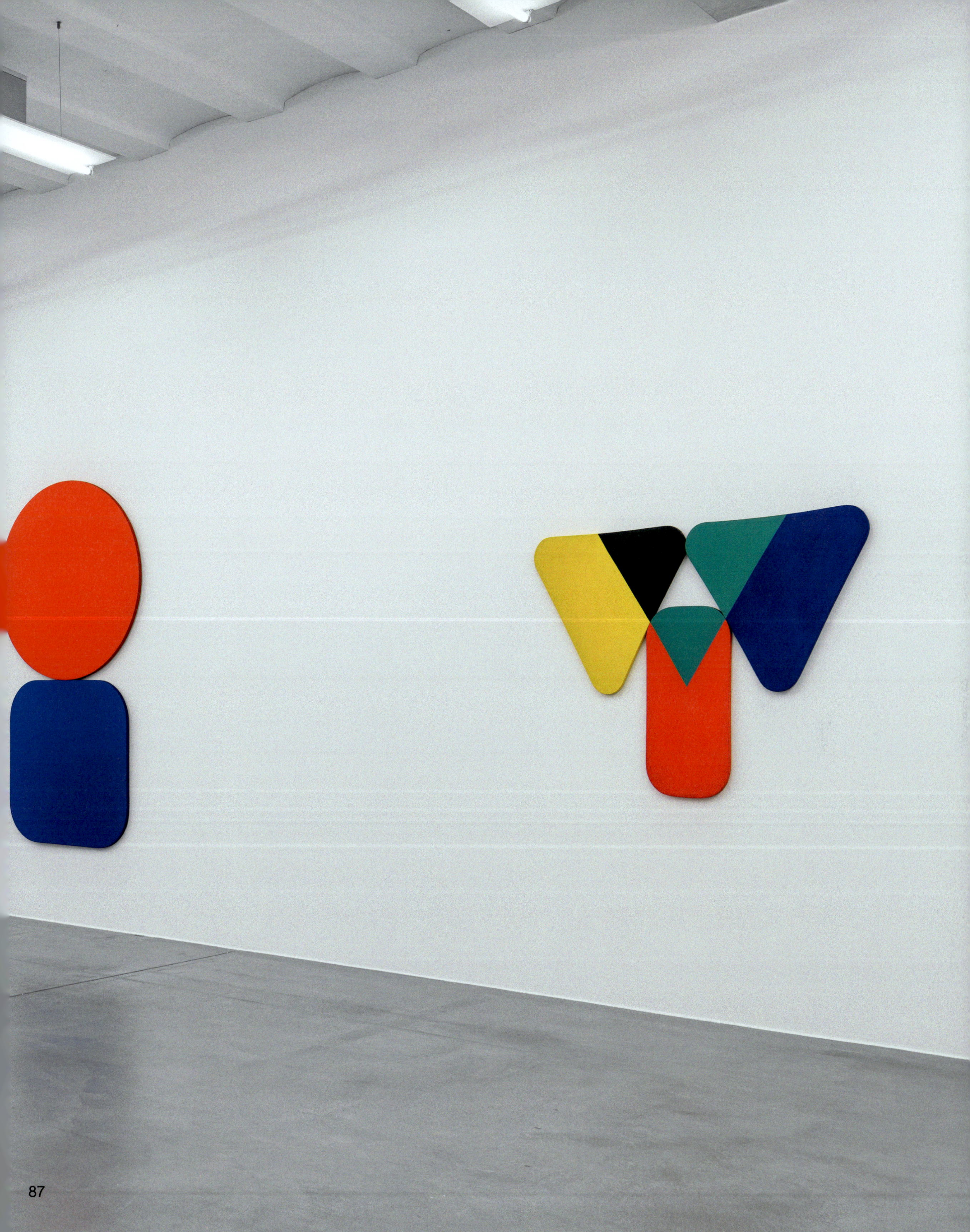

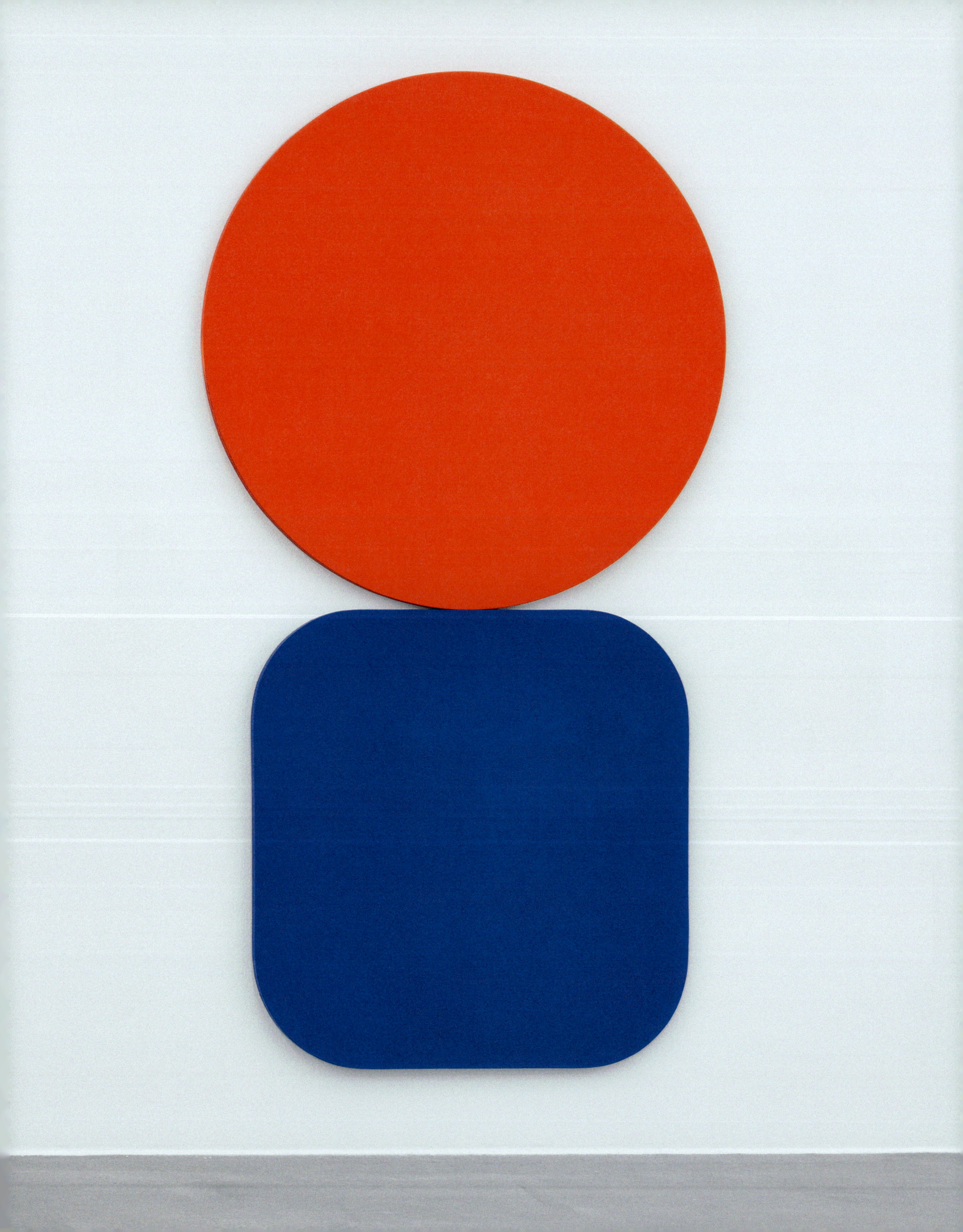

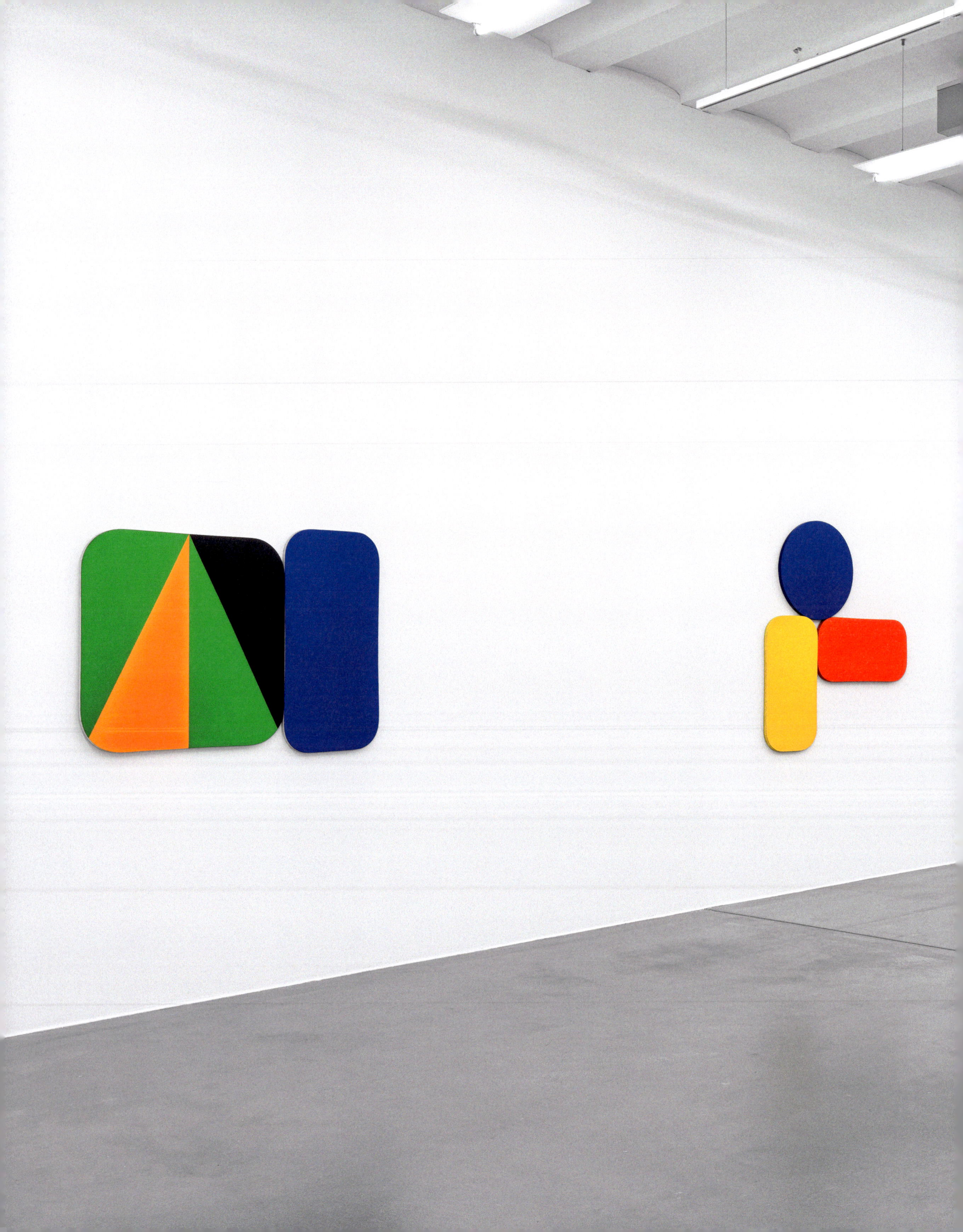

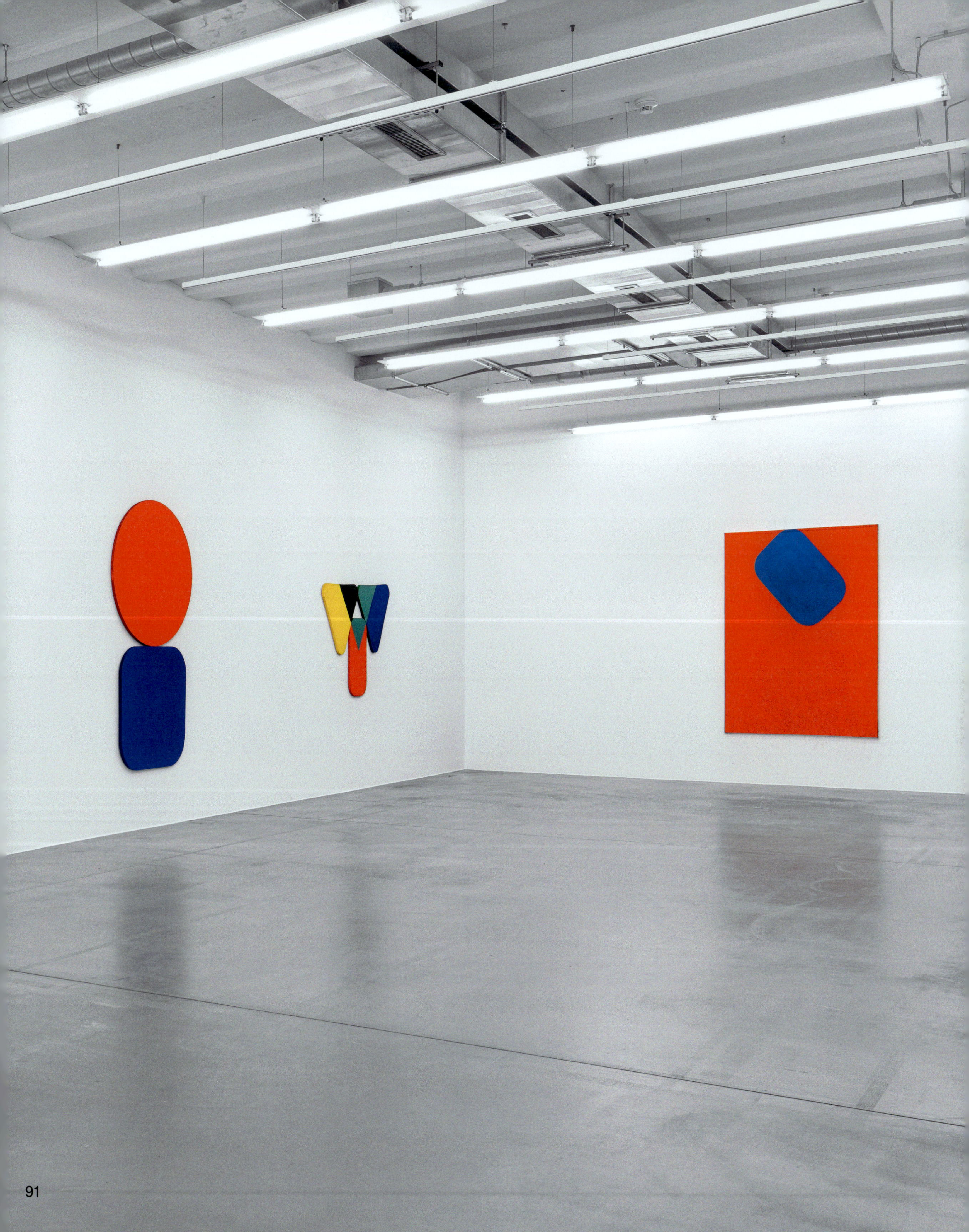

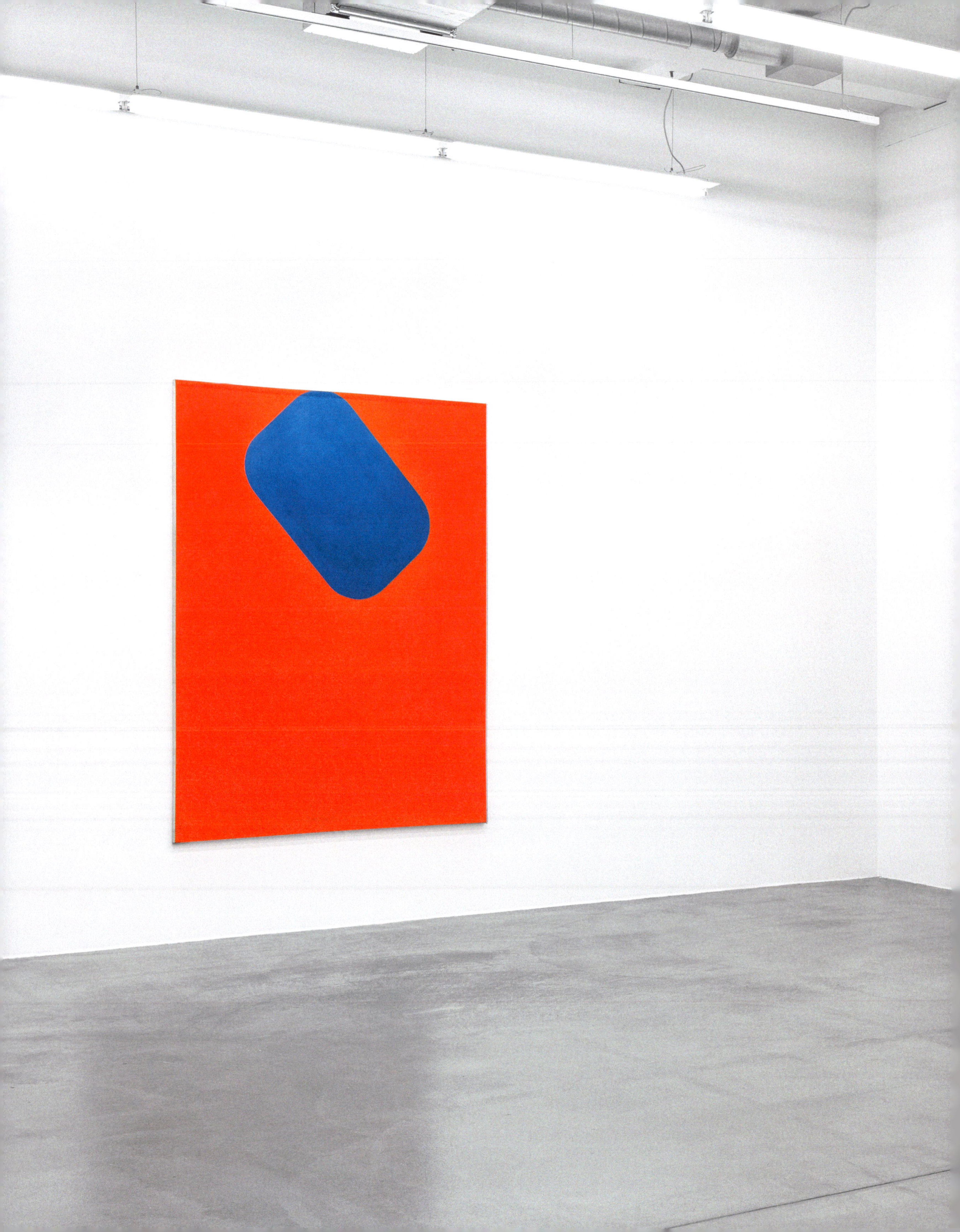

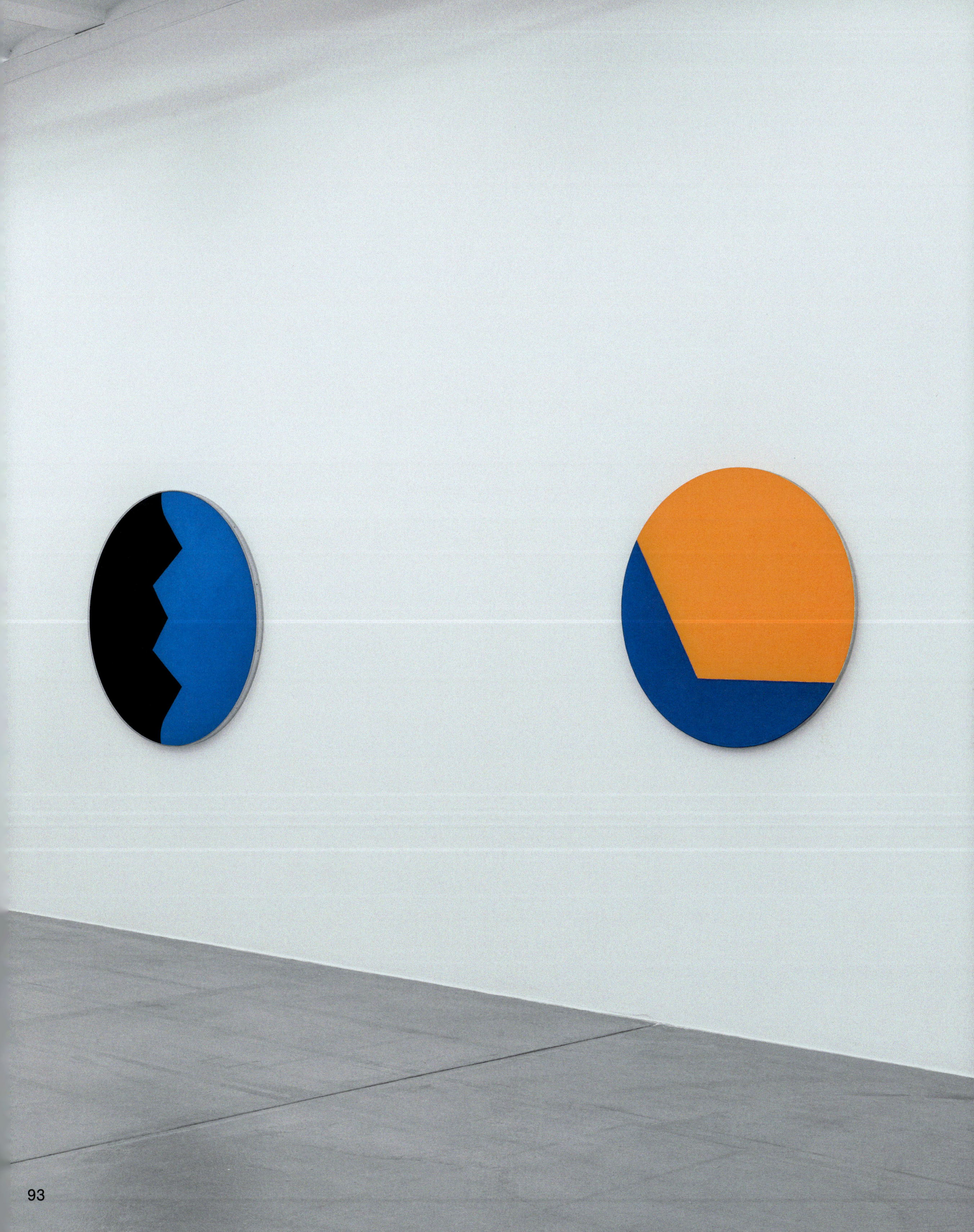

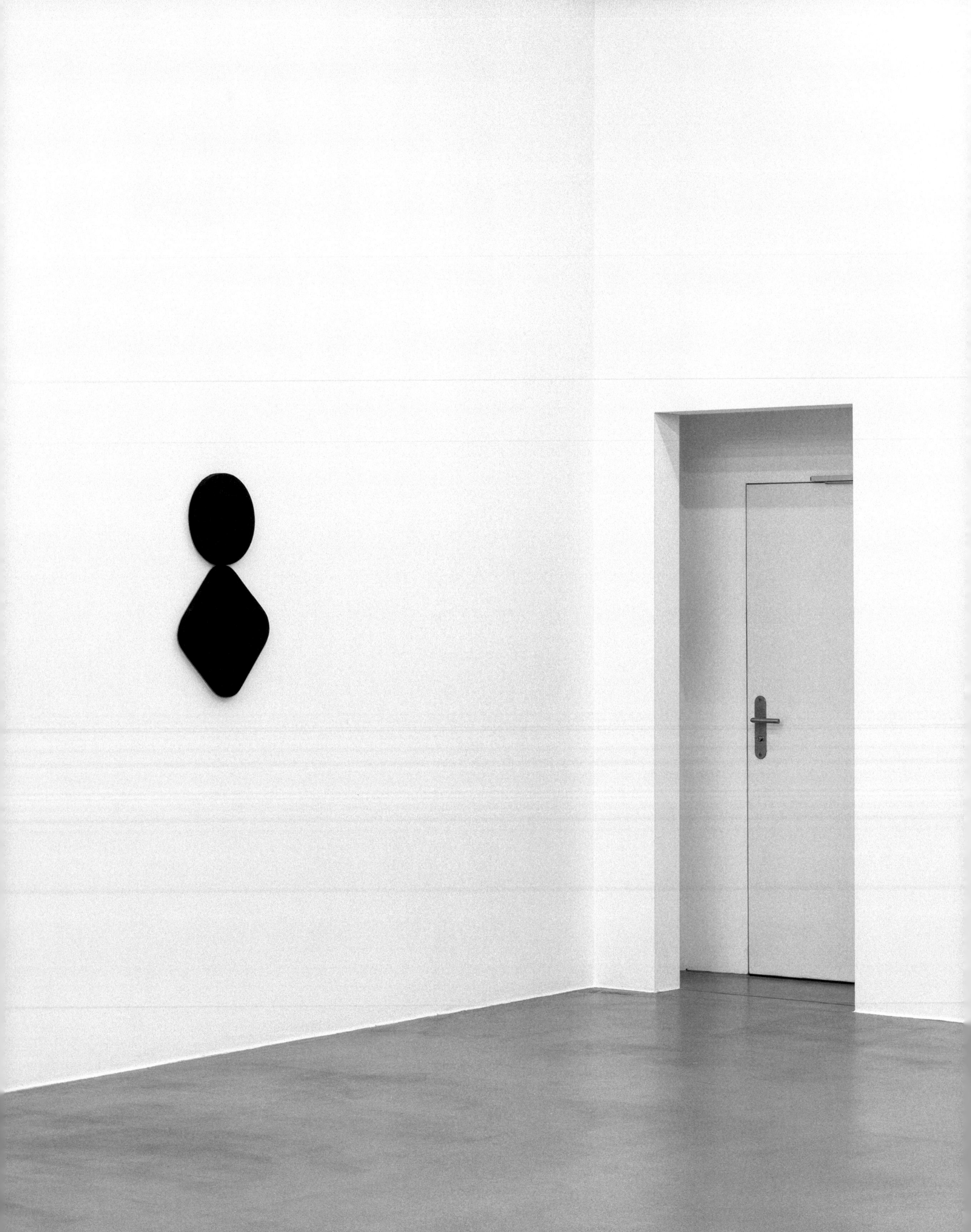

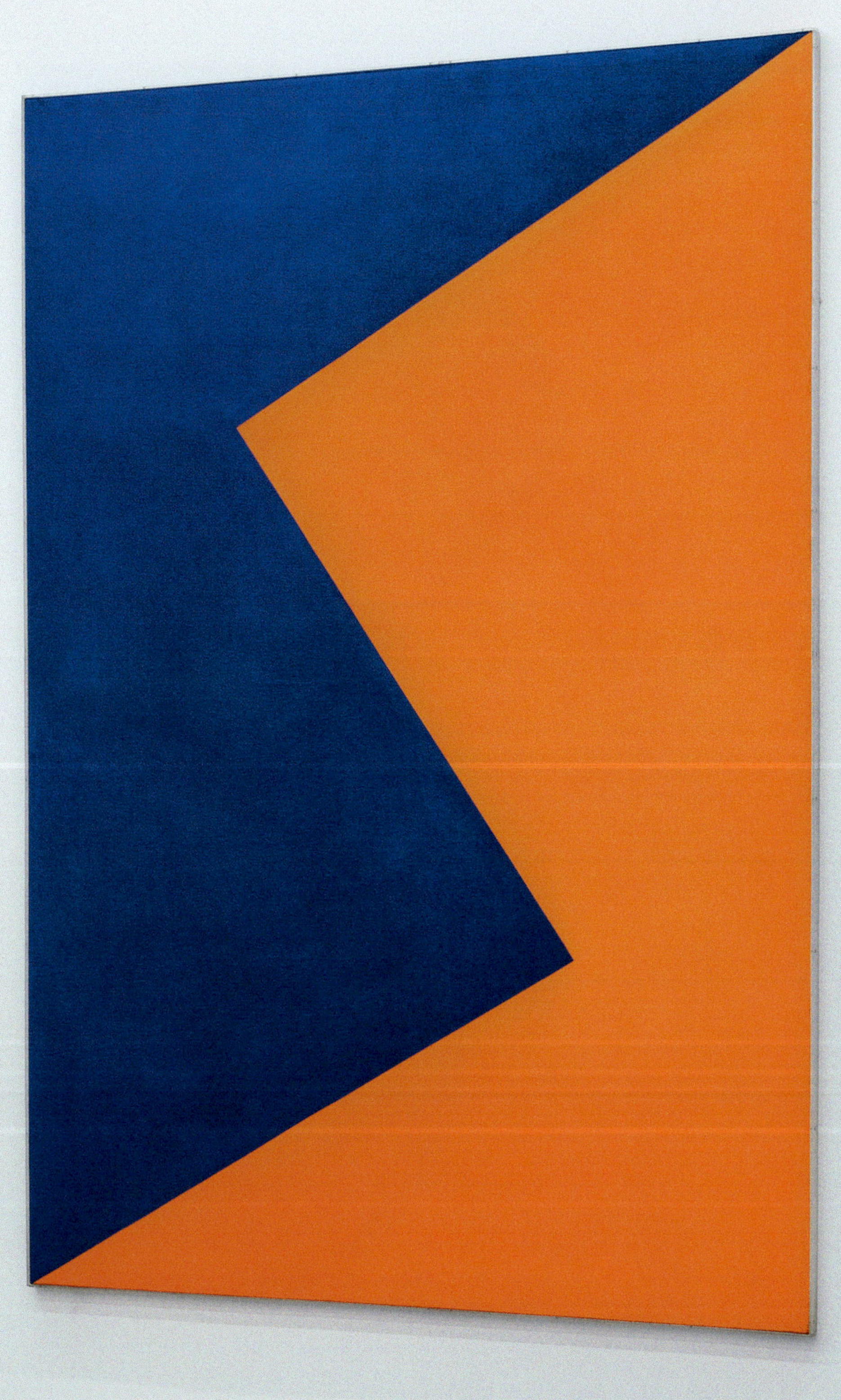

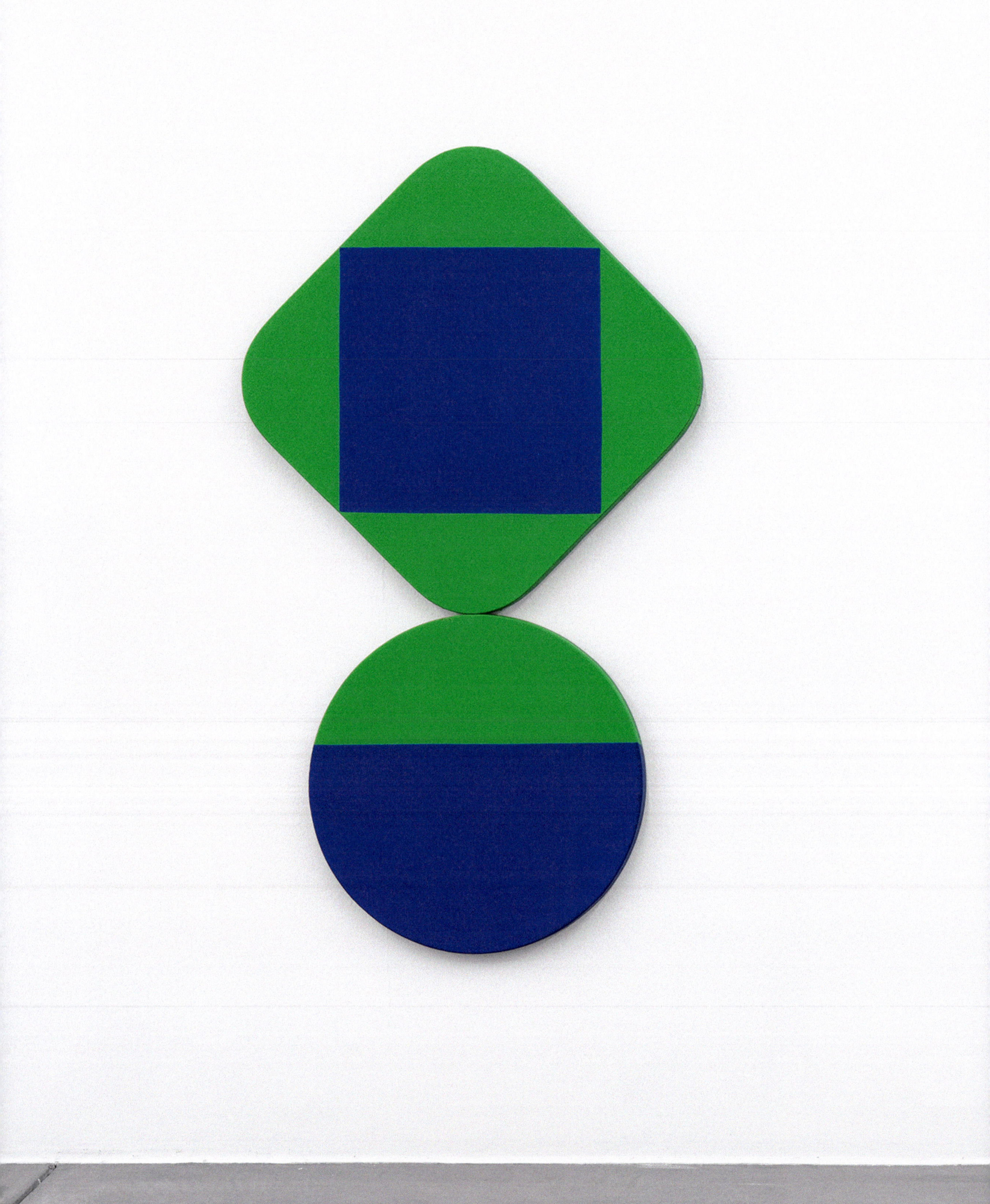

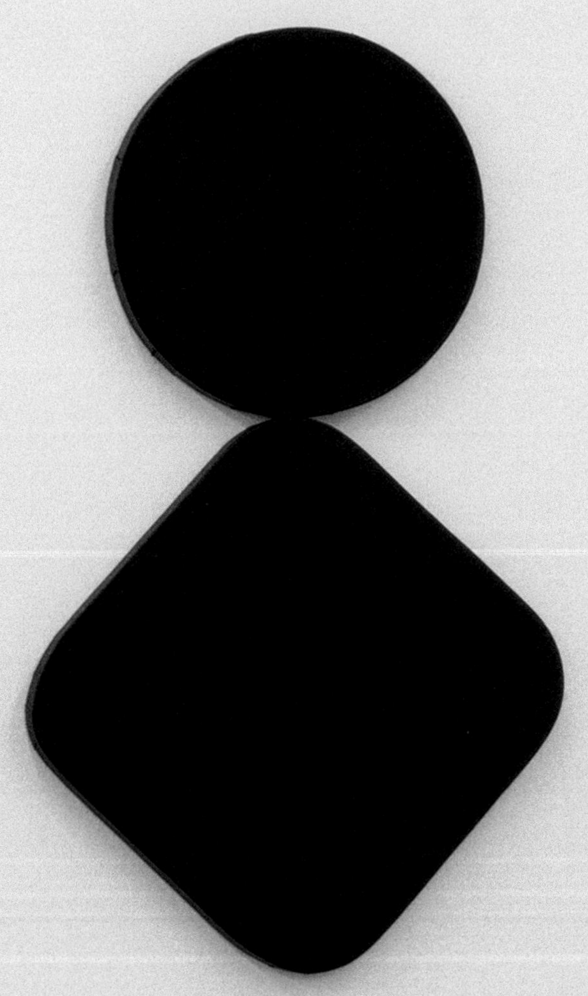

Leon Polk Smith

Margit Weinberg Staber

D

Auf der Titelseite des Katalogs, den das Brooklyn Museum 1996, im Todesjahr des Künstlers, publizierte, liest man: *Leon Polk Smith – American Painter.*[1] Er verstand sich bewusst als solcher und bezog sich dezidiert auf sein indigenes Erbe als Angehöriger der Native Americans. Wer war dieser Maler? Inspiriert durch die europäische Avantgarde und Mitspieler der New Yorker Szene in der Nachkriegszeit, ist er irgendwie unserem Kunstbewusstsein entglitten.

Von den 1960er-Jahren an gehörte Smith im Umfeld der aufblühenden Hard-Edge-Malerei und Minimal Art gemeinsam mit Ellsworth Kelly zu den Erfinderfiguren, die sich daranmachten, Gegengewichte zu setzen zur expressiven Wucht des Action Painting und des Abstrakten Expressionismus. In Europa brandeten damals die heftigen Wellen des Tachismus. Auch hierzu gab es Gegentendenzen, etwa die Zero-Gruppe in Deutschland. Fragt man Kenner der damaligen Szene, dann nennen sie die Namen Ellsworth Kelly und Frank Stella, vielleicht noch Kenneth Noland und Donald Judd. Auf die Frage nach Leon Polk Smith erntet man ein erstauntes Kopfschütteln.

Trotzdem ist sein Ausstellungsverzeichnis auch in Europa eindrücklich. Die Neue Nationalgalerie in Berlin zeigte 1984 die erste europäische Einzelausstellung; 1989 folgten das Wilhelm-Hack-Museum in Ludwigshafen und das Musée de Grenoble. Drei Jahre nach dem Tod des Malers liess Ludwigshafen 1999 eine *Hommage* folgen. Auch renommierte Galerien standen nicht hintenan, in New York, in Deutschland und in der Schweiz. Die Kunsthalle Bern, die Kunstmuseen Basel und Winterthur sowie St. Gallen wurden auf ihn aufmerksam.[2] Vor allem aber war er mit weiteren Beispielen der New Art aus Amerika bereits 1960 in der internationalen Übersichtsausstellung *konkrete kunst – 50 jahre entwicklung* im Helmhaus Zürich mit dabei.[3] Jahrelang hatte Max Bill auf diese retrospektive Schau hingearbeitet, die von der Avantgarde zu Beginn des 20. Jahrhunderts bis in die Gegenwart der 1960er-Jahre führte. Sie sollte ein Beweis sein für die Aktualität und Internationalität der Bewegung.

Die Ausstellung im Helmhaus (damals auch vom Kunsthaus Zürich genutzt) war meine erste umfangreiche kuratorische Aufgabe, an der ich im Auftrag von Max Bill mitwirken und den Katalog betreuen konnte: eine Chronologie, zurück bis zu Malewitsch, Kandinsky, Mondrian. In hohem, schmalem Format mit durchlaufendem Text entworfen, parallel zu allen reproduzierten Exponaten, war die Publikation ein beispielhaftes Produkt funktionaler Typografie. Im Kreis der Zürcher Konkreten blieb Bills unorthodoxe Sicht auf die von ihm auch theoretisch alimentierte konkrete Kunst nicht ohne Kritik. Für ihn gehörten Hard Edge und Minimal Art zu der sich anbahnenden Offenheit. Die Botschaft von jenseits des Atlantiks kam in erfrischend kreativer Energie mit ins Spiel. Leon Polk Smith einer der ihren. In den 1940er-Jahren hatte er nach figurativen Anfängen eine Bildergruppe im Stil von Mondrian geschaffen, er war mit van Doesburg vertraut, vom Theoriegebäude der bereits zur Klassik der Moderne zählenden Generation wollte er nichts wissen. Das Werk von Hans Arp und Constantin Brancusi, Bildhauern einer kurvilinearen organischen Formenwelt, bezeichnete er als kreativ erhellendes Vorbild.

Leon Polk Smith kam 1906 in Chickasha zur Welt, im damals noch unabhängigen «Indian Territory». Kurz darauf wurde es dem Bundesstaat Oklahoma einverleibt. Seine Familie war verwandt mit dem Stamm der Cherokee. Dieses indigene Erbe, so sagte er selbst, sei ihm eingeboren, habe ihn als Künstler unvergesslich geprägt. Es verband sich mit seiner Zugehörigkeit zur amerikanischen Avantgarde in der zweiten Hälfte des 20. Jahrhunderts. An allen einschlägigen Ausstellungen dieser Jahre in Amerika nahm er teil. Ich erinnere mich an *The Responsive Eye* 1965 im Museum of Modern Art in New York und 1966 *Systemic Painting* im Guggenheim Museum; 1968 *Plus by Minus: Today's Half Century* in der Albright-Knox Art Gallery in Buffalo. Als junge Kritikerin reiste ich Mitte der 1960er-Jahre nach New York. Selbstverständlich war auch die zur gleichen Zeit die Kunstwelt aufschreckende Pop-Art ein Objekt meiner Neugier. Die Querverbindungen beider Tendenzen, wie man sie auch bei Leon Polk Smith erahnen kann, forderten mein Interesse heraus. Ein spannendes Thema, bis heute kaum erforscht. Niemand war damals schon berühmt; man war ein gerne gesehener Gast aus der Schweiz auf der Suche nach Neuem, eine Empfehlung führte zur nächsten. So konnte ich auch in die legendäre Factory von Andy Warhol am Union Square einen Blick werfen. Aber Leon Polk Smith ist mir entgangen. Rückblickend

E The title page of the catalogue published by the Brooklyn Museum in 1996, the year of the artist's death, reads *Leon Polk Smith: American Painter.*[1] This was how Smith consciously saw himself, while decidedly making reference to his Indigenous heritage as a Native American. Who was this painter? Inspired by the European avant-garde, he was a player on the New York scene in the post-war period, yet he somehow slipped off our art radar.

From the 1960s onward, Smith, along with Ellsworth Kelly, was among the inventive figures in the milieu of the burgeoning Hard-edge Painting and Minimal Art movements, setting out to counterbalance the expressive force of Action Painting and Abstract Expressionism. Back then, Tachisme was making waves in Europe. There were also opposing movements, such as the Zero group in Germany. When those who knew the scene at the time are asked, they mention the names Ellsworth Kelly and Frank Stella, then perhaps Kenneth Noland and Donald Judd. Questions about Leon Polk Smith yield only bewildered head-shaking.

Nevertheless, Smith's list of exhibitions, even European ones, is impressive. Neue Nationalgalerie in Berlin presented his first European solo exhibition in 1984; the Wilhelm-Hack-Museum in Ludwigshafen and Musée de Grenoble followed in 1989. Three years after the painter's death, the museum in Ludwigshafen added a homage in 1999. Renowned galleries also did not shy away—not in New York, Germany, or Switzerland. Kunsthalle Bern, Kunstmuseum Basel, Kunstmuseum Winterthur, and Kunstmuseum St. Gallen all paid attention to him.[2] Most importantly, though, he had taken part in the international survey exhibition *konkrete kunst – 50 jahre entwicklung* (concrete art: 50 years of development) at Helmhaus in Zurich in 1960 with other examples of new art from the US.[3] Max Bill had spent years working on this retrospective show, which led from the avant-garde at the beginning of the twentieth century to the present day, meaning the 1960s. It was intended as evidence of how current and international the movement was.

The exhibition at Helmhaus (a venue also used by Kunsthaus Zürich at the time) was my first comprehensive curatorial undertaking. Max Bill had asked me to take over this duty and to oversee the catalogue: a chronology going back to Malevich, Kandinsky, and Mondrian. Designed in a tall narrow format with text running parallel to all the reproduced exhibited works throughout, the publication was an exemplary product of functional typography. In the Zurich Concretists' milieu, Bill's unorthodox view of Concrete Art, which he also supported with theory, did not go uncriticized. For him, Hard-edge and Minimal Art were part of an emerging openness. The message from across the Atlantic, which was incorporated as refreshingly creative energy, also played a role. Leon Polk Smith was part of this. After figurative beginnings, he had produced a group of paintings in the style of Mondrian in the 1940s. He was also familiar with van Doesburg, and he did not want to know anything about the body of theory from the generation already categorized as the classic modernists. He described the work of Hans Arp and Constantin Brancusi, who each sculpted a curvilinear organic world of forms, as models of creative enlightenment.

Leon Polk Smith was born in 1906 in Chickasha in what was then still independent Indian Territory. Shortly thereafter, it was incorporated into the State of Oklahoma. His family was related to the Cherokee tribe. This Indigenous heritage, as he said himself, unforgettably shaped him as an artist. In the second half of the twentieth century, this heritage and his affiliation with the American avant-garde intertwined. During those years, he took part in all relevant exhibitions in the US. I remember *The Responsive Eye* in 1965 at the Museum of Modern Art in New York, *Systemic Painting* in 1966 at the Guggenheim Museum, and *Plus by Minus: Today's Half Century* in 1968 at the Albright-Knox Art Gallery in Buffalo. I traveled to New York in the mid-1960s as a young critic. Naturally, I was also curious about Pop Art, which was rocking the art world at that time. The links between the two movements, which can also be glimpsed in Leon Polk Smith's work, piqued my interest. It is a fascinating topic that has still been little explored to this day. Nobody was famous yet. I was a welcome guest from Switzerland in search of something new. One recommendation led to the next. I was even able to take a look inside Andy Warhol's legendary Factory in Union Square, for instance. But Leon Polk Smith eluded me. Looking back, I wonder what it would have been like to be able to visit him in his studio and hear his opinion about his typical blend of different influences. Criticized as so-called cultural appropriation

frage ich mich, wie es wohl gewesen wäre, ihn in seinem Studio besuchen zu können und seine Sicht der für ihn typischen Verschmelzung verschiedener Einflüsse kennenzulernen. Heute in die Kritik sogenannter kultureller Aneignung geraten, ging es doch immer schon ganz selbstverständlich um inspirative Energien aus Gegenwart und Vergangenheit: Leon Polk Smith ein typischer Fall.

Bekannte Kritiker haben früh schon über ihn geschrieben, sowohl in seiner Heimat Amerika wie auch in Europa und insbesondere in Deutschland.[4] Smith selbst wies auf die Embleme und die Ornamentik seines Native America hin, auf deren intensive und direkte Koloristik, die Eigenart der geometrisierten Symbolik. Ich habe bei Wikipedia nachgeschaut und erstaunlich viel erfahren über die visuelle Kraft dieser Kultur. Die Berührungspunkte mit Leon Polk Smiths künstlerischer Identität sind unübersehbar.

Er erlebte eine im familiären Stammeskreis geborgene Jugend, gefolgt von harter, körperlicher Arbeit auf dem Acker oder im Strassenbau. Er war schon fast dreissig Jahre alt, als er zur Malerei fand. Er konnte sich zum Lehrer ausbilden und in entsprechenden Positionen tätig werden. 1939 reiste er zum ersten Mal nach Europa, lernte die Avantgarde kennen. Auch Mexiko war ein Reiseziel, was man seinen frühen figurativen Bildern ansieht. Im Stil von Mondrian schuf er Mitte der 1940er-Jahre eine Bildergruppe. New York wurde zu seinem Wohnsitz und er tauchte ein in die Kunstszene der als internationaler Hotspot sich etablierenden Metropole. New York wurde sein Lebensmittelpunkt: «New York hat ganz sicher meiner Seele und meinem Geist Freiheit gegeben [...]».[5] Auf seine Art blieb er ein Aussenseiter und verstand sich selbst in diesem Sinn.

Ohne Vorzeichnungen, direkt auf die Leinwand in perfekter, unmodulierter Flächigkeit aufgetragen, arbeitete er zunächst mit Ölfarbe, später wechselte er zu Acryl. Er habe vor der leeren Leinwand einfach den Pinsel in die Hand genommen und angefangen zu malen. Alle seine Bilder sind rahmenlos. Und er fügte hinzu, dass ihn eine Spiritualität getragen habe, die er auf seine Herkunft zurückführte. So äusserte er sich später sehr selbstbestimmt und auch persönlich bescheiden. Der amerikanische Kritiker Carter Ratcliff nannte es «The Geometry of Optimism».[6]

Das bildnerische Repertoire, das Smith im Lauf seiner langen künstlerischen Laufbahn entwickelt hat, zieht vor dem inneren Auge vorbei: der Kreis, das Oval und die Ellipse, Quadrat und Rechteck, auch in angeschnittener oder vom Maler erfundener, oft abgerundeter Form und oft mehrteilig aneinandergefügt zu einem Shaped Canvas. Die Nähe zu Ellsworth Kelly ist offensichtlich. Nachtwandlerisch präzis gesetzte, gerade, gebogene und abgewinkelte Linien in Schwarz auf weisser Fläche als alleinige Bildgrössen faszinierten ihn immer wieder von Neuem. Das intensive Kolorit bleibt lebenslang bestimmend. Eine späte Bildergruppe von 1994 heisst *Event in Blue,* auch *Event in Red* und *Event in Orange.* Zudem liebte er das Tondo als Bildformat. Man wundert sich, dass in der Literatur über Smith der Name von Fritz Glarner nicht auftaucht, dem Meister des Tondo, der in diesen Jahren in New York lebte. Smiths Bilderwelt liest sich wie eine Fortsetzungsgeschichte, die mit einem sich wiederholenden Vokabular immer wieder neue Kapitel aufschlägt. Kombinatorik versteht sich von selbst im Wirkungsfeld des Konstruktiv-Konkreten. Descartes fällt mir ein, hat der Philosoph doch schon vor Jahrhunderten lapidar festgehalten: Alles ist schon da, aber die Anordnung ist neu. Wo würde diese Sentenz besser passen als bei den Spielregeln der konstruktiv-konkreten Kunst? Leon Polk Smith macht da keine Ausnahme. Drei Elemente hätten ihn in der Kunst interessiert, erklärte er 1961: Linie, Farbe und das «concept of space».[7] Ja, was meint er mit «space», gehört doch zu seiner Malerei dezidiert die Flächigkeit auf der Leinwand? Er meint, so darf man annehmen, die von ihm angesprochene Spiritualität, die die Materialität eines Bildes über sich selbst hinaus beseelt.

Naheliegend – beim Betrachten seiner Bilder fällt die wiederkehrende kompositionelle Zweigeteiltheit auf: Die auf der einen Bildseite angelegten und angeschnittenen Elemente antworten auf ihr Gegenüber wie ein Echolot, das sich zurückmeldet. Die Teilformen können auch von aussen ins Bildfeld eindringen und regen den Betrachter zum Weiterdenken und Weiterspinnen der vom Maler vorgegebenen Fragmente an. Ich denke an ein Liebesgedicht von Goethe, in welchem er das zweigeteilte Blatt des Ginkgo-Baumes als Gleichnis für die innere Zwiesprache und das Unausgesprochene zwischen zwei Menschen heranzieht: «Fühlst

today, this has always been quite naturally about inspirational energy from the past and the present; Leon Polk Smith is a typical example.

Well-known critics wrote about him early on, both in his Native America and in Europe, particularly in Germany.[4] Smith referred to Native American emblems and ornamentation, their intense and direct coloring, and the distinctiveness of their geometrized symbolism. I took a look on Wikipedia and learned a surprising amount about how visually powerful this culture is. The points of contact with Leon Polk Smith's artistic identity are impossible to overlook.

Smith lived a sheltered life in the family tribe as a youth, followed by hard physical labor in the fields or in road construction. It was not until he was almost thirty years old that he discovered painting. He was able to train as a teacher and worked in several such positions. In 1939, he traveled to Europe for the first time and became acquainted with the avant-garde. Mexico was also a travel destination, as is evident in his early figurative paintings. In the mid-1940s, he produced a group of paintings in the style of Mondrian. New York was establishing itself as an international hotspot and he made this metropolis his home, immersing himself in its art scene. It became central to his life. "New York certainly gave freedom to my mind and spirit," he said.[5] In his own way, he remained an outsider, and that is how he saw himself.

At first, he worked with oil paint without any preliminary drawings, applying it directly to the canvas in perfect, unmodulated flatness. Later, he switched to acrylic. He said that he simply picked up a brush in front of the empty canvas and started to paint. All of his paintings are frameless. He also claimed to be carried by a spirituality, which he put down to his origins. He thus went on to express himself in a very self-determined way, yet with personal modesty. American critic Carter Ratcliff called this "the geometry of optimism."[6]

The visual repertoire that Smith developed over the course of his long career as an artist passes before my mind's eye: the circle, oval, ellipse, square, and the rectangle, the latter also in a truncated form or in one invented by the painter, often rounded and often comprising several parts joined together as shaped canvases. The closeness to Ellsworth Kelly is obvious. Straight, curved, and angled black lines placed as the sole visual parameters on a white field with somnambulistic precision continued to fascinate him anew. Intense coloring remained a determining factor throughout his life: One late group of paintings from 1994 includes works called *Event in Blue*, *Event in Red*, and *Event in Orange*. He also loved the tondo as a painting format. It is surprising that the name of Fritz Glarner, a master of the tondo who lived in New York during those years, does not appear in the literature on the artist. Smith's imagery reads like a serial that keeps opening new chapters with a repeating vocabulary. Combinatorics is a matter of course in the Constructivist-Concrete domain, and the philosopher Descartes comes to mind, who succinctly remarked centuries ago something similar to how everything is already there, but the arrangement is new. Where could this maxim be more at home than in the rules of Constructivist-Concrete Art? Leon Polk Smith is no exception. In 1961, he explained that three elements interested him in art: line, color, and the "concept of space."[7] But what did he mean by "space," since his paintings are decidedly two-dimensional on the canvas? It can be assumed that he meant the aforementioned spirituality, which transcends a painting's materiality.

One thing is obvious upon examination of his paintings: the recurring compositional dichotomy. The elements laid out and truncated on one side of the image respond to their counterparts like the return signals of an echo sounder. The partial forms can also penetrate the picture field from the outside and encourage the beholder to extrapolate the fragments provided by the painter, taking them further. I am reminded of a love poem by Goethe in which he uses the two-part leaf of the ginkgo tree as a metaphor for the inner dialogue and for what is unsaid between two people: "Is it not my songs' suggestion / That I'm one and also two?"[8] Yin-yang, the Chinese symbol for the notion that everything also has an opposite with which it forms a whole, may also be incorporated into this mental exercise. Is it not the case that every artwork has its own inherent virtual reality? Years ago, Susan Sontag said something about how images, when viewed, grow beyond themselves and open up perceptual spaces that we wander through, experience, consider, and make our

du nicht an meinen Liedern / Dass ich Eins und doppelt bin?»[8] Yin-Yang, das chinesische Symbol, das sagt, alles besitze auch sein Gegenteil und bilde so ein Ganzes, darf man ebenfalls in dieses Gedankenspiel miteinbeziehen. Hat nicht jedes Kunstwerk seine eigene, ihm innewohnende Virtual Reality? Susan Sontag hat vor Jahren beschrieben, wie Bilder beim Betrachten über sich selbst hinauswachsen und Wahrnehmungsräume öffnen, die wir durchwandern, erleben, bedenken und uns zu eigen machen. Imaginäre Entdeckungsreisen, auch und besonders im Universum des Abstrakten und Konstruktiven. Leon Polk Smith ein schönes Beispiel und zugleich ein Künstler, der Bilder als Objekte down to earth malte.

Er war ein aufmerksamer Beobachter des amerikanischen Everyday Life, dessen plakative Symbole und Signale mitsamt ihrem Kolorit er als unwiderstehliche Anregungen verstand und als geometrisierte Abstraktion in sein bildnerisches Vorhaben einfliessen liess. Eine unvermutete Beobachtung traf ihn 1954 blitzartig in sein malerisches Herz; zehn Jahre später erzählte er von diesem Moment:

> Ich war gerade dabei, mir einen Sport-Katalog anzusehen, in dem Zeichnungen von Tennisbällen, Fussbällen, Baseballs und Basketbällen abgebildet waren. Es handelte sich dabei um einfache Kreise, auf deren Oberfläche die jeweilige Naht der Bälle gezeichnet war. Ich war fasziniert von dem Raum, der zwischen den Linien entstanden war. Es fesselte mich derartig, daß ich mich sofort hinsetzte und ebenfalls einige dieser Bälle zeichnete, wobei ich dieses Raum-Konzept nachahmte. Ich malte ungefähr zwölf große, kreisförmige Gemälde, ehe ich in der Lage war, diese Konzeption, bei der ich zwei oder drei Formen und ebenso viele Farben verwendet habe, auf das Rechteck zu übertragen. Und ich weiß bis heute nicht, welche Bildräume auf diese Weise entstehen. Es sind gewiß nicht nur die erdbezogenen Räume, mit denen wir seit Jahrhunderten vertraut sind. In meinen Augen handelt es sich dabei um andere Räume, die sich der gesamten Welt erst im letzten Jahrzehnt erschlossen haben.[9]

Insbesondere hat ihn der aus Leder gefertigte Baseball inspiriert mit seinen von Hand eingenähten, ringsum verlaufenden roten Fäden.

Es ist ein scheinbar widersprüchliches und doch homogenes ästhetisches Gemenge, das seine Bilder prägt und den Betrachter fasziniert. Die kunsthistorische Schublade Hard Edge ist rasch bei der Hand. Und doch senden die scheinbar so einfachen und klar erfassbaren Bilder von Leon Polk Smith sowohl in Form wie Farbe ganz eigene Stimmungswerte und in ihnen verborgene Botschaften aus, eine ganze Kulturlandschaft aus High and Low, Avantgarde und Tradition tut sich auf. Man kann seine Kompositionen immer wieder anschauen und staunt.

own. Imaginary journeys of discovery also occur within the abstract and constructivist universe in particular. Leon Polk Smith serves as a fine example of this, while at the same time, he was an artist who painted pictures as objects in a down-to-earth manner.

Smith was an attentive observer of American everyday life. He saw its eye-catching symbols and signals together with their coloring as irresistible stimuli and integrated these into his artwork as geometrized abstraction. In 1954, an unexpected observation struck his painterly heart in a flash—a moment that he described ten years later as follows: I was looking at an athletic catalog and the illustrations in this catalog were drawings, rather than photographs, of the tennis ball, football, baseball and basketball. They were just line circles with a drawing of the seams on the covering of the balls.

> I was fascinated by the space that was between these lines and felt bound to them and started immediately drawing some of my own, taking off from this space concept. I did about twelve large circular paintings before I was able to carry this particular space concept, using two or three forms and two or three colors, over into the rectangle. And I still don't know what this space is. It isn't just the earthy space that we have been familiar with for centuries, but I think that it has something to do with the other spaces that the whole world has really been interested in for the past decade.[9]

He was especially inspired by the leather baseball with hand-sewn red threads running around it.

A seemingly contradictory yet homogeneous aesthetic mixture characterizes his paintings and fascinates the beholder. Art history's Hard-edge pigeonhole is immediately at the ready. However, in terms of both form and color, Leon Polk Smith's seemingly simple and clearly comprehensible paintings convey their very own moods and hidden messages within them; a whole cultural landscape of high and low, of avant-garde and tradition, opens up. You can look at his compositions again and again and never cease to be amazed.

D

1 *Leon Polk Smith – American Painter,* Ausst.-Kat. Brooklyn Museum 1996. Texte: Carter Ratcliff, «Leon Polk Smith: The Geometry of Optimism»; Brooke Kamin Rapaport, «An Interview with Leon Polk Smith»; Arthur C. Danto, «Leon Polk Smith and Real Space»; John Alan Farmer, «Leon Polk Smith: A Life in Abstraction».
2 Vgl. Dieter Honisch, Jens Christian Jensen (Hrsg.), *Amerikanische Kunst von 1945 bis heute,* Köln 1976, S. 114 f. Das Buch erschien als Katalog zu den Ausstellungen *New York in Europa* (Berlin) und *Amerikanische Druckgrafik aus öffentlichen Sammlungen der Bundesrepublik Deutschland* (Kiel).
3 Zürcher Kunstgesellschaft und Verwaltungsabteilung des Stadtpräsidenten, *konkrete kunst – 50 jahre entwicklung,* Ausst.-Kat. Helmhaus Zürich 1960, Einleitungstext: Max Bill, Texte und Dokumentation: Margit Staber. Leon Polk Smith: Abb 117, Biografie S. 70.
4 In den USA u. a.: Lawrence Alloway, Dore Ashton, Arthur C. Danto, Carter Ratcliff, Barbara Rose. In Europa u. a.: Klaus Honnef, Dieter Honisch, Max Imdahl, Jean Leering, Serge Lemoine, Franz Meyer, Antje von Graevenitz.
5 Leon Polk Smith in einem Statement von 1979, siehe: *Leon Polk Smith,* hrsg. von Richard W. Gassen und Jean-Paul Monery, Ausst.-Kat. Wilhelm-Hack-Museum, Ludwigshafen 1989, S. 98.
6 Carter Ratcliff, «Leon Polk Smith: The Geometry of Optimism» (wie Anm. 1), S. 1–14.
7 Leon Polk Smith in einem Statement, siehe: *Leon Polk Smith* (wie Anm. 5), S. 98.
8 Siehe Siegfried Unseld, *Goethe und der Gingko,* Frankfurt 1998, S. 58.
9 Leon Polk Smith im Gespräch mit d'Arcy Hayman, abgedruckt in: Ina Prinz (Hrsg.), *Leon Polk Smith im Arithmeum,* Ausst.-Kat. Arithmeum Bonn, Bonn 2001, S. 6–17, hier S. 8.

E

1 *Leon Polk Smith: American Painter,* exh. cat. Brooklyn Museum (New York: Brooklyn Museum, 1996), featuring "An Interview with Leon Polk Smith" by Brooke Kamin Rapaport and essays by Carter Ratcliff, "Leon Polk Smith: The Geometry of Optimism"; Arthur C. Danto, "Leon Polk Smith and Real Space"; and John Alan Farmer, "Leon Polk Smith: A Life in Abstraction."
2 See Dieter Honisch and Jens Christian Jensen (eds.), *Amerikanische Kunst von 1945 bis heute* (American Art from 1945 to Today) (Cologne: DuMont Buchverlag, 1976), 114 f. The book was published as a catalogue for the exhibitions *New York in Europa* (New York in Europe) (Berlin) and *Amerikanische Druckgrafik aus öffentlichen Sammlungen der Bundesrepublik Deutschland* (American Prints from Public Collections in the Federal Republic of Germany) (Kiel).
3 Zürcher Kunstgesellschaft and the Department of Administration of the Mayor of Zurich, *konkrete kunst – 50 jahre entwicklung* (concrete art: 50 years of development), exh. cat. Helmhaus Zurich (Zurich: 1960), with an introduction by Max Bill and essays and documentation by Margit Staber. For Leon Polk Smith, see fig. 117, biography 70.
4 This included Lawrence Alloway, Dore Ashton, Arthur C. Danto, Carter Ratcliff, and Barbara Rose in the US; in Europe, Klaus Honnef, Dieter Honisch, Max Imdahl, Jean Leering, Serge Lemoine, Franz Meyer, and Antje von Graevenitz.
5 Leon Polk Smith in a statement from 1979 published in *Leon Polk Smith,* exh. cat. Wilhelm-Hack-Museum Ludwigshafen (Ludwigshafen: Wilhelm-Hack-Museum, 1989), 98, https://leonpolksmithfoundation.org/research-resources/artist-statements/.
6 Carter Ratcliff, "Leon Polk Smith: The Geometry of Optimism," in *Leon Polk Smith: American Painter,* 1–14.
7 Leon Polk Smith in a statement, *Leon Polk Smith,* exh. cat. Wilhelm-Hack-Museum Ludwigshafen (Ludwigshafen: Wilhelm-Hack-Museum, 1989), 91, https://leonpolksmithfoundation.org/research-resources/artist-statements/.
8 See Siegfried Unseld, *Goethe and the* Gingko (Chicago: University of Chicago Press, 2003).
9 Leon Polk Smith in an interview with d'Arcy Hayman, printed in Ina Prinz (ed.), *Leon Polk Smith im Arithmeum* (Leon Polk Smith at the Arithmeum), exh. cat. Arithmeum Bonn (Bonn: Bouvier Verlag, 2001), 19–27, here 20, https://leonpolksmithfoundation.org/research-resources/interviews/darcy-hayman/.

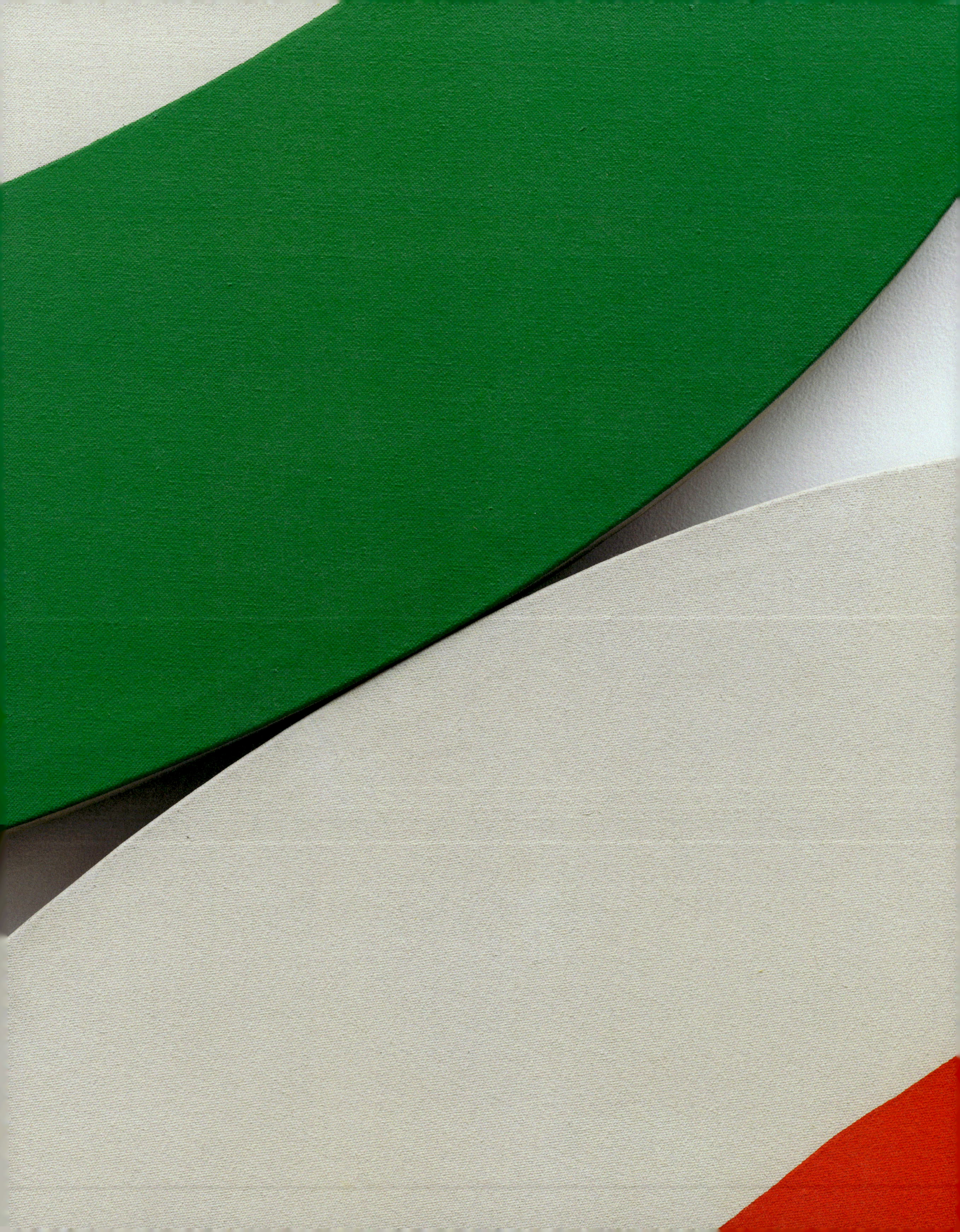

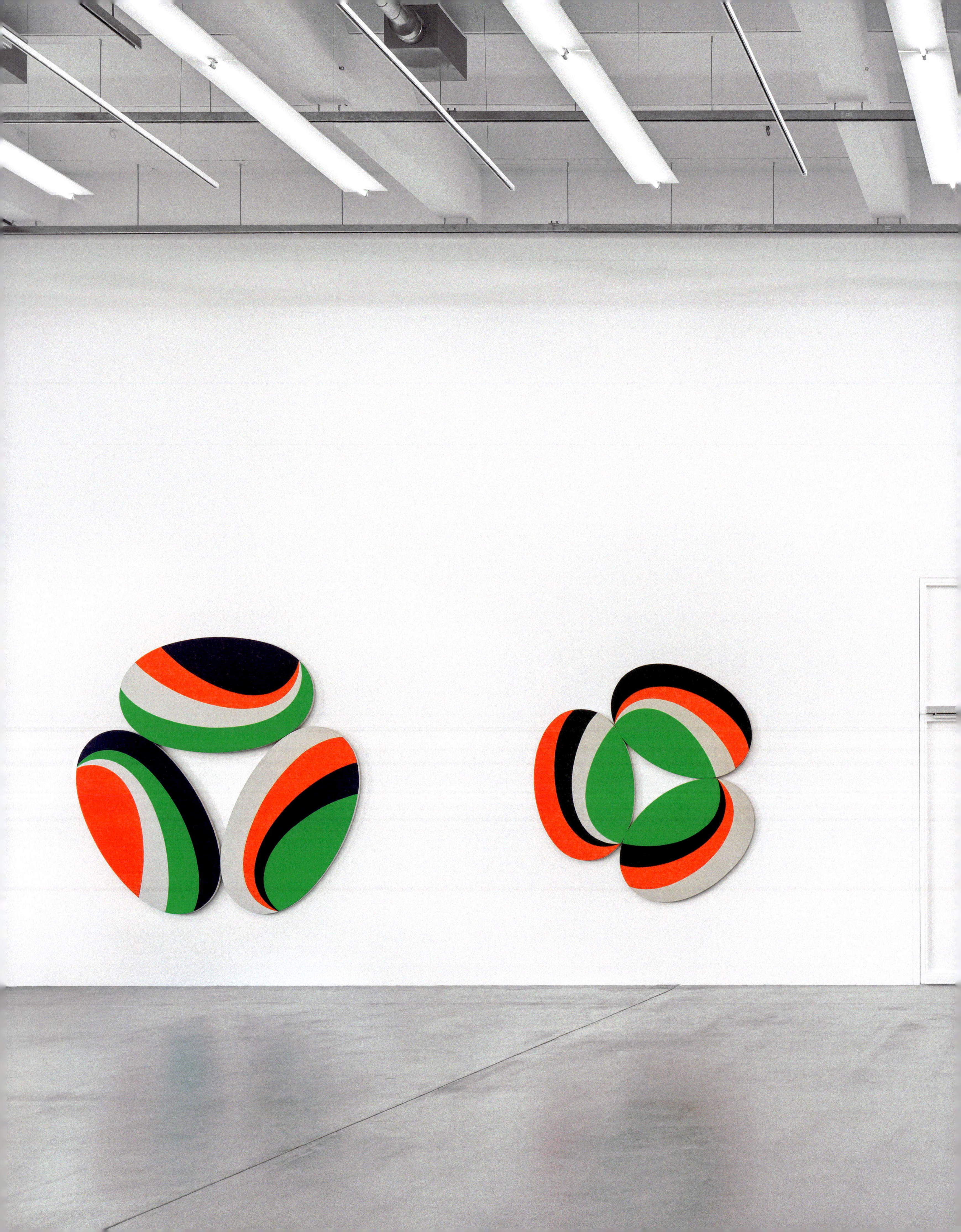

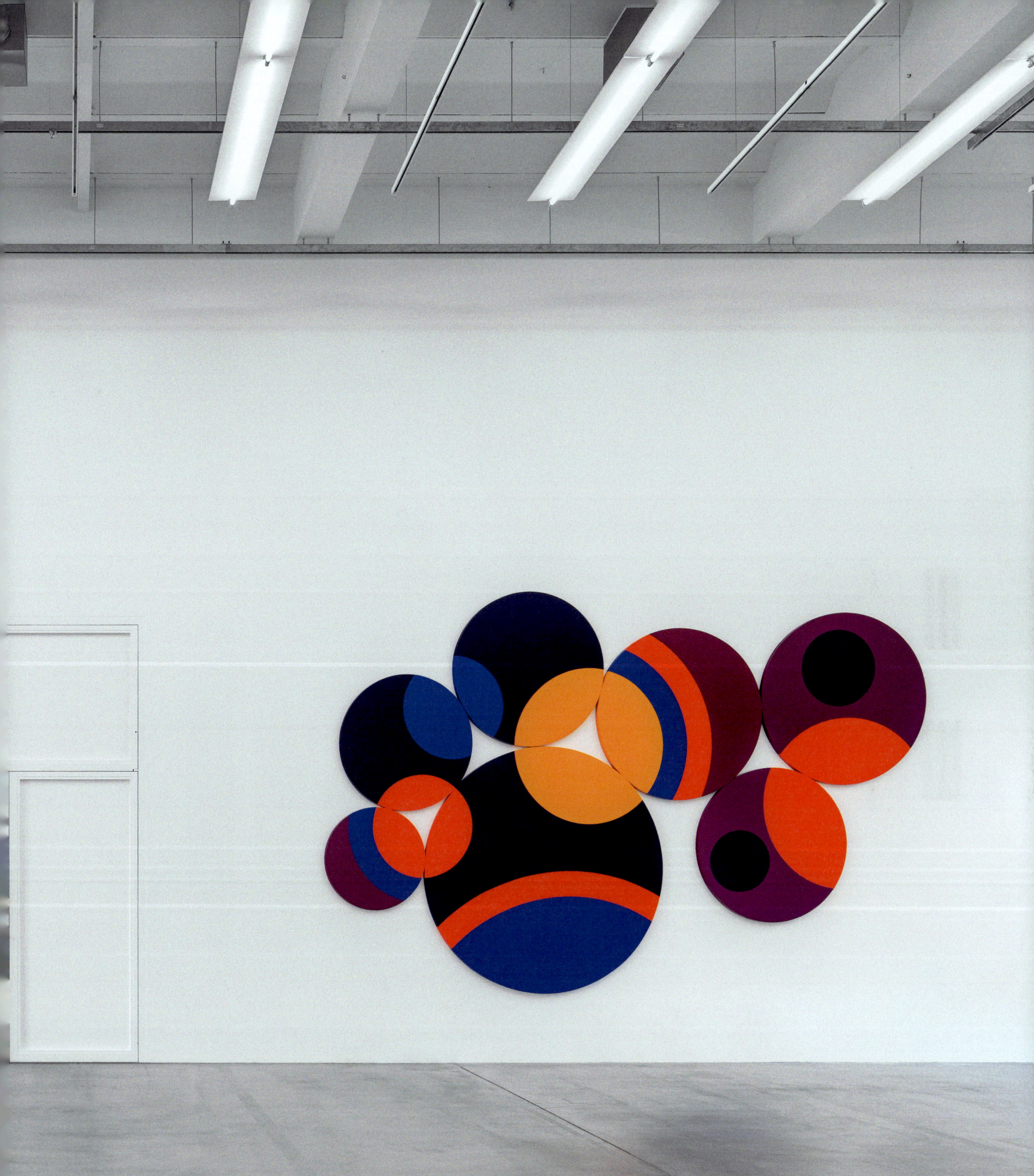

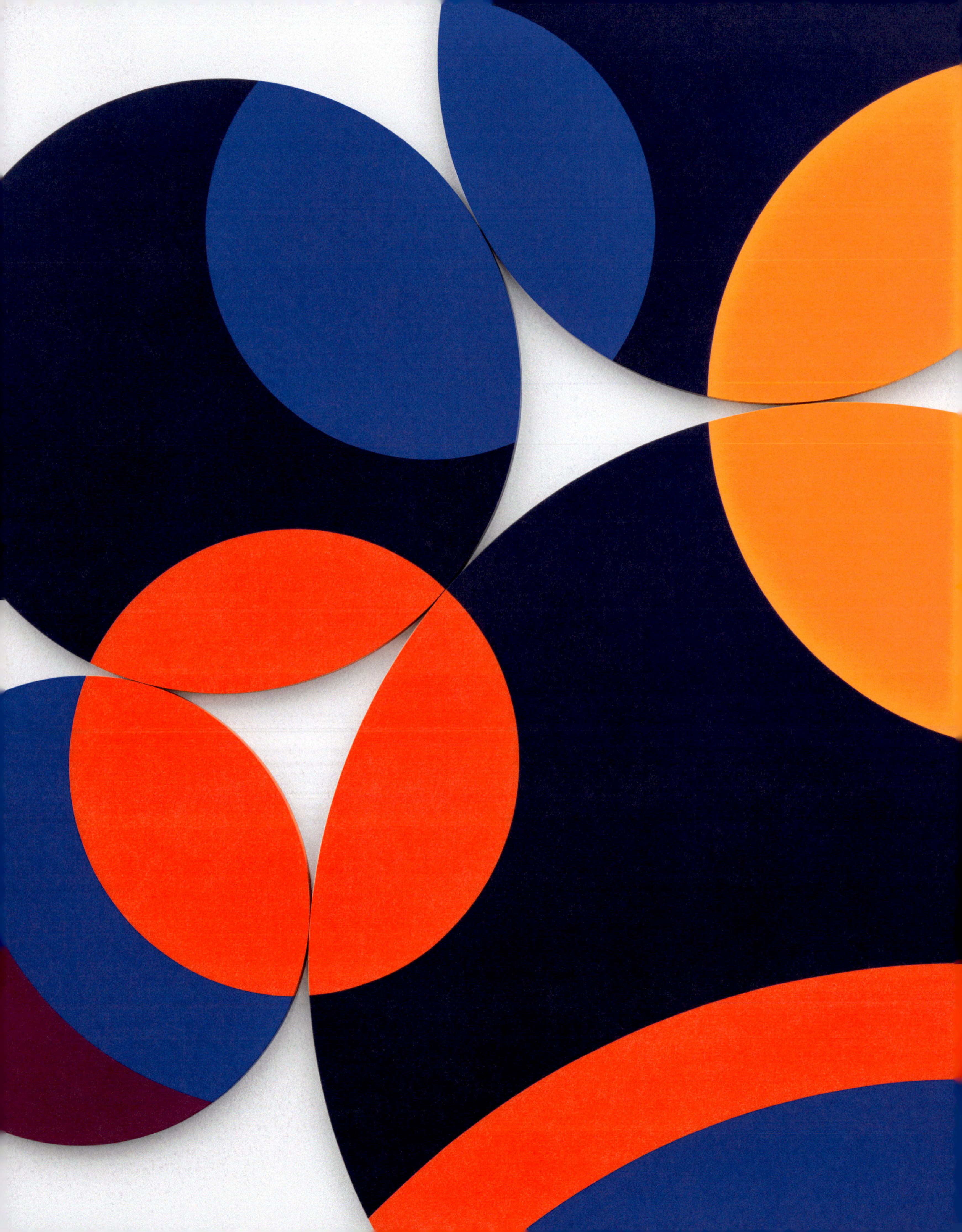

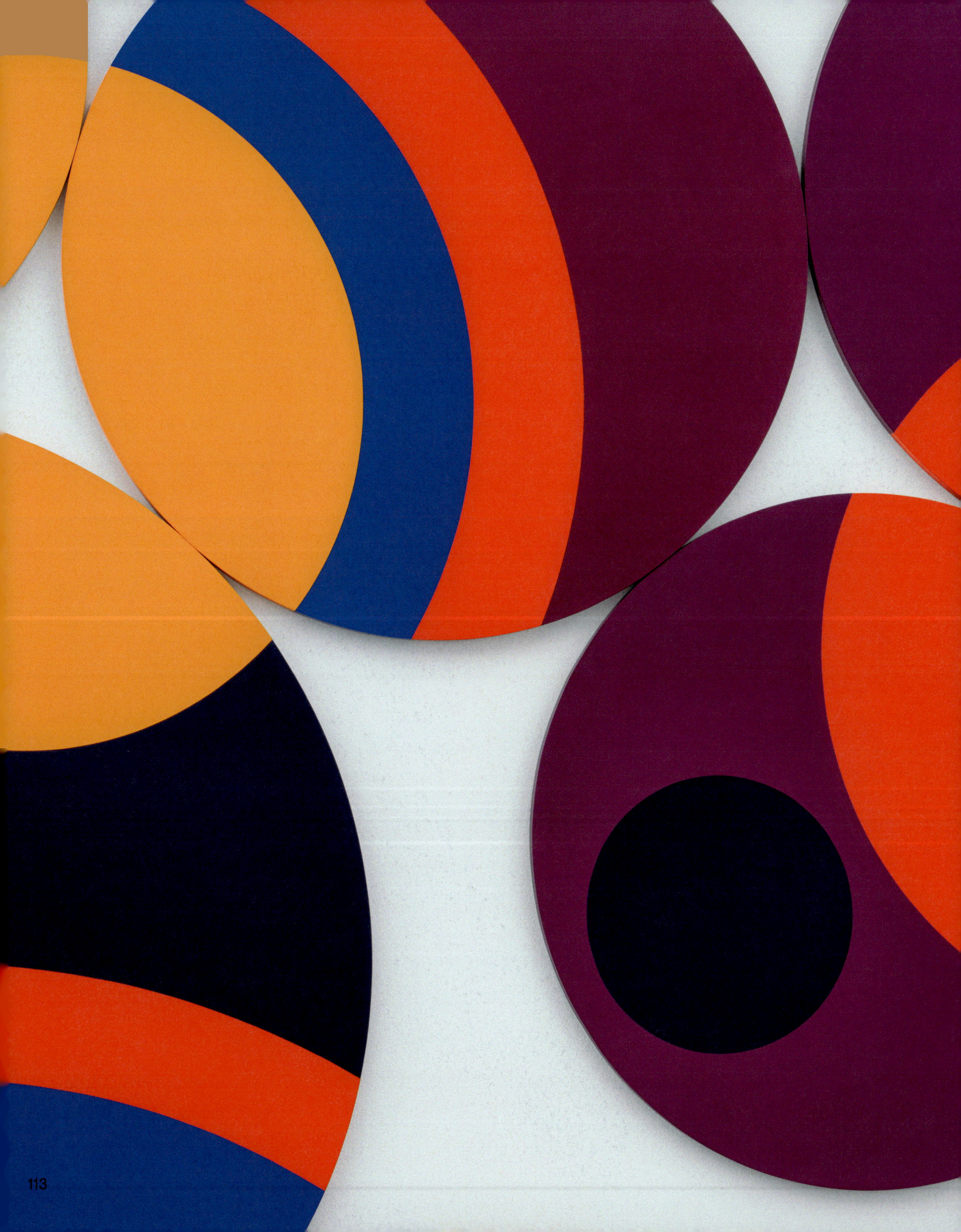

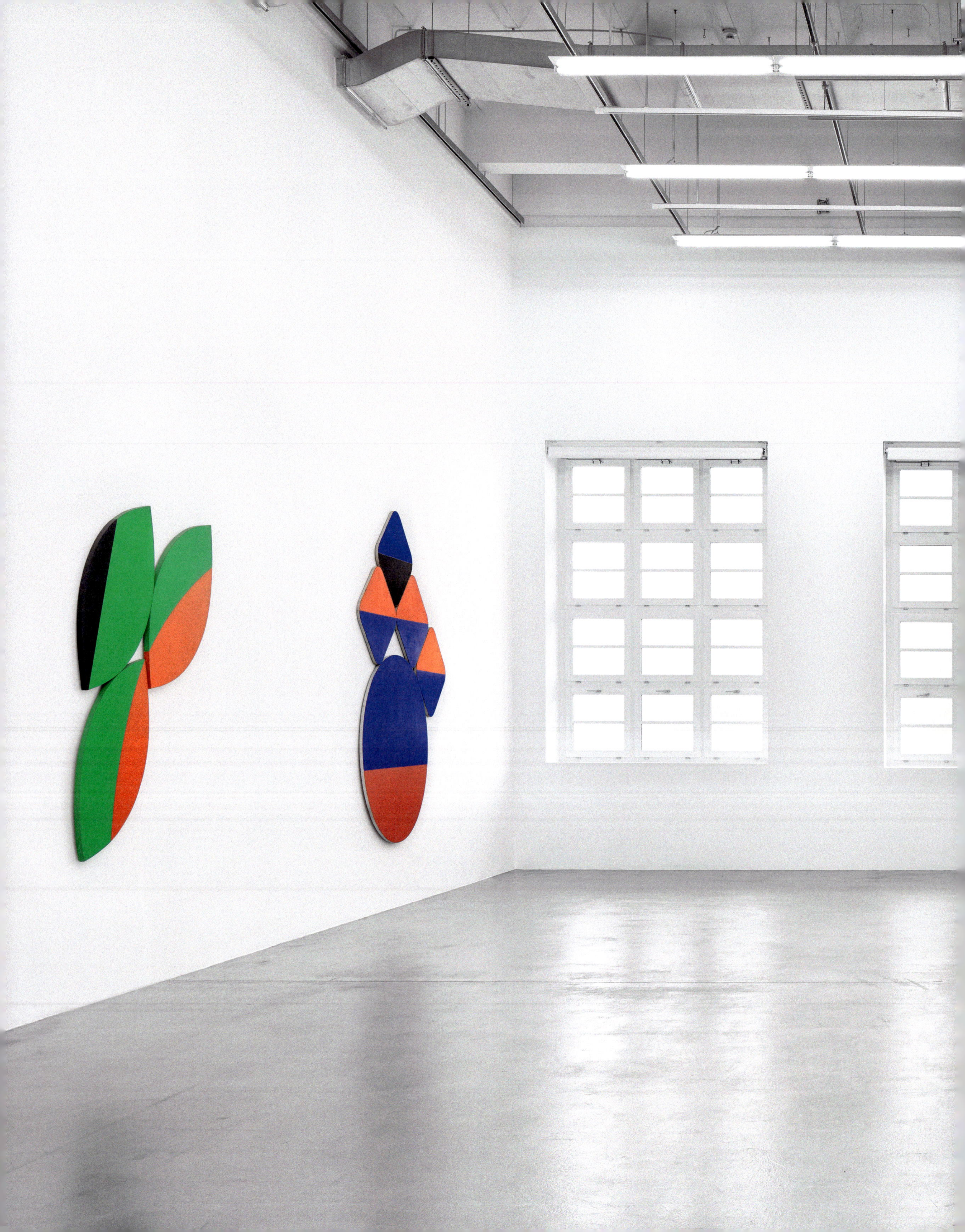

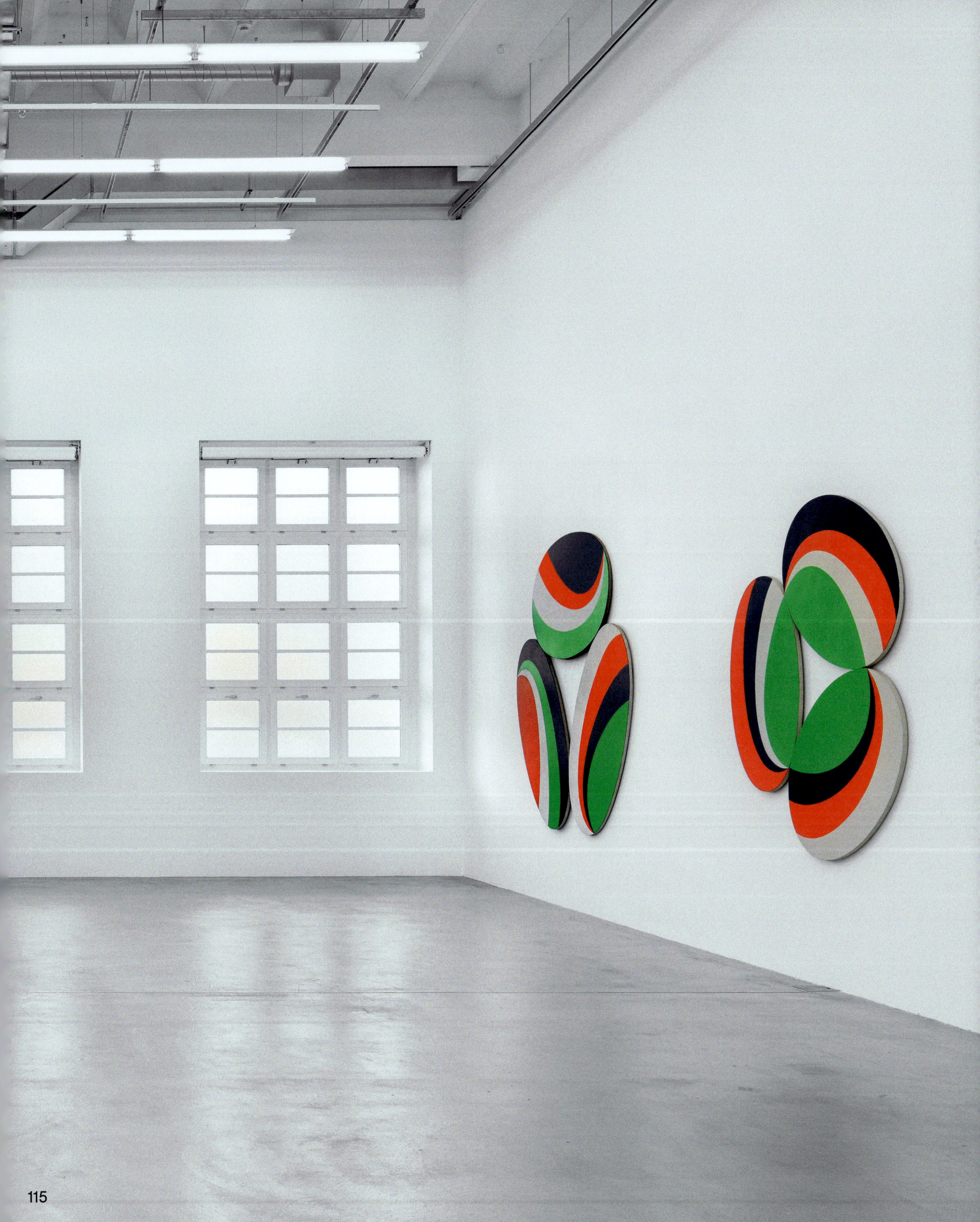

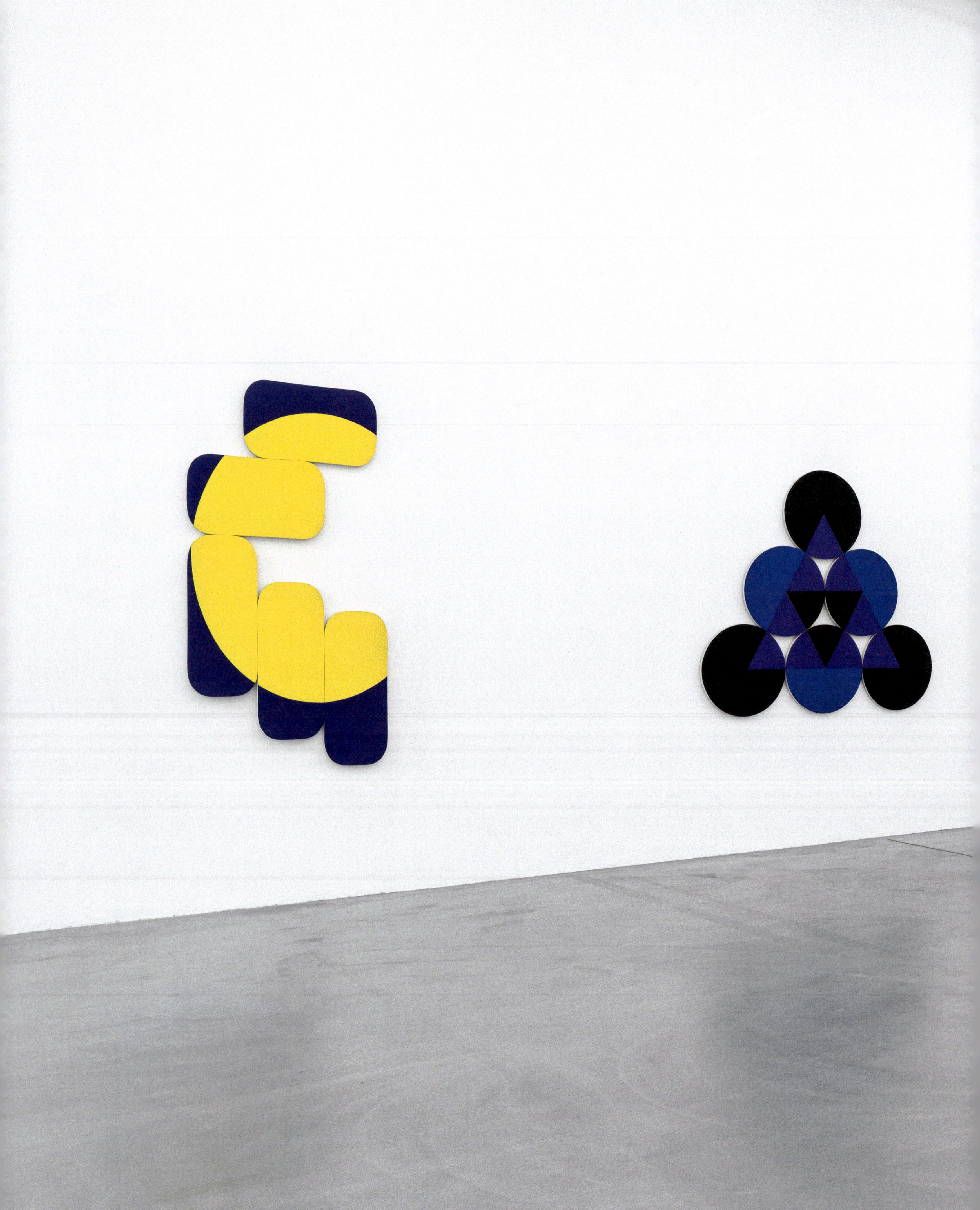

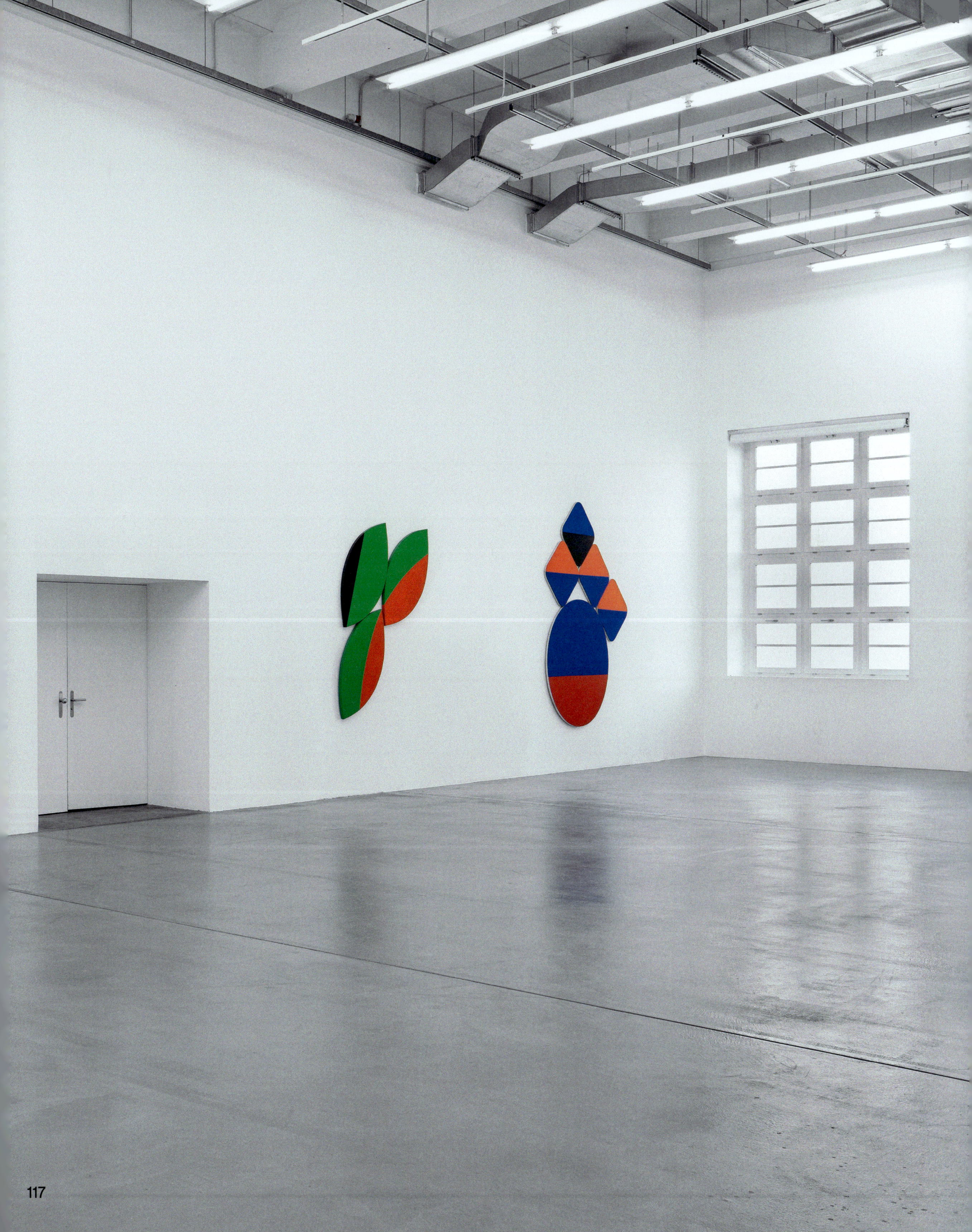

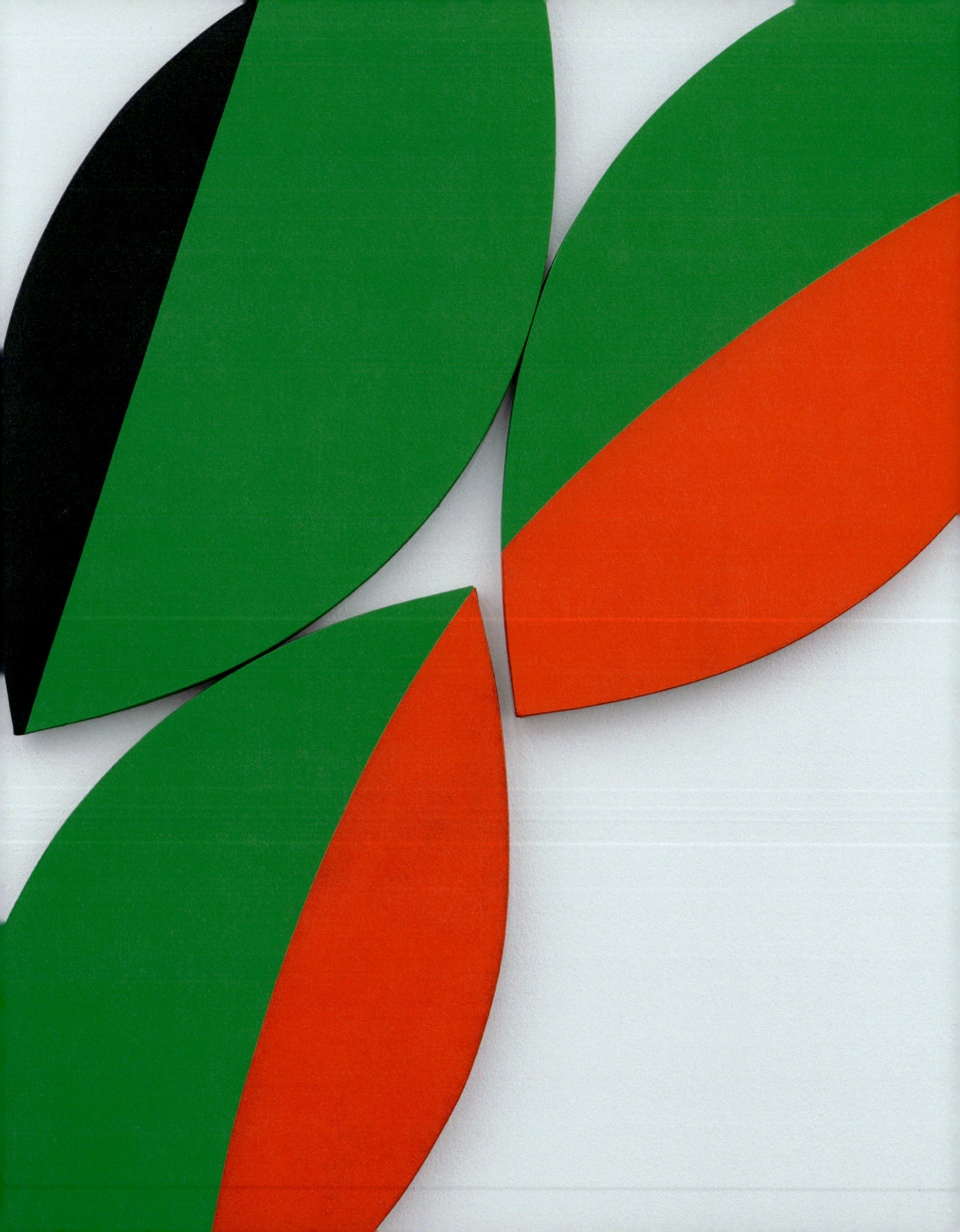

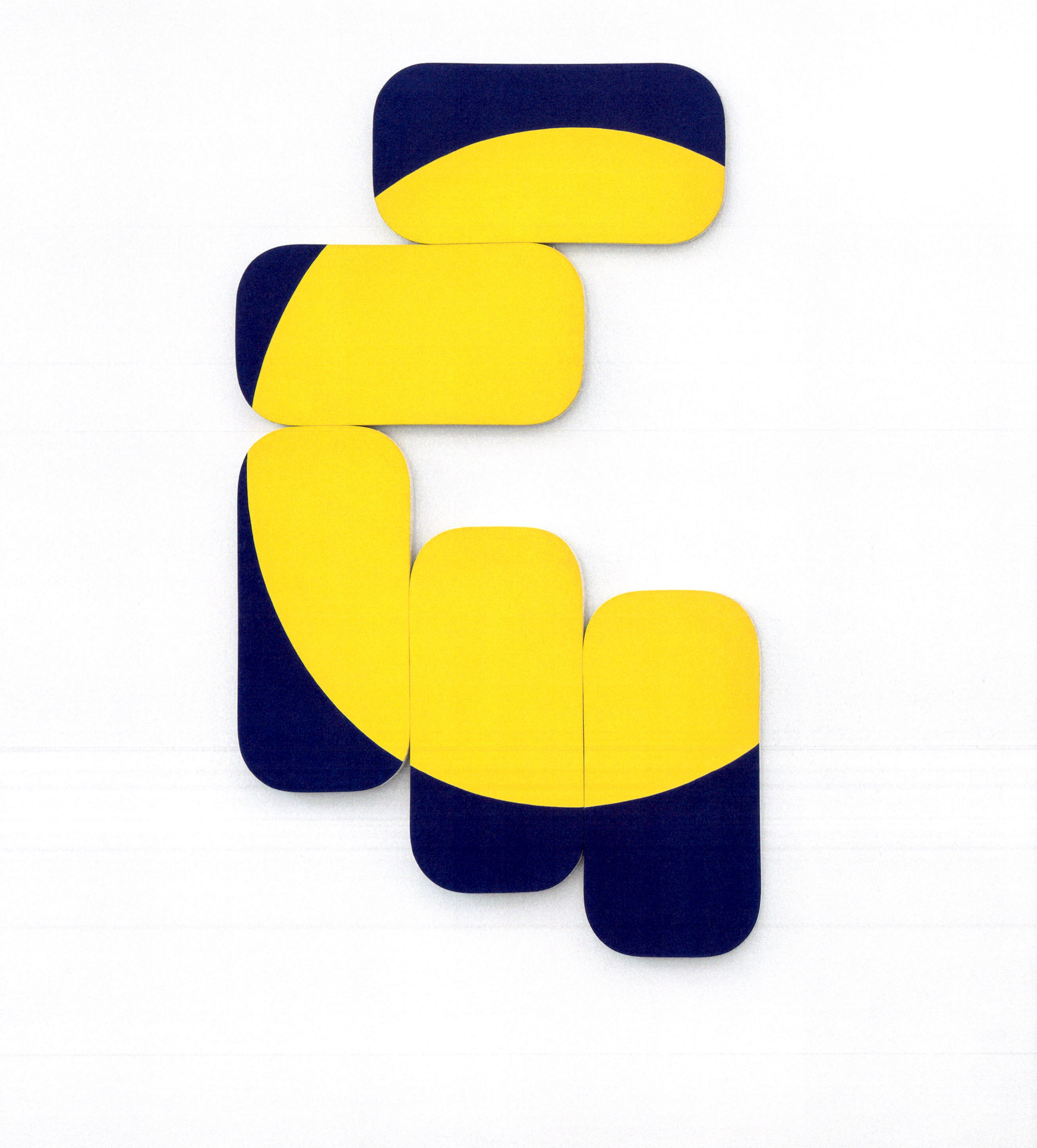

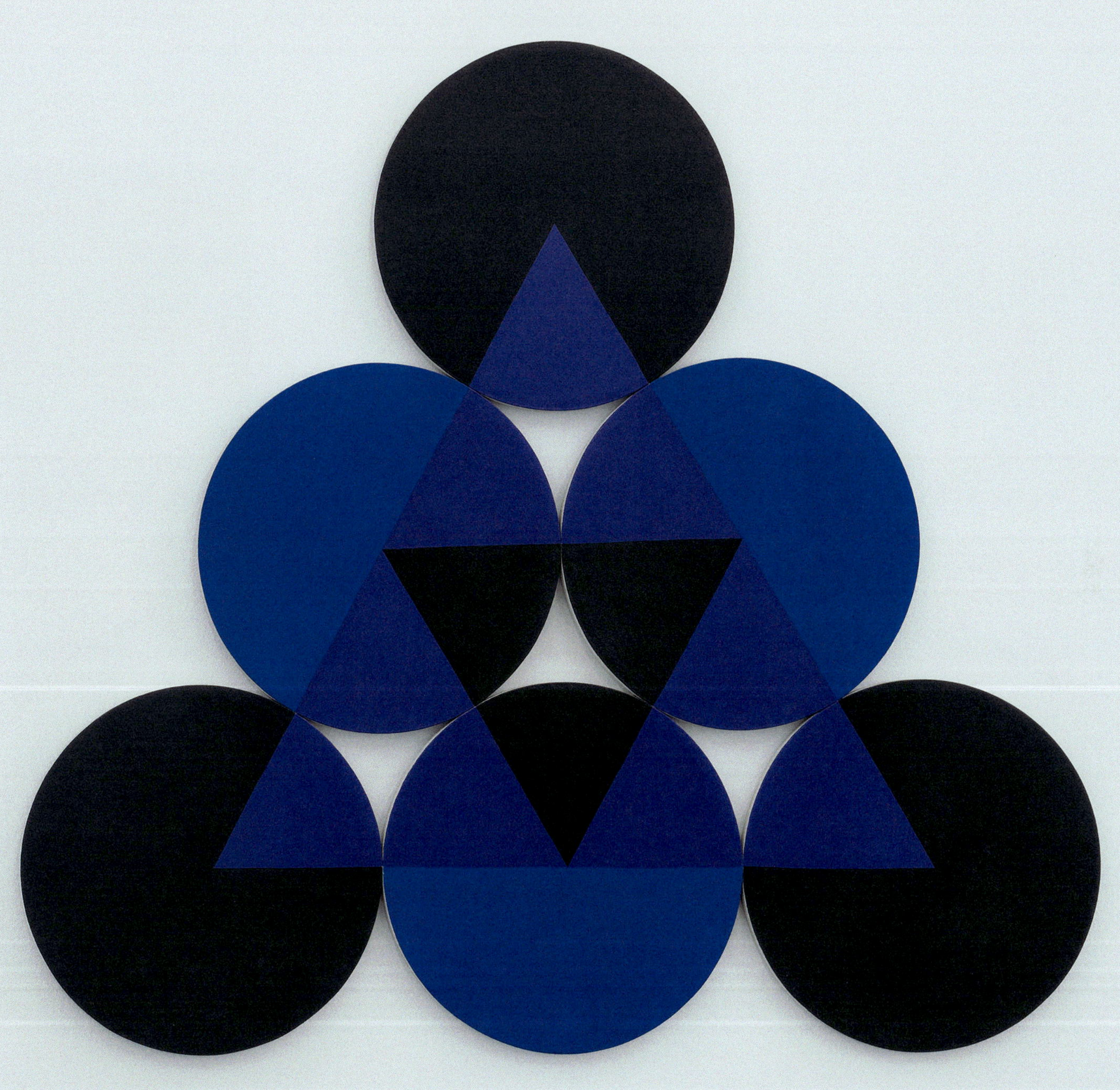

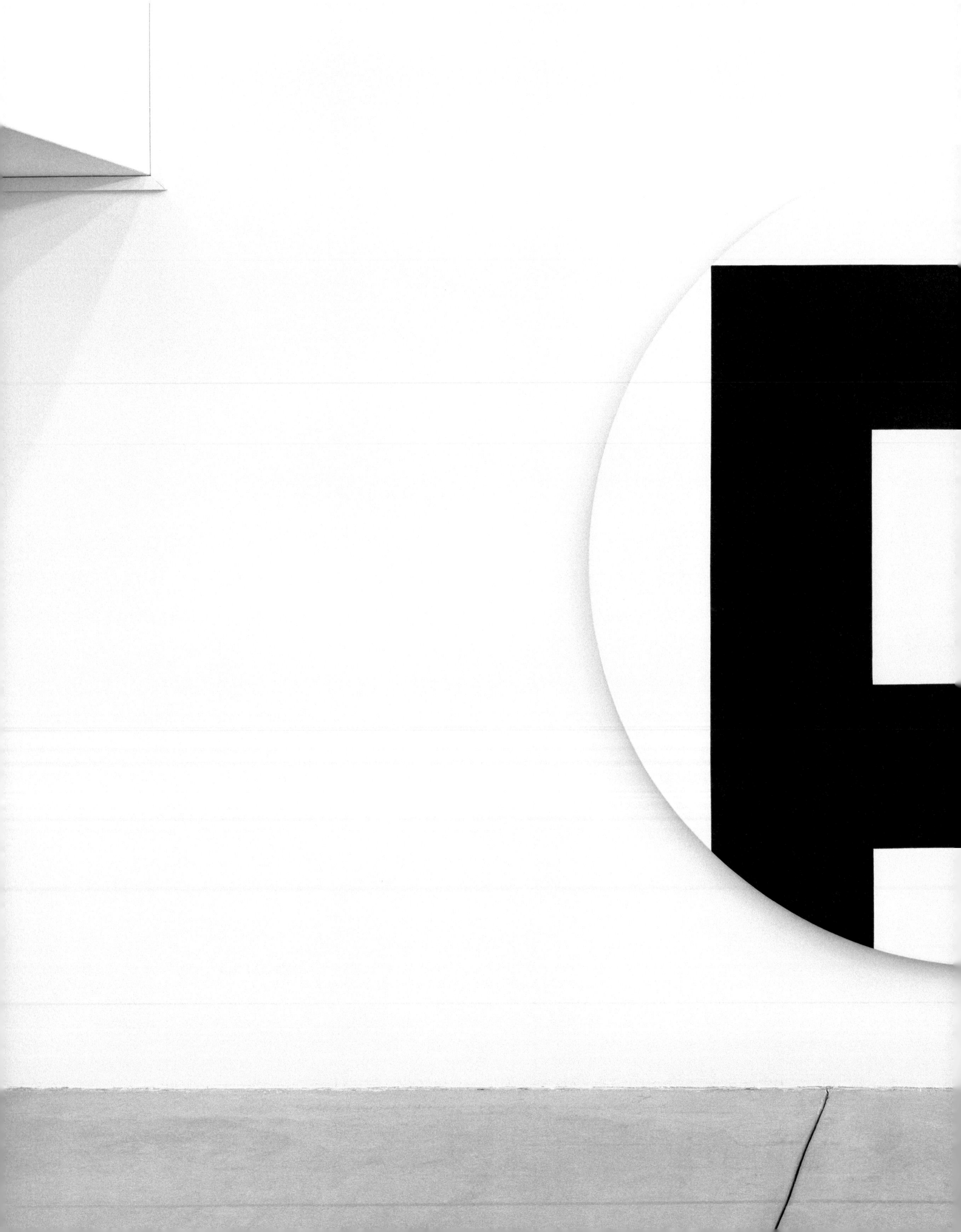

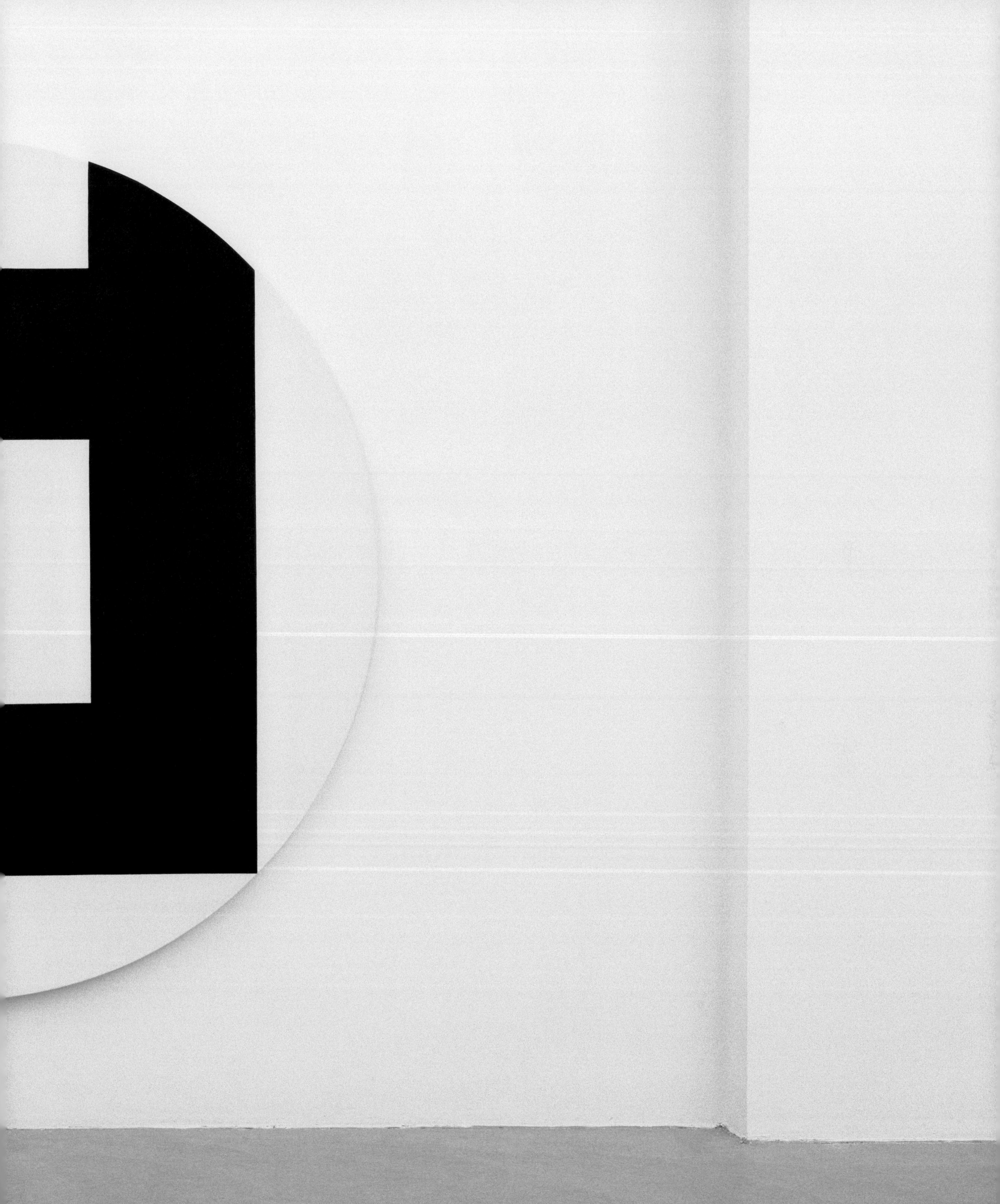

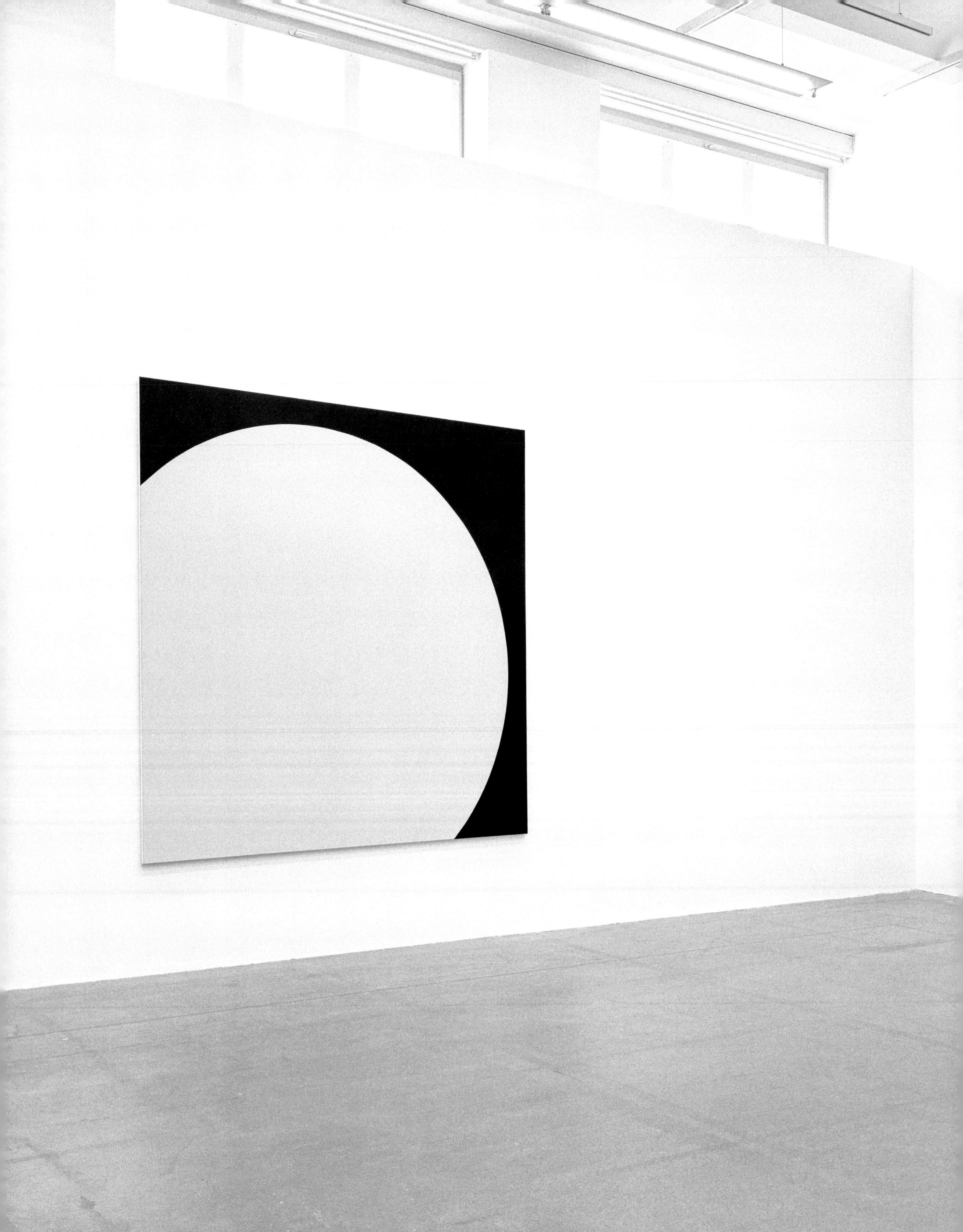

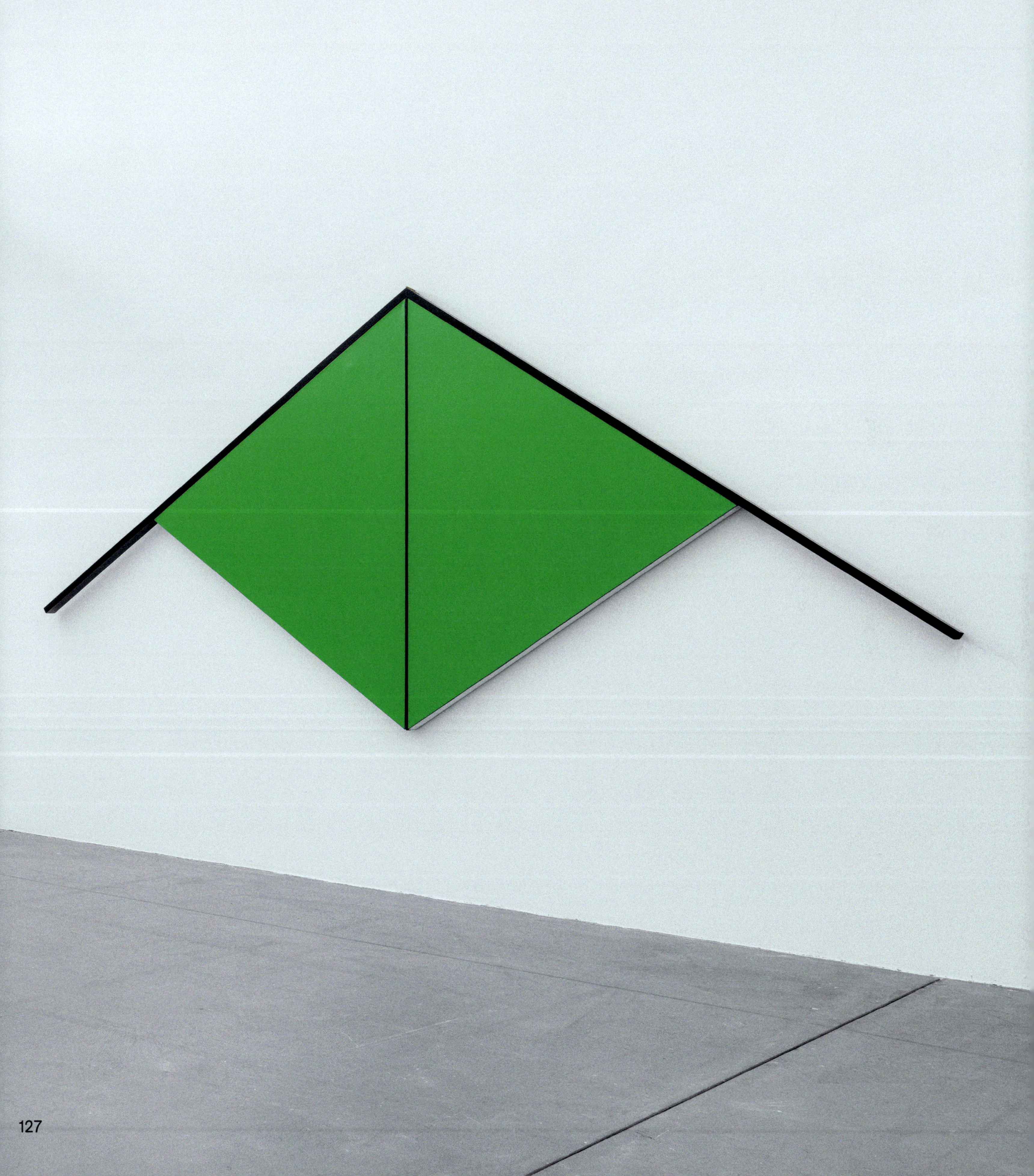

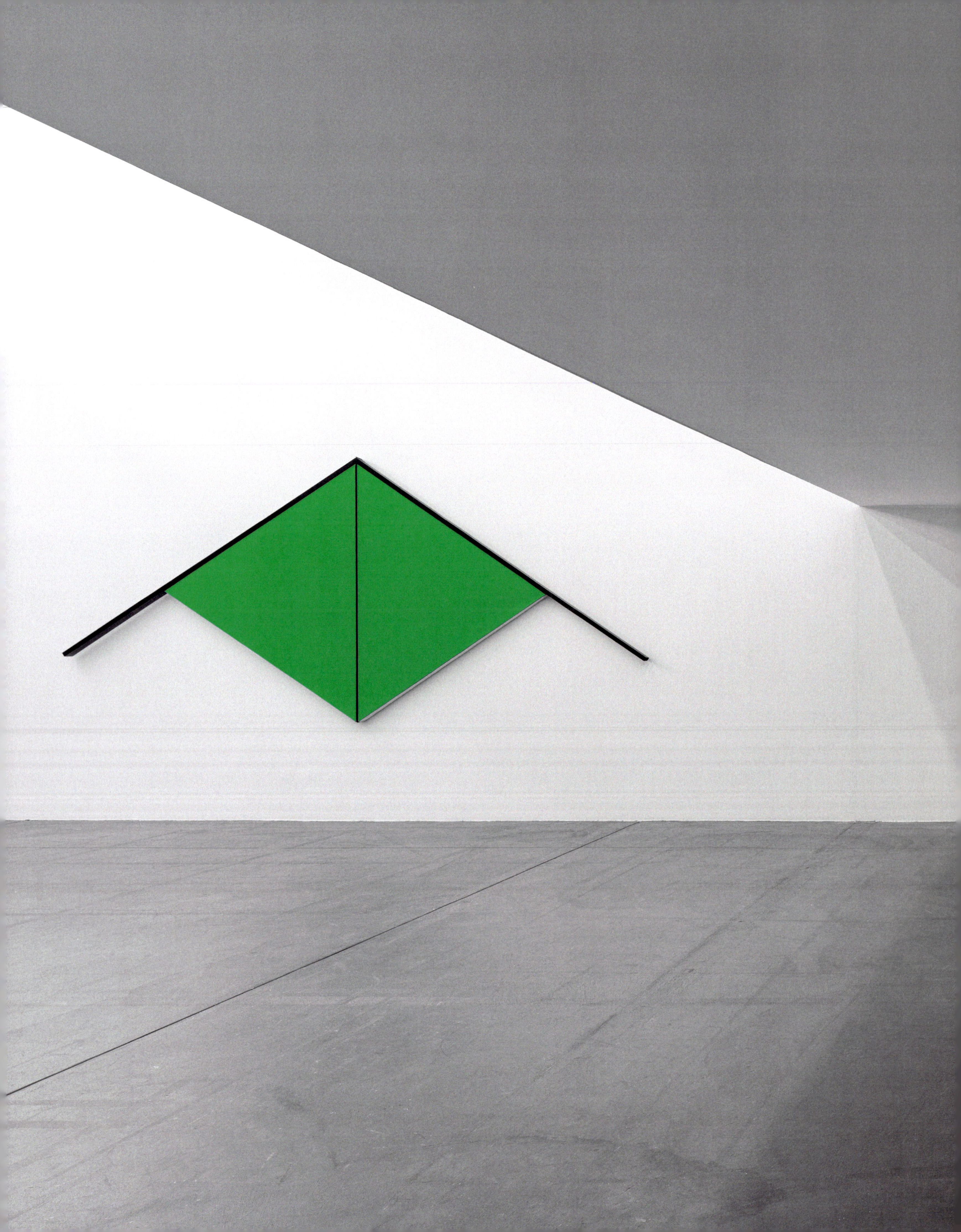

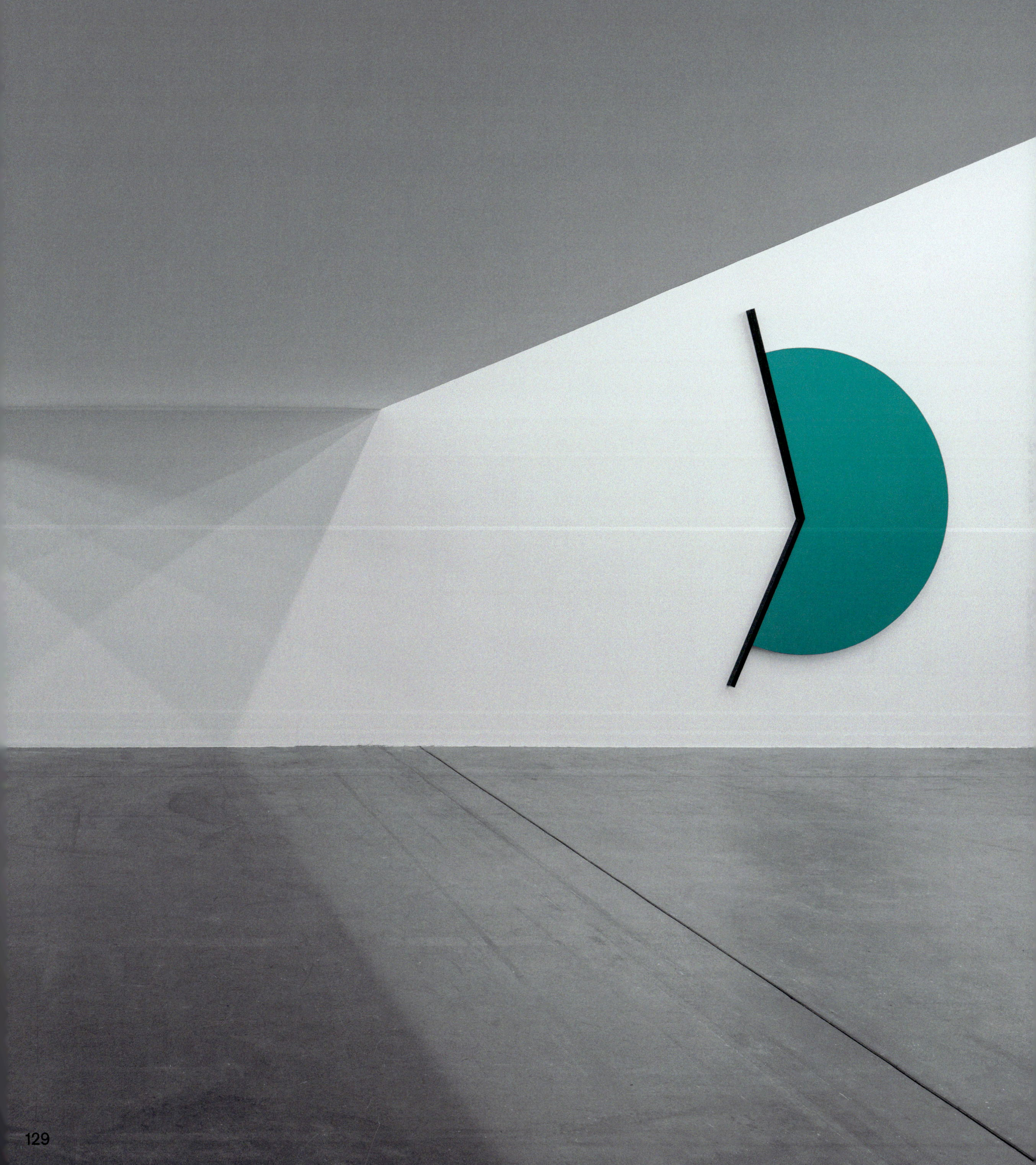

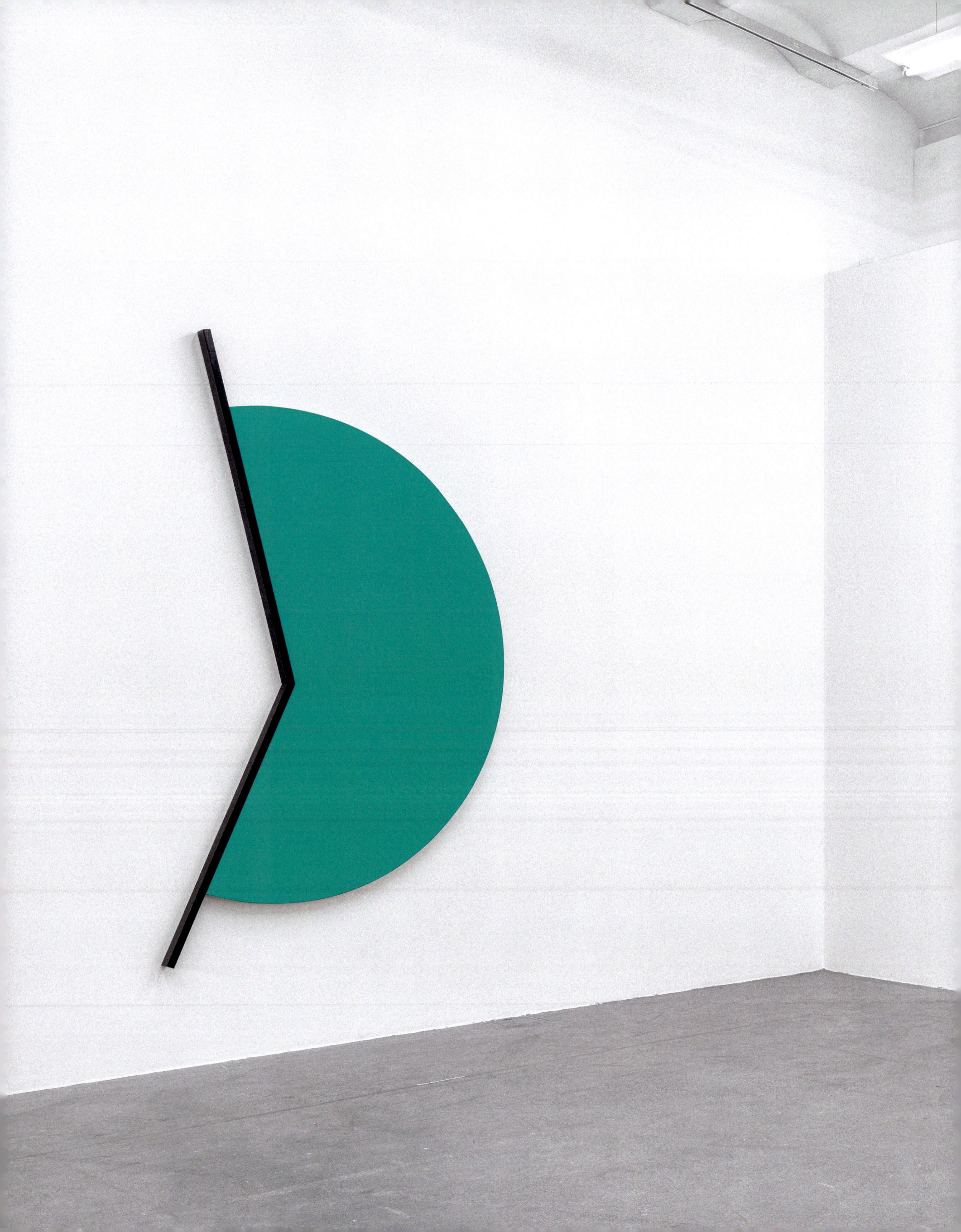

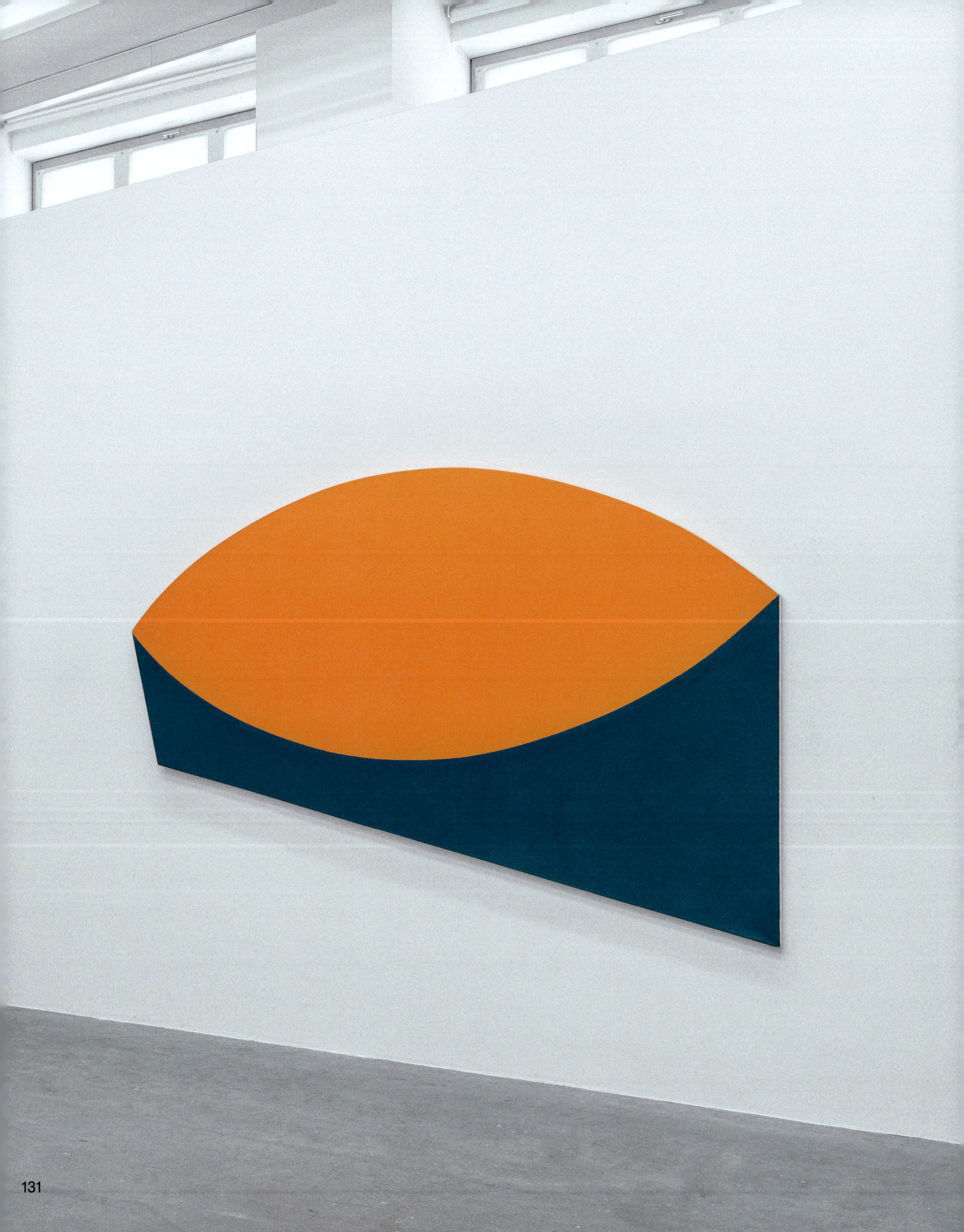

Leon Polk Smith: Schockt noch immer

Leon Polk Smith: Still Shocking

David M. Roche

D Grosse Künstler:innen werden oft mit bestimmten Landschaften in Verbindung gebracht – Georgia O'Keeffe zum Beispiel mit New Mexico oder Richard Diebenkorn mit Kalifornien. Bei Leon Polk Smith ist es Oklahoma. Smith kam 1906 nahe der im «Indian Territory» gelegenen Stadt Chickasha zur Welt, kurz bevor Oklahoma die Eigenstaatlichkeit erhielt. Er wuchs auf den Ranches und Farmen des ländlichen Oklahoma auf, besuchte die Pocasset High School und anschliessend das Oklahoma State College in Ada. Auch wenn Smith Oklahoma verliess und nach Europa und Mexiko reiste, bevor er 1944 nach New York City übersiedelte, um sich ganz der Kunst zu widmen, scheint seine Imagination die Landschaft seiner Jugend nie verlassen zu haben. Seine gesamte Laufbahn hindurch blieben die Kiamichi-Bergkette im Osten, die Hochgrasprärie im Westen und Norden und der weite Himmel über Oklahoma wichtige Inspirationsquellen für ihn. Smith selbst sagte dazu: «Ich habe vierzig Jahre meines Lebens in Oklahoma verbracht, und es hat einen warmen Platz in meinem Herzen, und es ist überall in [meiner] Malerei ... Ich schulde Oklahoma alles.»[1]

Im Jahr 2021 organisierte das Heard Museum in Phoenix, Arizona, eine Ausstellung mit dem Titel *Leon Polk Smith: Hiding in Plain Sight.* Die Ausstellung unternahm den Versuch, die Deutung von Smiths Werk über die gängigen eurozentrischen Besprechungen hinaus zu erweitern und seine Verbundenheit mit dem indigenen Amerika miteinzubeziehen. Seine Kindheit und Jugend auf dem Land der Chickasaw im Oklahoma der Depressionszeit brachte Smith nicht nur in unmittelbaren Kontakt mit Angehörigen verschiedener indigener Kulturen, sondern ermöglichte ihm auch, an Ereignissen, Aktivitäten und Festen teilzuhaben, die die Kunst und Kultur der indigenen Bevölkerung in den Alltag einbetteten.

Zu den in der Ausstellung gezeigten Beispielen indigenen Kunsthandwerks gehörten Bandolier-Taschen, Wiegenbretter, Pfeifentaschen, bemalte Tierhäute und Schilde sowie mit Seidenbändern besetzte Kleidung. Deren geometrische Muster und leuchtenden Farbkombinationen sind den Form- und Farb-Arrangements verwandt, die häufig in Smiths Werken zu finden sind. So wurden in der Ausstellung beispielsweise eine lederne, mit Perlen besetzte Pfeifentasche der Chayenne ❶ mit Smiths *N.Y. City* (1945) ❷, ein Schild und eine Decke der Comanchen ❸ mit der *Constellation Yellow-Blue-Violet* (1970) ❹ und *Dusty Miller Leaf* (1953) ❺ mit einem mit Bänderapplikationen versehenen Rock des Sac- und Fox-Volkstammes verglichen ❻. Smith bemerkte:

> Ich war immer beeindruckt von der hohen ästhetischen Qualität der Gestaltung und handwerklichen Verarbeitung in ihrer Kunst. 1938 malte ich mein bis dahin abstraktestes Gemälde. Es hiess *A Stroll in the Forest* [Ein Spaziergang im Wald] und ich glaube, das war sehr stark von der indianischen Kunst beeinflusst – von deren Einfachheit und deren Direktheit, davon, nichts hinzuzutun, was nicht gebraucht wird. Es ist nichts da ausser diesen vertikalen Baumstämmen. Ich hatte auch nie irgendwelche Hemmungen, was Farbe angeht. Ich hatte nie Angst vor ihr. Ich glaube, diese Freiheit der Farbe rührte aus meiner Beziehung zu den Indianern.[2]

Der Einfluss des indigenen Oklahoma zeigt sich auch vielfach in Smiths Werktiteln, etwa in *Okemah* (1955), *Kanawa* (1956), *Cherokee* (1958) und *Pontotoc* (1958). Dass Smith viele seiner abstrakten Gemälde mit indigenen Namen versah, blieb zu seinen Lebzeiten weitgehend unbemerkt, offenbart jedoch seine Verbindung mit seinem Leben in Oklahoma und mit der Cherokee-Sprache, die seine erste Sprache war.[3] Diane Fraher, eine Osage/Cherokee und Gründerin von American Indian Artists Inc. (Amerinda), erklärt: «Leons Eltern waren beide halbe Cherokee, also war er zur Hälfte Cherokee. Sie sprachen Cherokee.»[4]

Fünfundzwanzig Jahre vor der Ausstellung im Heard Museum organisierte das Brooklyn Museum eine Retrospektive mit dem Titel *Leon Polk Smith: American Painter.* Diese Ausstellung war aus mehreren Gründen bemerkenswert, in Bezug auf den vorliegenden Essay aber vor allem deshalb, weil Smith sich öffentlich als Angehöriger der Cherokee zu erkennen gab. In ihrem Interview für den Ausstellungskatalog – dem vermutlich ersten aufgezeichneten Gespräch Smiths über seine Arbeit und deren Bezug zu seinem indigenen Erbe überhaupt – bemerkte Brooke Kamin Rapaport, «das war ein grosser Teil Ihres Lebens». Smith antwortete zustimmend: «Ein sehr grosser sogar.»[5] Ohne diesen offiziellen Beleg wäre die Ausstellung im Heard Museum nicht tragfähig gewesen.

E Great artists are often associated with specific landscapes—for example, Georgia O'Keeffe and New Mexico, or Richard Diebenkorn and California. For Leon Polk Smith, it is Oklahoma.

Smith was born near the town of Chickasha in Indian Territory in 1906, just before Oklahoma achieved statehood. He grew up on the ranches and farms of rural Oklahoma, attending Pocasset High School and then Oklahoma State College in Ada. Although Smith left Oklahoma and traveled to Europe and Mexico before settling in New York City in 1944 to commit full-time to making art, his imagination never seemed to have left the landscape of his youth. The Kiamichi Mountains to the east, the tallgrass prairie to the west and north, and the vast Oklahoma sky were significant sources of inspiration for him throughout his career. Smith stated, "I spent forty years of my life in Oklahoma, and it has a warm place in my heart, and it is everywhere in [my] painting ... I give all the credit to Oklahoma."[1]

In 2021, the Heard Museum in Phoenix, Arizona, organized an exhibition titled *Leon Polk Smith: Hiding in Plain Sight*. The exhibition sought to expand the interpretation of Smith's work beyond the predominant Eurocentric criticism to include his ties to Indigenous America. Growing up on Chickasaw lands in Depression-era Oklahoma not only brought Smith in direct contact with people from several Indigenous cultures; it also afforded him the opportunity to participate in events, activities, and celebrations that incorporated Indigenous cultural arts as a part of daily life.

The examples of Indigenous cultural arts in the exhibition included bandolier bags, cradleboards, pipe bags, painted hides and shields, and clothing trimmed with silk ribbon work. Their geometric patterns and bright color combinations echo the forms and color-blocking often encountered in Smith's work. For example, the exhibition cross-referenced a Cheyenne beaded hide pipe bag ❶ with Smith's *N.Y. City* (1945) ❷, a Comanche shield ❸ and cover with *Constellation Yellow-Blue-Violet* (1970) ❹, and *Dusty Miller Leaf* (1953) ❺ with a Sac and Fox skirt with cut ribbon appliqué ❻. Smith noted:

> I was always impressed by the high quality of aesthetics in design and craftsmanship in their art. In 1938 I did my most abstract painting to date. It was called *A Stroll in the Forest*, and I think that was very much influenced by Indian art—the simplicity of it and the directness of it, and not putting in anything that wasn't needed. Nothing there but these vertical tree trunks. I also never had any inhibitions about color. I was never afraid of it. I think that freedom of color came out of my relationship with the Indians.[2]

The influence of Indigenous Oklahoma is also evident in the titles of Smith's works, many of which bear Indigenous names. These include *Okemah* (1955), *Kanawa* (1956), *Cherokee* (1958), and *Pontotoc* (1958). Smith's practice of applying Indigenous names to many of his abstract paintings went largely unnoticed in his lifetime, yet it reveals the connection of Smith's experiences with his life in Oklahoma and possibly to the Cherokee language, which was his first language.[3] Diane Fraher, an Osage/Cherokee and founder of American Indian Artists Inc. (Amerinda), further states that, "Leon's parents were both one-half Cherokee so he was half Cherokee. They were Cherokee speakers."[4]

Twenty-five years prior to the Heard Museum exhibition, the Brooklyn Museum organized a career retrospective titled *Leon Polk Smith: American Painter*. The exhibition was noteworthy for several reasons, but perhaps—for the purposes of this essay—for no greater reason than Smith's public self-identification as being of Cherokee heritage. In her interview for that exhibition's catalogue, which included what is thought to be the first recorded conversation with Smith about his work within the context of his Indigenous heritage, Brooke Kamin Rapaport noted that "it was much a part of the fabric of your life." Smith agreed, saying, "Very much so."[5] Without this public record, the Heard Museum exhibition would not have been viable.

Smith's self-identification as Cherokee in the Brooklyn Museum exhibition catalogue was not particularly surprising at the time. His identity was something that he had openly discussed with friends, Indigenous and non-Indigenous alike, and it was commonly accepted. Smith openly and generously supported the burgeoning contemporary American Indian art movement in New York City. According to David Bunn Martine,

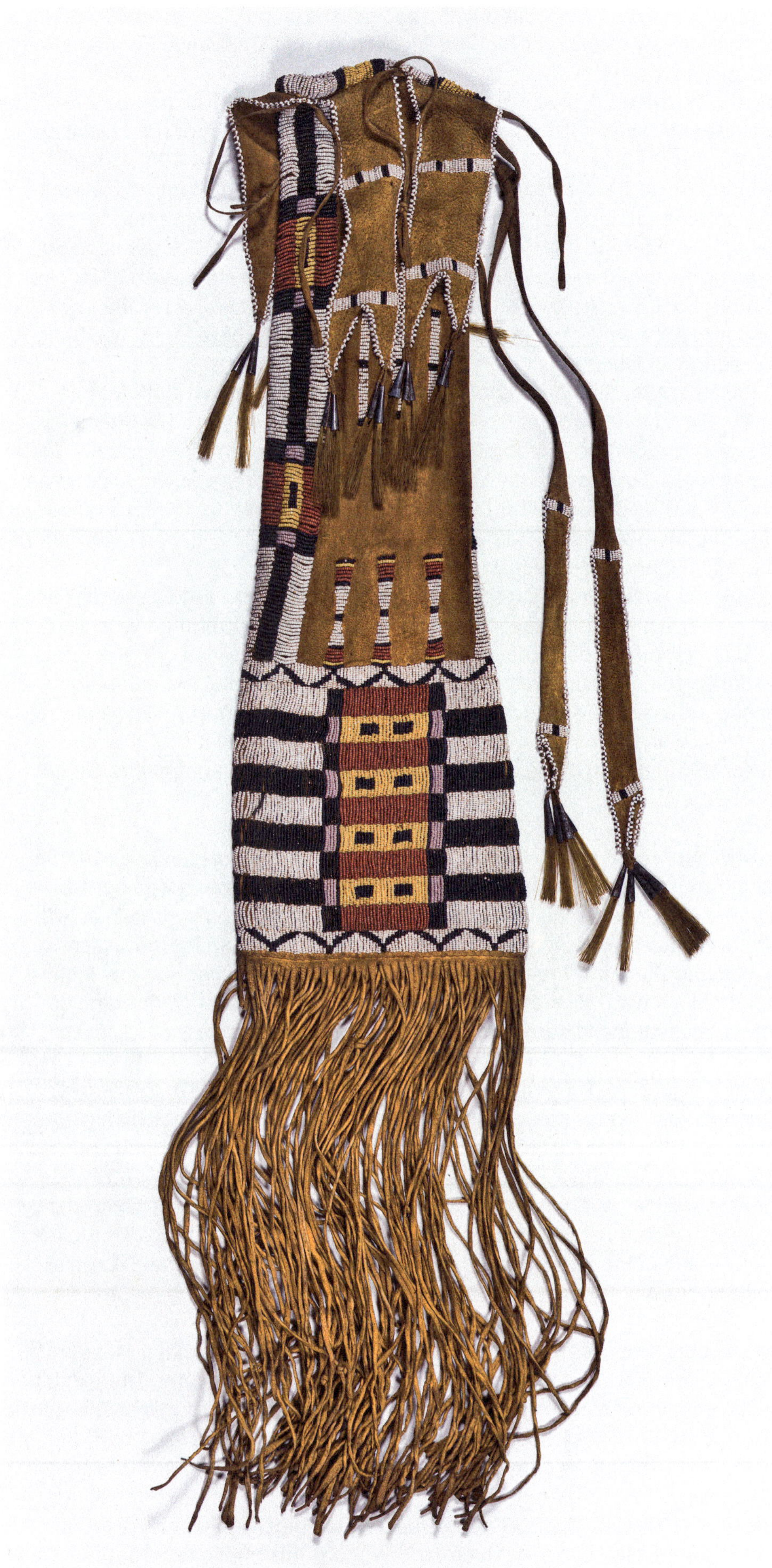

❶ Unbekannter Künstler | Unidentified artist, Pfeifentasche der Cheyenne | Cheyenne pipe bag, Heard Museum Collection, Phoenix, Nachlass | Estate of Carolann Smurthwaite, Foto | Photo: Craig Smith

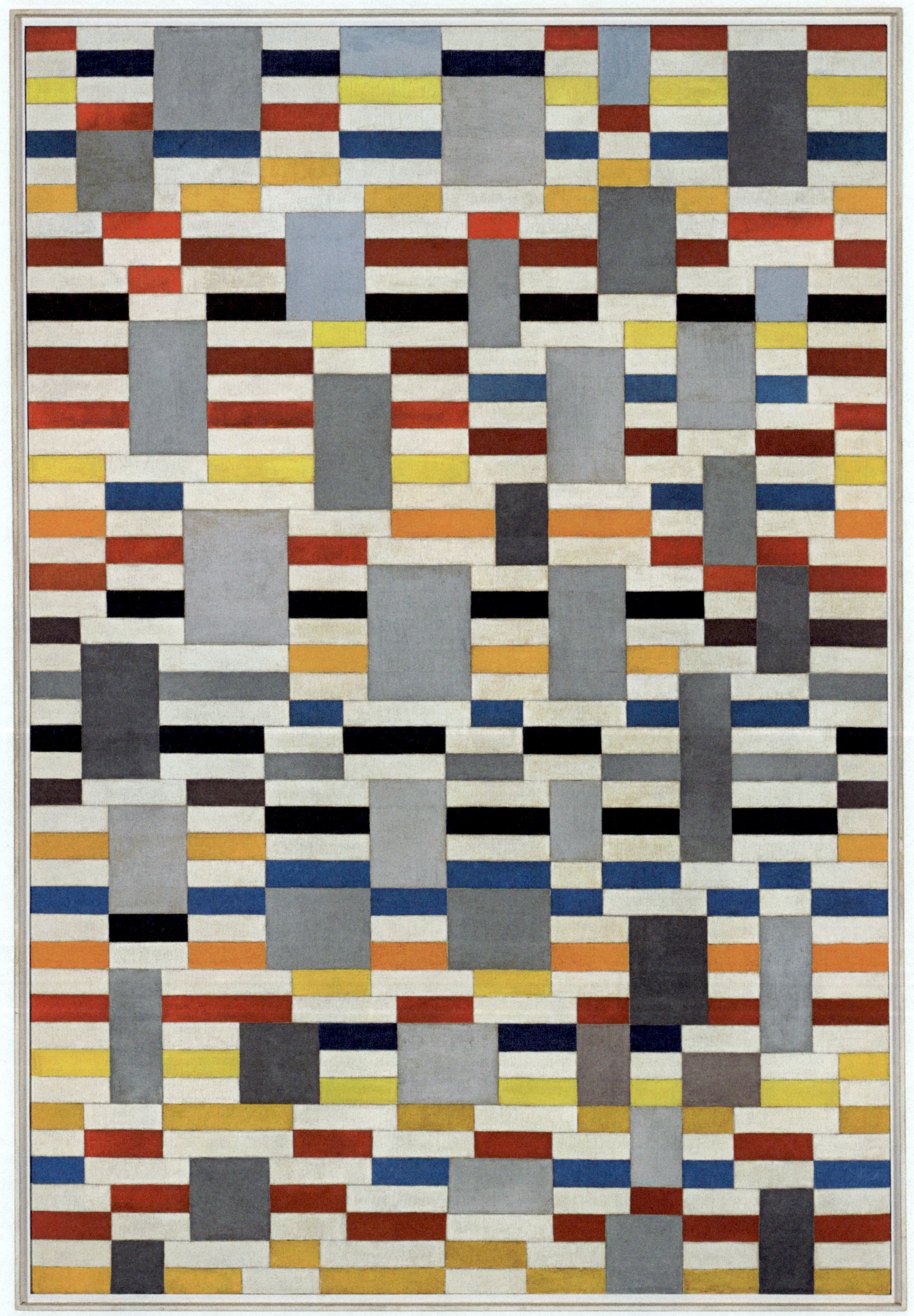

❷ Leon Polk Smith, *N.Y. City*, 1945, Öl und Farbstift auf Leinen | Oil and pencil on linen, 118,7 × 83,2 cm, Whitney Museum of American Art, New York, Ankauf ermöglicht durch | Purchase with funds from the Edward R. Downe, Jr. Purchase Fund and the National Endowment for the Arts in honor of the Museum's 50th Anniversary, © 2023, ProLitteris, Zürich

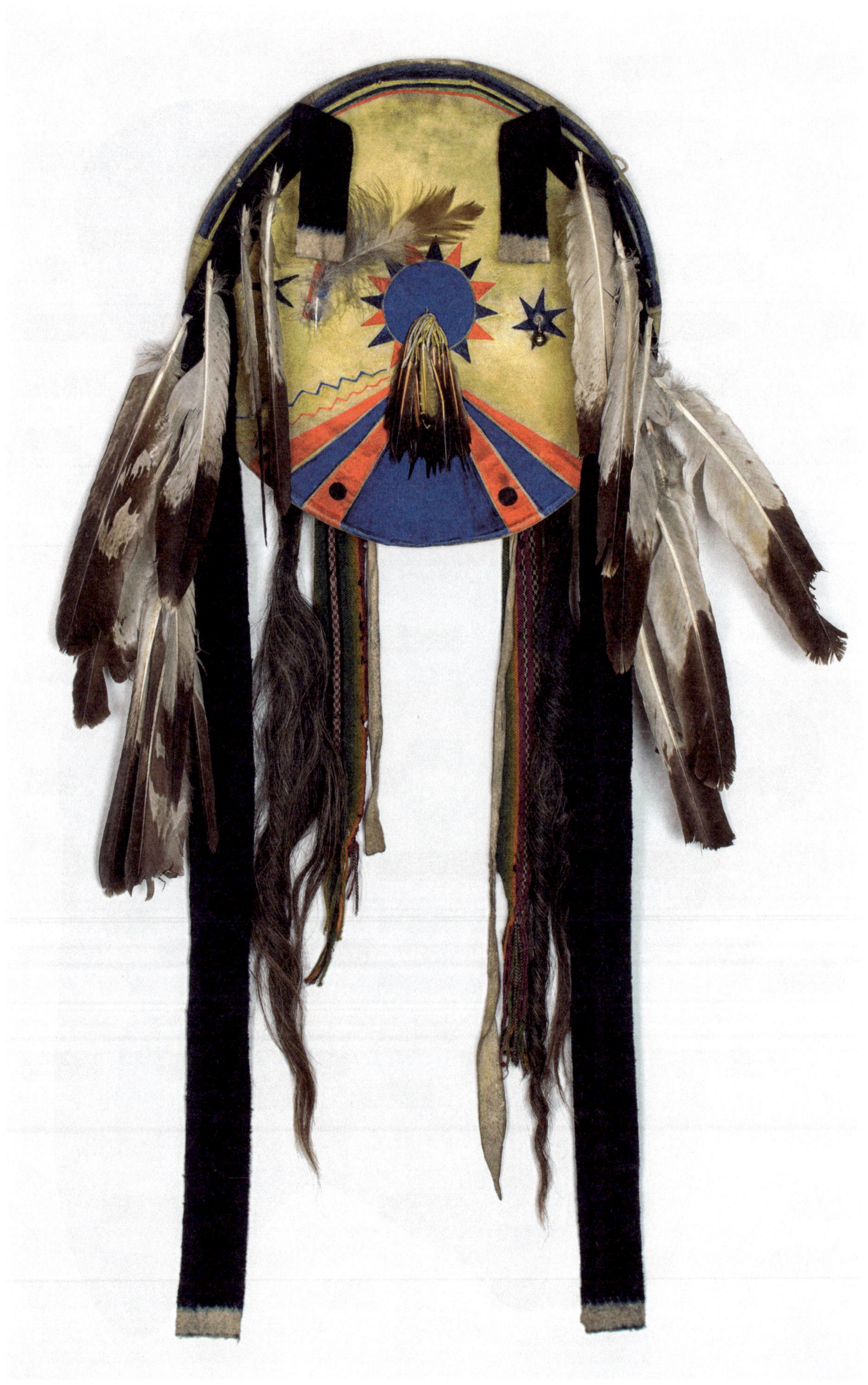

❸ Unbekannter Künstler | Unidentified artist, Schild der Comanchen | Comanche schield, Fred Harvey Fine Arts Collection, Heard Museum, Phoenix, Foto | Photo: Craig Smith

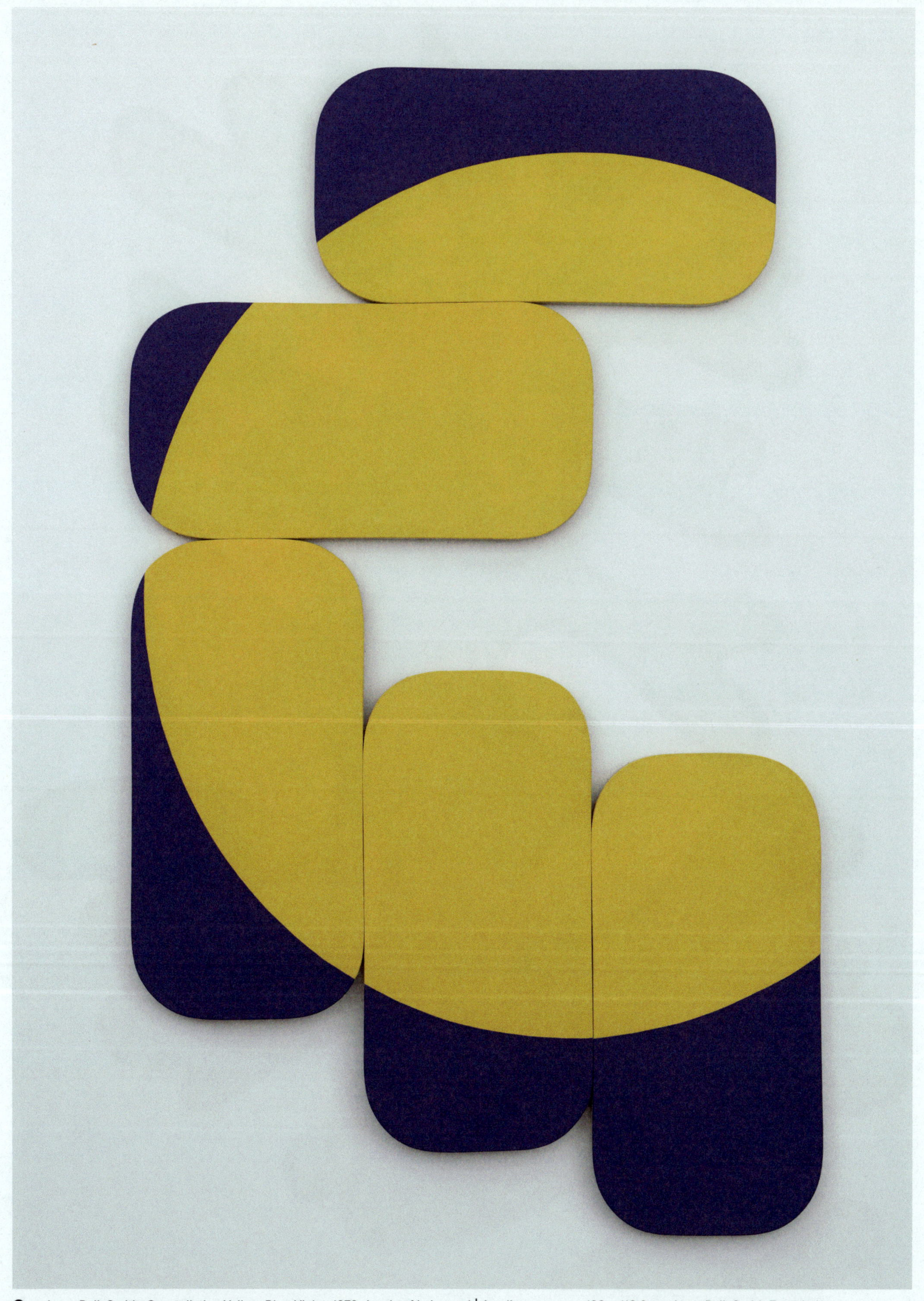

❹ Leon Polk Smith, *Constellation Yellow-Blue-Violet*, 1970, Acryl auf Leinwand | Acrylic on canvas, 193 × 116,8 cm, Leon Polk Smith Foundation, Courtesy of Lisson Gallery, © 2023, ProLitteris, Zürich

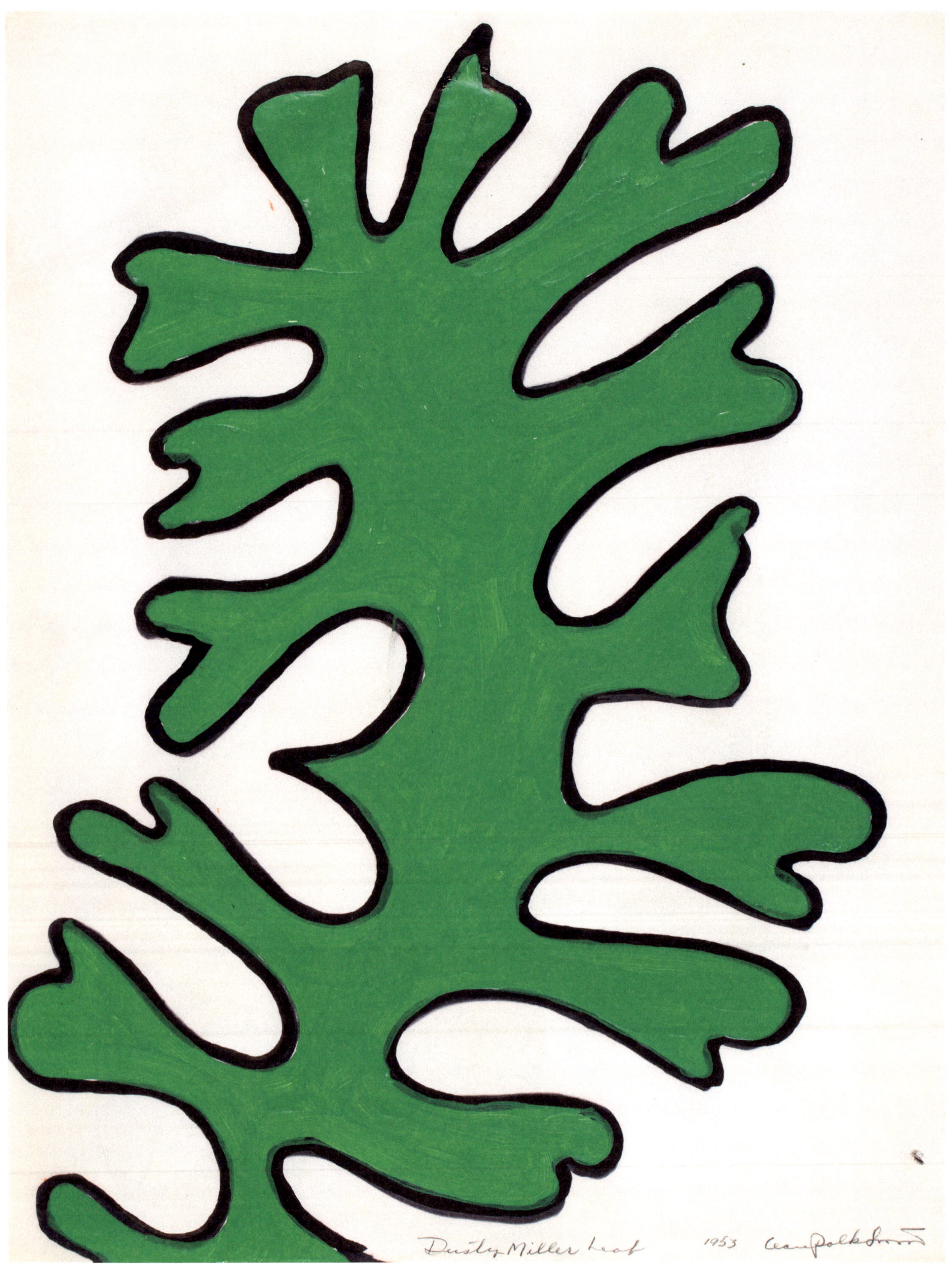

5 Leon Polk Smith, *Dusty Miller Leaf*, 1953, Farbe auf Papier | Paint on paper, 45,7 × 35,2 cm, Courtesy of Heard Museum, Phoenix, © 2023, ProLitteris, Zürich

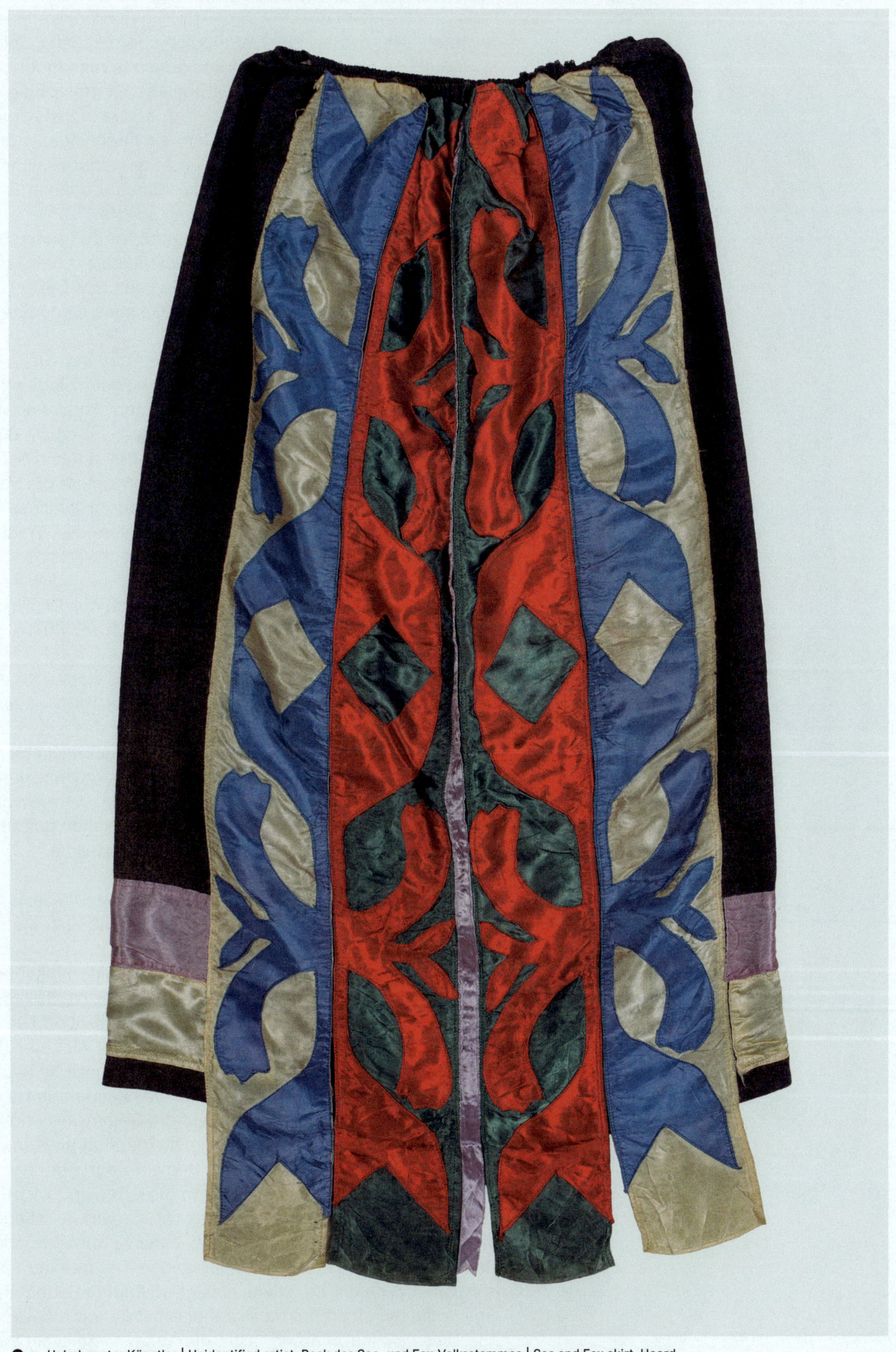

❻ Unbekannter Künstler | Unidentified artist, Rock des Sac- und Fox-Volksstammes | Sac and Fox skirt, Heard Museum Collection, Phoenix, Schenkung von Herr & Frau | Gift of Mr. & Mrs. Harvey III, Foto | Photo: Craig Smith

Dass Smith sich im Ausstellungskatalog des Brooklyn Museum als Cherokee bezeichnete, war damals nicht sonderlich überraschend. Seine Herkunft hatte er sowohl mit indigenen als auch mit nicht-indigenen Freund:innen offen besprochen und sie wurde allgemein akzeptiert. Unverhohlen und grosszügig unterstützte Smith die damals aufkeimende Bewegung der American Indian Art in New York. David Bunn Martine zufolge war er «insbesondere ein intellektueller und finanzieller Mentor von Lloyd R. Oxendine (Lumbee), der sich selbst ebenfalls und auf neue Weise als ein von den Native Americans abstammender Künstler definierte und damit eine wichtige Rolle hinsichtlich der Wurzeln der Bewegung spielte.»[6]

Dieses Bekenntnis zu einem essenziellen Teil seiner selbst mag für Smith nicht besonders berichtenswert gewesen sein, bedenkt man, wie die Lage in dem Oklahoma war, in dem er geboren wurde und aufwuchs. Joe Baker (Lenape), Co-Kurator der Ausstellung im Heard Museum und selbst Künstler, sagte über diese Zeit:

> Als Smith im sogenannten Indian Territory aufwuchs – einem Auffanggebiet für Indianerstämme, die im Zuge der Zwangsumsiedlung dorthin kamen – gab es 39 Stämme, die da Seite an Seite lebten. Anders als im Südwesten wurde den Stammesmitgliedern das Land zugeteilt. Innerhalb des Territoriums gab es nur wenige Reservate. Die jeweilige Identität stand in der frühen Entwicklungsphase des Staates nicht im Vordergrund. Man kannte die Menschen durch ihre Familien und die kleinen Gemeinschaften, die sie ihr Zuhause nannten. Indianer kamen zu Gesellschaftstänzen und Powwows zusammen. Traditionelle religiöse Praktiken waren illegal.[7]

Lynette Perry, eine 1914 geborene Angehörige des Delaware-Stammes, lebte in ihrer Jugend im ländlichen Oklahoma, ganz ähnlich wie Smith. Sie schrieb:

> Delaware, Cherokee, Weisse, Osage, das spielte für uns keine grosse Rolle. Wir haben unsere Nachbarn als Volk schon ziemlich akzeptiert, es gab sogar viele Mischehen. Wir haben nie gedacht, dass das, was wir da machen, Delaware ist. [...] Wir lebten ein Leben, das uns ganz natürlich erschien, und nie machten wir uns Gedanken darüber, was einheimisch und was europäisch sein könnte, genauso wenig wie wir bei den Pflanzen, die in unseren Wäldern und Feldern wuchsen, einen Unterschied machten. Die Wälder sahen gut aus; unser Leben fühlte sich richtig an; das war alles, was ich wissen musste.[8]

Diese Erinnerung an ihre Kindheit offenbart eine fluide, ja wohlwollende Sicht auf Identität und steht in scharfem Kontrast zu dem eher starren Denken, das derzeit in den Vereinigten Staaten um sich greift.

Ein weiterer Grund, warum Smiths Selbstidentifikation als Cherokee damals keine überraschende Mitteilung gewesen sein dürfte, ist, dass seine Eigenschaft als Künstler nicht von seinem indigenen Hintergrund herrührte und er auch nicht den Anspruch erhob, die Cherokee Nation durch seine Kunst zu vertreten. Carter Ratcliff schreibt in seinem Essay «New World View»: «Sein Erbe brachte ihn weder mit dem zeitgenössischen Amerika noch mit der Moderne in Konflikt; vielmehr hatte er das Gefühl, dass ihn die Spiritualität der Native Americans auf die Gegenwart und ihre Möglichkeiten einstimmte».[9] Damals wie heute wird seine Identität als Künstler eher damit verbunden, dass er ein Schüler Piet Mondrians und ein Begründer der Hard-Edge-Malerei war.

Identität war noch nie ein so kompliziertes und wichtiges Thema im Bereich der indigenen Kunst wie heute. Das liegt daran, dass künstlerische Arbeit unmittelbar mit der Wahrung und Weiterentwicklung einer Kultur verbunden wird. Wenn eine Kultur in Gefahr ist, so wie das bei vielen indigenen Kulturen der Fall ist, kann die Identität eines Künstlers oder einer Künstlerin eine gewichtigere Bedeutung erlangen. Jede Bekundung einer indigenen Identität muss daher ernst genommen werden.

Dieser Aufsatz verfolgt nicht die Absicht, die Leser:innen von Smiths Cherokee-Erbe zu überzeugen. Smiths Entscheidungen, insbesondere sein Selbstverständnis als Cherokee, werfen in der aktuellen kulturellen Dynamik Fragen auf – Fragen, die ihn wiederum zu einer polarisierenden, komplizierten und sympathischen Persönlichkeit gemacht haben. Sollten wir ignorieren, dass Smiths Herkunft aus Oklahoma und seine Selbstidentifikation als Cherokee ein wesentlicher Bestandteil seiner Kunst war – oder

"Importantly, he was a mentor both intellectually and financially to Lloyd R. Oxendine (Lumbee), who also self-defined in a new way as a Native artist, thereby playing a pivotal role in nurturing the movement's roots."[6]

This acknowledgment of an essential part of himself might not have felt newsworthy to Smith, considering the context of the Oklahoma in which he was born and raised. Of that time, Joe Baker (Lenape), co-curator of the Heard Museum exhibition and artist, stated,

> When Smith was growing up in what was known as Indian Territory—a holding space for Indian tribes relocated through forced removal—there were 39 tribes existing side by side. Unlike [in] the Southwest, lands were distributed to tribal members through allotment. Few reservations existed within the territory. Individual identity was not top of mind in the early development of the state. Individuals were known by their families and the small communities they called home. Indian people gathered around social dances and powwows. Traditional religious practices were illegal.[7]

Lynette Perry, a member of the Delaware tribe who was born in 1914, lived her early life in rural Oklahoma, much like Smith did. She wrote:

> Delaware, Cherokee, white, Osage, it didn't much matter to us. We pretty much accepted our neighbors as folks, even did a lot of intermarrying. We never thought, this thing we're doing now is Delaware. [...] We lived a life that seemed natural to us and never considered what might be Native and what European, any more than we made that distinction about plants that grew in our woods and fields. The woods looked fine; our life felt right; that was all I needed to know.[8]

This recollection of her childhood reveals a fluid, if not sympathetic, view on identity and stands in marked contrast to the more rigid thinking that is currently pervasive in the United States.

Another reason why Smith's self-identification as Cherokee might not have felt like a surprising announcement at that time is that his identity as an artist did not derive from his Indigenous background; nor did he claim to represent the Cherokee Nation through his art. According to Carter Ratcliff in his essay "New World View," "His heritage would put him at odds neither with contemporary America nor with Modernism; in fact, the spirituality of the Native Americans, he felt, attuned him to the present and its possibilities."[9] Then, as now, his artistic identity is more closely aligned with being a disciple of Piet Mondrian and a founder of the Hard-edge Painting movement.

Identity has never been a more complicated or important issue in the field of Indigenous art than it is today. This is because artistic practice is directly related to the preservation and advancement of culture. When a culture is at risk, as so many Indigenous cultures are, an artist's identity can take on heightened significance. Any claim of Native identity must therefore be taken seriously.

It is not the intention of this essay to convince the reader of Smith's Cherokee heritage. Smith's choices, especially his self-identification as Cherokee, raise questions in today's current cultural dynamic—questions that have made him, in turn, a polarizing, complicated, and sympathetic figure. Should we ignore that Smith's Oklahoma heritage and self-identification as Cherokee was a major part of his art, or should we show that this is where it came from? University of Texas at Austin Professor Randolph Lewis suggests the following:

> Trapped in a racist, homophobic society, Smith had to make difficult decisions about his public identity. Some of his decisions may disappoint us today, but the "Indianness" of this significant artist was present in his work whether he intended it to be or not, whether he always announced it to the world or not. Even when he seemed to minimize the Indian aspects of his work, the influence of Indian cultures still made its way onto his canvas, sometimes blatantly, sometimes cryptically.[10]

To date, there is no evidence that Smith was an enrolled member of the Cherokee Nation. Currently, only individuals who are descended from those whose names appear

sollten wir zeigen, dass da ihre Ursprünge liegen? Randolph Lewis, Professor an der University of Texas in Austin, behauptet:

> Gefangen in einer rassistischen, homophoben Gesellschaft, musste Smith bezüglich seiner öffentlichen Identität schwierige Entscheidungen treffen. Einige seiner Entscheidungen mögen uns heute enttäuschen, aber die «Indianness» dieses bedeutenden Künstlers war in seinem Schaffen präsent, ob er es wollte oder nicht, ob er es der Welt wieder und wieder verkündete oder nicht. Selbst dann, wenn er die indianischen Aspekte seines Werks zu minimieren schien, fand der Einfluss der indianischen Kulturen immer noch – mal offensichtlich, mal kryptisch – den Weg auf seine Leinwand.[10]

Bis heute gibt es keinen Beleg dafür, dass Smith ein eingetragenes Mitglied der Cherokee Nation war. Derzeit kommen nur Personen für die Staatsbürgerschaft der Cherokee Nation infrage, die von Menschen abstammen, deren Namen auf der entsprechenden Dawes-Rolle zu finden sind.[11] Viele von denen, die berechtigt waren, die Dawes-Rolle zu unterzeichnen und die Stammesregistrierung und -anerkennung zu erhalten, verweigerten dies aufgrund der langen Geschichte der Vertragsbrüche zwischen den Stämmen und der Bundesregierung. Andere, die sich ausserhalb der Cherokee Nation in Orten wie Texas und Arkansas niedergelassen hatten, waren nicht befugt, die Dawes-Rolle zu unterschreiben, da sie bereits Bürger:innen der Vereinigten Staaten waren. Die Frage der Aufnahme betrifft die Souveränität der Stämme unmittelbar und muss respektiert werden. Für diejenigen, die eine bundesstaatliche Anerkennung und die Stammesregistrierung als wichtigste Kriterien zur Festlegung der Indigenität erachten, ist Smith kein Cherokee.

Die Anwendung dieser Standards zur Begründung indigener Authentizität legt jedoch keinen Wert auf unmittelbare, persönliche Erfahrungswerte und ignoriert die mündliche Überlieferung der Native Americans, die traditionell das wichtigste Medium für die Weitergabe kultureller Informationen ist. Dwanna L. McKay von der Muscogee (Creek) Nation und Assistenzprofessorin im Programm für Rassen-, Ethnizitäts- und Migrationsstudien am Colorado College schreibt:

> Die Forschung zeigt, dass die Institutionalisierung von Legitimitätskriterien umstrittene Bedeutungen von Indigenität in den Vereinigten Staaten hervorgebracht hat, was unter Indigenen sowie unter indigenen Gemeinschaften zu einer hartnäckigen Debatte über authentische Indigenität führt. Der Tropus des «echten Indianers», der durch die kolonisierende Bundespolitik eingeführt wurde, ist heute für American Indians ein soziales Faktum. Daher stösst die Behauptung, indigen zu sein, in den Vereinigten Staaten häufig auf Widerstand, selbst innerhalb indigener Gemeinschaften.[12]

Es gibt viele Künstler:innen, die Stämmen angehören, die von der Bundesregierung nicht anerkannt sind. Andere zelebrieren ein gemischt indigenes und nicht-indigenes Erbe oder einen gemischten Stammeshintergrund. Manche sind registriert, andere nicht. Auch wenn sie herausfordernd sein kann, führt die Komplexität dieser Gegebenheiten häufig zu einem wachen Diskurs und zu einem tieferen Verständnis nicht nur für die Kunst und Geschichte der American Indians, sondern auch für den Kampf, dem sich viele kunstschaffende People of Color heute stellen müssen. heather ahtone (Chickasaw), leitende Kuratorin am American Indian Cultural Center and Museum in Oklahoma, meint: «Es ist so wichtig zu berücksichtigen, dass Gemeinschaften der Native Americans Teil eines grösseren Spektrums von indigenen Kulturen sind. Die Erkundung der gesamten Bandbreite dieses Spektrums, dieses Regenbogens, ermöglicht uns, Respekt und Verständnis für die Kulturen zu erlangen, die näher an Daheim sind.»[13] Smiths Aussage, er stamme von den Cherokee ab, sollte in diesem Licht gesehen werden.

Es ist klar, dass Oklahoma ein Teil von Smiths kreativer DNA war. Smith erkannte seine Beziehung zu den Landschaften und Menschen Oklahomas als wesentlich für seine Identität und Entwicklung als Künstler an. Er erklärte: «Ich bin im Südwesten aufgewachsen, wo die Farben der Natur rein und überbordend waren und wo meine indianischen Nachbarn und Verwandten Farben einsetzten, um zu vibrieren und schocken.»[14] Diese Auskunft sollte das Verständnis dafür, welche Rolle die Farbe bei der

on the Dawes Roll are considered eligible for Cherokee Nation citizenship.[11] Many who were eligible to sign the Dawes Roll and receive tribal enrollment and recognition refused to do so because of the long history of broken treaties between the tribes and the federal government. Others who had settled outside the Cherokee Nation in places like Texas and Arkansas were ineligible to sign the Dawes Roll because they were already United States citizens. Enrollment is an issue that speaks directly to the sovereignty of tribes and must be respected. For those who use federal recognition and tribal enrollment as the primary criteria for determining Indigeneity, Smith is not Cherokee.

Using these standards to establish Indigenous authenticity, however, does not place value on direct, first-person experience and ignores Native oral history, which has traditionally been the primary means by which cultural information was shared. Dwanna L. McKay of the Muscogee (Creek) Nation and Assistant Professor in the Race, Ethnicity, and Migration Studies Program at Colorado College writes:

> Research shows that the institutionalization of legitimacy criteria has created contested meanings of being indigenous to the United States, which leads to an unrelenting debate about authentic indigeneity among indigenous people and between indigenous communities. While instituted through colonizing federal Indian policy, the "real Indian" trope is now a social fact for American Indians. Thus, indigeneity claims commonly encounter resistance in the United States, even within indigenous communities.[12]

There are many artists who are members of tribes that are not recognized by the federal government. Others celebrate mixed Native and non-Native heritage, as well as mixed tribal backgrounds. Some are enrolled, and some are not. Though it can be challenging, the complexity of this reality often leads to thoughtful discourse and a deeper understanding of American Indian art and history as well as the struggle that many artists of color face today. heather ahtone, (Chickasaw), senior curator at the American Indian Cultural Center and Museum in Oklahoma, suggests, "It is so important to consider that Native American communities are part of the larger spectrum of Indigenous cultures. Exploring the full breadth of that spectrum, like a rainbow, allows us to gain respect and understanding about the cultures closer to home."[13] Smith's assertion of Cherokee heritage merits consideration within this framework.

It is clear that Oklahoma was part of Smith's creative DNA. Smith acknowledged his relationship to the landscapes and peoples of Oklahoma as essential to his identity and development as an artist. He stated, "I grew up in the Southwest, where the colors in nature were pure and rampant, and where my Indian neighbors and relatives used color to vibrate and shock."[14] This information should serve to deepen the appreciation of the role it played in the creation of his art and, in turn, his important contributions to American modernism. Leon Polk Smith, a founder of the Hard-edge Painting movement, pioneered new abstracting ways of seeing our world and electrified his canvases with bright colors, shapes, and compositions. Today, they still vibrate and shock with unique personal meaning and visual force.

Entstehung seiner Kunst und damit auch bei seinen wichtigen Beiträgen zur amerikanischen Moderne gespielt hat, noch vertiefen. Leon Polk Smith, ein Begründer der Hard-Edge-Malerei, war ein Wegbereiter neuer, abstrakter Sichtweisen auf unsere Welt und elektrisierte seine Leinwände mit leuchtenden Farben, Formen und Kompositionen. Heute vibrieren und schocken sie noch immer mit einer unverwechselbar persönlichen Bedeutung und visueller Kraft.

D

1 Zit. n. Jenna Duncan, «Leon Polk Smith: Hiding in Plain Sight at Heard Museum», in: *Echo Magazine*, März 2021, S. 22–23.
2 Leon Polk Smith im Interview mit Brooke Kamin Rapaport, «An Interview with Leon Polk Smith», in: *Leon Polk Smith: American Painter*, Ausst.-Kat. Brooklyn Museum, New York 1996, S. 19.
3 David Bunn Martine, in: Ders., *No Reservation: New York Contemporary Native American Art Movement*, New York 2017, S. 60.
4 Diane Fraher, in: *No Reservation* (wie Anm. 3), S. 65.
5 Smith, «An Interview» (wie Anm. 2), S. 19.
6 Martine, *No Reservation* (wie Anm. 3), S. 64.
7 Joe Baker in einem fachlichen Austausch am 25. Juni 2020.
8 Lynette Perry und Manny Skolnick, *Keeper of the Delaware Dolls*, Lincoln 1999, S. 51 f.
9 Carter Ratcliff, «New World View», in: *Artforum*, März 1997, S. 14.
10 Randolph Lewis, «The Native Roots of Modern Art: Rereading the Paintings of Leon Polk Smith», in: *American Indian Quarterly* (Winter 2001), S. 108.
11 Bei den Dawes-Rollen handelt es sich um Listen aus den Jahren 1898–1914, in denen die anerkannten Mitglieder von fünf Stämmen – Cherokees, Creeks, Choctaws, Chickasaws und Seminolen – aufgeführt sind, die Anspruch auf eine Zuteilung von Land hatten. Siehe National Archives online: https://www.archives.gov/research/native-americans/dawes/tutorial/intro.html (zuletzt abgerufen: 5.1.2023).
12 Dwanna L. McKay, «Real Indians: Policing or Protecting Authentic Indigenous Identity?», in: *Sociology of Race and Ethnicity*, 2021, S. 12.
13 heather ahtone, «Redefining Images: Indigenous Photographers», in: *Art Focus Oklahoma*, Mai/Juni 2014, S. 16.
14 Lawrence Alloway, «Leon Polk Smith's Maverick Attitude», in: *The New York Times*, 8. Dezember 1973, S. 29.

E

1 Quoted in Jenna Duncan, "Leon Polk Smith: Hiding in Plain Sight at Heard Museum," *Echo Magazine* 32: 6 (March 2021): 22–23.
2 Leon Polk Smith interviewed by Brooke Kamin Rapaport, "An Interview with Leon Polk Smith," in *Leon Polk Smith: American Painter*, exh. cat. Brooklyn Museum (New York: Brooklyn Museum, 1996), 19.
3 David Bunn Martine, *No Reservation: New York Contemporary Native American Art Movement* (New York: Amerinda, Inc., 2017), 60.
4 Diane Fraher, quoted in ibid., 65.
5 Smith, "An Interview," 19.
6 Martine, *No Reservation*, 64.
7 Joe Baker, professional communication, 25 June 2020.
8 Lynette Perry and Manny Skolnick, *Keeper of the Delaware Dolls* (Lincoln: Bison Books, 1999), 51–52.
9 Carter Ratcliff, "New World View," *Artforum* (March 1997): 14.
10 Randolph Lewis, "The Native Roots of Modern Art: Rereading the Paintings of Leon Polk Smith," *American Indian Quarterly* (Winter 2001): 108.
11 The Dawes Rolls are lists from 1898 to 1914 of accepted members of five tribes—the Cherokees, Creeks, Choctaws, Chickasaws, and Seminoles—who were entitled to an allotment of land. See National Archives online at https://www.archives.gov/research/native-amer- icans/dawes/tutorial/intro.html.
12 Dwanna L. McKay, "Real Indians: Policing or Protecting Authentic Indigenous Identity?" *Sociology of Race and Ethnicity* (2021): 12.
13 heather ahtone, "Redefining Images: Indigenous Photographers," *Art Focus Oklahoma* (May/June 2014): 16.
14 Lawrence Alloway, "Leon Polk Smith's Maverick Attitude," *The New York Times*, 8 December 1973, 29.

Anhang

Appendix

Werke in der Ausstellung | Works on display

Ohne Titel | Untitled, 1946
Tinte und Filzstift auf Papier | Ink and marker on paper
49,5 × 34 cm, gerahmt | framed
Leon Polk Smith Foundation, Courtesy of Lisson Gallery
S. | p. 14

Ohne Titel | Untitled, 1946
Farbe und Tempera auf Karton | Paint and tempera on cardboard
34 × 24,8 cm, gerahmt | framed
Leon Polk Smith Foundation, Courtesy of Lisson Gallery
S. | p. 14

Diagonal Passage, 1947
Öl auf Leinwand | Oil on canvas
Ø 147 cm
Museum Ritter, Waldenbuch
S. | p. 17

Black-Black, 1950
Öl auf Leinwand | Oil on canvas
126,7 × 83,2 cm
Leon Polk Smith Foundation, Courtesy of Lisson Gallery
S. | p. 16

Diagonal Passage with Horizontal, 1950
Öl auf Leinwand | Oil on canvas
66,7 × 106,7 cm
Leon Polk Smith Foundation, Courtesy of Lisson Gallery
S. | pp. 20, 34

Black-White Repeat, 1953
Öl auf Leinwand | Oil on canvas
130 × 97 cm
Privatsammlung | Private collection, Berlin
S. | pp. 13, 14, 21

Chikasaw, 1953
Öl auf Leinwand | Oil on canvas
Ø 61 cm
Nicole Schlégl-Helbling
S. | pp. 15, 19

Ohne Titel | Untitled, 1954
Öl auf Leinwand | Oil on canvas
74,3 × 74,9 cm
Leon Polk Smith Foundation, Courtesy of Lisson Gallery
S. | pp. 59, 61

Blue Red Spheres, 1955
Öl auf Leinwand | Oil on canvas
60,3 × 60,3 cm
Leon Polk Smith Foundation, Courtesy of Lisson Gallery
S. | p. 55

Kanawa, 1956
Öl auf Leinwand | Oil on canvas
Ø 104,1 cm
Privatsammlung | Private collection, Berlin
S. | p. 27

Tapari, 1956
Öl auf Leinwand | Oil on canvas
81,4 × 40,7 cm
Privatsammlung | Private collection, Berlin
S. | pp. 15, 18

Nowata, 1956
Öl auf Leinwand | Oil on canvas
Ø 85,1 cm
Privatsammlung | Private collection, Berlin
S. | pp. 24, 27

Triptik, 1957–1959
Öl auf Leinwand | Oil on canvas
3 Teile | parts, je | each 40 × 132 cm
Novartis Art Collection
S. | p. 26

Caddo, 1958
Öl und Metallicfarbe auf Leinwand | Oil and metallic paint on canvas
63,5 × 50,8 cm
Privatsammlung | Private collection, Berlin
S. | pp. 21, 23

Over Easy, 1958
Öl auf Leinwand | Oil on canvas
109 × 84 cm
Städel Museum Frankfurt am Main, Eigentum des Städelschen Museums-Vereins e.V.
S. | pp. 20, 25, 43

N. 1469B, 1960
Öl auf Holz | Oil on wood
Ø 61 cm
Leon Polk Smith Foundation, Courtesy of Lisson Gallery
S. | pp. 54, 57

Relief No. 1469, 1960
Öl auf Holz | Oil on wood
Ø 61 cm
Leon Polk Smith Foundation,
Courtesy of Lisson Gallery
S. | pp. 54, 56

Correspondence Black and Blue, 1960
Öl auf Leinwand | Oil on canvas
Ø 120 cm
Leon Polk Smith Foundation,
Courtesy of Lisson Gallery
S. | pp. 93, 95

Cumulus A, 1961
Öl auf Holz | Oil on wood
200,7 × 40,6 cm
Leon Polk Smith Foundation,
Courtesy of Lisson Gallery
S. | p. 55

Prolonged Echo, 1961
Öl auf Leinwand | Oil on canvas
89 × 83,8 cm
Novartis Art Collection
S. | pp. 24/25

Wood Relief 1100 Black-Silver, 1961
Öl auf Holz | Oil on wood
Ø 28 cm
Leon Polk Smith Foundation,
Courtesy of Lisson Gallery
S. | pp. 53, 54

Correspondence Blue-Orange, 1962
Acryl und Collage auf Leinwand |
Acrylic and collage on canvas
Ø 100,3 cm
Leon Polk Smith Foundation,
Courtesy of Lisson Gallery
S. | p. 93

Ohne Titel | Untitled, 1965
Gerissenes Papier | Torn paper
39,5 × 32 cm, gerahmt | framed
Musée de Grenoble
S. | p. 58

Ohne Titel | Untitled, 1965
Gerissenes Papier | Torn paper
39,5 × 32 cm, gerahmt | framed
Musée de Grenoble
S. | p. 58

Ohne Titel | Untitled, 1965
Gerissenes Papier | Torn paper
39,5 × 32 cm, gerahmt | framed
Musée de Grenoble
S. | p. 58

Ohne Titel | Untitled, 1965
Gerissenes Papier | Torn paper
39,5 × 32 cm, gerahmt | framed
Musée de Grenoble
S. | p. 58

Ohne Titel | Untitled, 1965
Gerissenes Papier | Torn paper
39,5 × 32 cm, gerahmt | framed
Musée de Grenoble
S. | p. 58

Seven Involvements in One, 1966
Paravent
Öl auf Leinwand | Oil on canvas
220 × 400 × 4 cm
Leon Polk Smith Foundation,
Courtesy of Lisson Gallery
S. | pp. 64–68

Constellation Leveling Blue – Green, 1967
Öl auf Leinwand | Oil on canvas
2 Teile | parts, gesamt | overall
106,7 × 61,1 cm
Privatsammlung | Private collection,
Berlin
S. | p. 98

Constellation Red-Green-Black, 1967
Acryl auf Leinwand | Acrylic on canvas
3 Teile | parts,
gesamt | overall 243,8 × 132,1 cm
Leon Polk Smith Foundation,
Courtesy of Lisson Gallery
S. | pp. 114, 117, 119

Ohne Titel | Untitled, 1968
Bleistift und Farbe auf Papier |
Pencil and paint on paper
102,2 × 65,4 cm
Leon Polk Smith Foundation,
Courtesy of Lisson Gallery
S. | p. 63

Constellation: Untitled, 1968
Acryl auf Leinwand | Acrylic on canvas
2 Teile | parts, gesamt | overall
72 × 43 cm
Leon Polk Smith Foundation,
Courtesy of Lisson Gallery
S. | pp. 96, 99

Correspondence Blue-Yellow Zig Zag,
1968
Acryl auf Leinwand | Acrylic on canvas
147,3 × 233,7 cm
Leon Polk Smith Foundation,
Courtesy of Lisson Gallery
S. | pp. 86, 97

Constellation Q, 1968
Acryl auf Leinwand | Acrylic on canvas
3 Teile | parts, gesamt | overall
140 × 120 cm
Leon Polk Smith Foundation,
Courtesy of Lisson Gallery
S. | pp. 86, 90

Red Circle Blue Square, 1968
Farbe auf Leinwand | Paint on canvas
2 Teile | parts, gesamt | overall
220 × 121 cm
Leon Polk Smith Foundation,
Courtesy of Lisson Gallery
S. | pp. 87, 89, 91

Constellation Y, 1968
Acryl auf Leinwand | Acrylic on canvas
3 Teile | parts, gesamt | overall
115 × 160 cm
Leon Polk Smith Foundation,
Courtesy of Lisson Gallery
S. | pp. 46, 87, 91

Correspondence Orange-Blue, 1968
Acryl auf Leinwand | Acrylic on canvas
215 × 168 cm
Musée de Grenoble
S. | pp. 91, 92

Constellation Blue-Black-Purple – Six Circles, 1968
Acryl auf Leinwand | Acrylic on canvas
6 Teile | parts, gesamt | overall
165,1 × 184,2 cm
Leon Polk Smith Foundation,
Courtesy of Lisson Gallery
S. | pp. 116, 121

Ohne Titel | Untitled, 1969
Farbpapier, Grafit und Tinte auf Papier |
Colored paper, graphite and ink on paper
84,5 × 62,2 cm, gerahmt | framed
Leon Polk Smith Foundation,
Courtesy of Lisson Gallery
S. | p. 62

Constellation O, 1969
Acryl auf Leinwand | Acrylic on canvas
2 Teile | parts, gesamt | overall
139,7 × 100,3 cm
Leon Polk Smith Foundation,
Courtesy of Lisson Gallery
S. | pp. 86, 90

Constellation A, 1969
Acryl auf Leinwand | Acrylic on canvas
5 Teile | parts, insgesamt | overall
264,2 × 195,6 cm
Leon Polk Smith Foundation,
Courtesy of Lisson Gallery
S. | pp. 114, 117

Constellation Twelve Circles, 1969–1988
Latex auf Aluminium | Latex on aluminum
7 Teile | parts,
gesamt | overall 518,2 × 370,8 cm
Novartis Art Collection
S. | pp. 111, 112/113

Constellation Yellow-Blue-Violet, 1970
Acryl auf Leinwand | Acrylic on canvas
5 Teile | parts,
gesamt | overall 196,5 × 120 cm
Leon Polk Smith Foundation,
Courtesy of Lisson Gallery
S. | pp. 116, 120, 139

Constellation Up and Away, 1970
Acryl auf Leinwand | Acrylic on canvas
3 Teile | parts,
gesamt | overall 239 × 259 cm
Leon Polk Smith Foundation,
Courtesy of Lisson Gallery
S. | pp. 109, 110, 115

Constellation Happy Day, 1971
Acryl auf Leinwand | Acrylic on canvas
3 Teile | parts,
gesamt | overall 206 × 197 cm
Leon Polk Smith Foundation,
Courtesy of Lisson Gallery
S. | pp. 110, 115

No. 7809, 1978
Acryl auf Leinwand | Acrylic on canvas
Ø 202 cm
Privatsammlung | Private collection,
Zürich
S. | pp. 122/123

Sunset Caribe, 1983
Acryl auf Leinwand | Acrylic on canvas
152 × 284 cm
Leon Polk Smith Foundation,
Courtesy of Lisson Gallery
S. | pp. 50/51, 131

Green – Two Black Edges, 1984
Acryl auf Leinwand, Holz |
Acrylic on canvas, wood
188 × 432 cm
Neues Museum Nürnberg,
Leihgabe der | Loan of Stadt Nürnberg
S. | pp. 82, 127, 128

Curve for Blue Green, 1984
Acryl auf Leinwand, Holz |
Acrylic on canvas, wood
254 × 147,3 cm
Leon Polk Smith Foundation,
Courtesy of Lisson Gallery
S. | pp. 129, 130

Prairie Moon, 1988
Acryl auf Leinwand |
Acrylic on canvas
213,4 × 214 cm
Leon Polk Smith Foundation,
Courtesy of Lisson Gallery
S. | pp. 125, 126

Leon Polk Smith: Kurzbiografie

1906
Leon Polk Smith wird am 20. Mai als achtes von neun Kindern in Chickasha im damaligen «Indian Territory» geboren, das im Jahr darauf in den neu gegründeten US-Bundesstaat Oklahoma integriert wird. Smiths Eltern waren vermutlich beide halbe Cherokee; er wächst in einem vornehmlich von der Kultur der Chickasaw und Choctaw Native Americans geprägten Umfeld auf.

1912
Umzug der Familie in die ebenfalls ländlich geprägte Kleinstadt Franks südlich von Ada, Oklahoma

1925–1930
Nach dem Highschool-Abschluss verdient Smith sein Geld als Rancharbeiter in Oklahoma, bevor er nach Arizona übersiedelt, wo er im Strassenbau tätig ist und Telefonkabel verlegt. Auch als 1929 die Weltwirtschaft einbricht und in den USA die Grosse Depression einsetzt, unterstützt er seine Familie und deren Farm mit regelmässigen Zahlungen. Daneben lässt er sich in Ada zum Lehrer ausbilden und besucht Zusatzkurse in Kunst und Psychologie.

1931
Zwangsversteigerung der familieneigenen Farm

1934
Studienabschluss mit einem Bachelor of Arts in Pädagogik

1934–1940
Arbeit als Primar- und Sekundarlehrer in Franks und im benachbarten Fittstown, Oklahoma

1936–1938
Smith belegt die Sommerkurse am renommierten Teachers College der Columbia University in New York City. Im ersten Jahr besucht er A.E. Gallatins Museum of Living Art an der New York University, wo er zum ersten Mal Werken von Piet Mondrian, Constantin Brancusi und Hans Arp begegnet.

1938
Studienabschluss mit einem Master of Arts in Kunst und pädagogischer Psychologie

1939–1940
Reisen nach Europa und Mexiko

1940–1942
Arbeit als Assistenzprofessor für Kunst am Georgia Teachers College in Collegeboro, Georgia

1941
Erste Einzelausstellung in der Uptown Gallery in New York City mit vom Surrealismus inspirierten Gemälden und Aquarellen; erste Teilnahme an einer institutionellen Gruppenausstellung im Brooklyn Museum, New York City

1942
Umzug in den Bundesstaat Delaware, wo er den Posten als State Supervisor of Art Education übernimmt; erste institutionelle Einzelausstellung an der Telfair Academy of Arts and Sciences in Savannah, Georgia

1943
Smith fertigt seine ersten rein geometrischen Malereien, darunter *OK Territory*.

1944
Kündigung der Stelle in Delaware und Umzug nach New York City. Smith beginnt, am Museum of Non-Objective Painting in New York City als Assistent von Hilla Rebay zu arbeiten, die später Gründungsdirektorin des Solomon R. Guggenheim Museum wird. Ein Stipendium der Solomon R. Guggenheim Foundation ermöglicht ihm einen längeren Aufenthalt in Santa Fe, New Mexico, wo er weitere geometrisch-abstrakte Leinwand- und Papierarbeiten erstellt.

1945
Zurück in New York City entstehen Malereien, die stark von der Bildsprache Piet Mondrians beeinflusst sind, darunter *Diagonal Passages*.

1949
Smith nimmt an der Gruppenausstellung *Post Mondrian Painters* in der Sidney Janis Gallery in New York City teil, in der auch Arbeiten von Josef Albers, Ilya Bolotowsky und Fritz Glarner gezeigt werden.

Leon Polk Smith: Short Chronology

1906
Leon Polk Smith, the eighth of nine children, is born on May 20 in Chickasha within so-called Indian Territory, which becomes integrated into the newly formed state of Oklahoma in the following year. Smith's parents, probably both half Cherokee, raise him in an environment imbued with the culture of the Chickasaw and Choctaw Native American people.

1912
The family moves to another rural town in Oklahoma called Franks, south of Ada.

1925–1930
After graduating from high school, Smith works as a ranch hand in Oklahoma before moving to Arizona, where he works in road construction and lays telephone cable. He supports his family and their farm with regular payments. These continue when the world economy collapses in 1929 and the Great Depression begins in the US. He also trains as a teacher in Ada and attends supplementary courses in art and psychology.

1931
His family's farm is foreclosed.

1934
Graduates with a Bachelor of Arts in education.

1934–1940
Works as a primary and secondary school teacher in Franks and neighboring Fittstown, Oklahoma.

1936–1938
Smith takes summer courses at the renowned Columbia University Teachers College in New York City. During his first year, he visits A.E. Gallatin's Museum of Living Art at New York University, where he first encounters artworks by Piet Mondrian, Constantin Brancusi, and Hans Arp.

1938
Graduates with a Master of Arts in art and educational psychology.

1939–1940
Travels to Europe and Mexico.

1940–1942
Works as Assistant Professor of Art at Georgia Teachers College in Collegeboro, Georgia.

1941
First solo exhibition is held at Uptown Gallery in New York City and features paintings and watercolors inspired by Surrealism; first participation in an institutional group exhibition held at the Brooklyn Museum, New York City.

1942
Moves to the state of Delaware, where he takes the position of State Supervisor of Art Education; first institutional solo exhibition at the Telfair Academy of Arts and Sciences in Savannah, Georgia.

1943
Smith produces his earliest purely geometric paintings, including *OK Territory*.

1944
Quits his job in Delaware and moves to New York City. Smith begins working at the Museum of Non-Objective Painting in New York City as an assistant to Hilla Rebay, who would later become the cofounder and first director of the Solomon R. Guggenheim Museum. A grant from the Solomon R. Guggenheim Foundation enables an extended stay in Santa Fe, New Mexico, where he produces more geometric abstract works on canvas and paper.

1945
Back in New York City, he produces paintings that are strongly influenced by the visual language of Piet Mondrian, including *Diagonal Passages*.

1949
Smith participates in the group exhibition *Post-Mondrian Painters* at the Sidney Janis Gallery in New York City, which also presents works by Josef Albers, Ilya Bolotowsky, and Fritz Glarner.

1951–1952
Spends seven months in Varadero, Cuba.

1952
Is appointed Professor of Art at Mills College of Education in New York City. Smith meets his future life partner, Robert Jamieson.

1951–1952
Siebenmonatiger Aufenthalt in Varadero, Kuba

1952
Berufung zum Professor für Kunst am Mills College of Education in New York City. Smith trifft seinen künftigen Lebenspartner Robert Jamieson.

1954
Inspiriert durch Bilder von Baseball- und Basketball-Bällen, die er in einem Sportartikelkatalog entdeckt, entwickelt Smith auf kreisrunden Leinwänden Werke wie *First-One*. Insbesondere die räumliche Wirkung der runden Leinwände interessiert ihn.

1955
Beginn der umfangreichen Serie von Collagen aus zerrissenem farbigem Papier

1960
Beginn der mehrjährigen Beschäftigung mit den zweifarbigen organisch-abstrakten *Correspondences*, mit denen er seine Art der (von ihm mitbegründeten) Hard-Edge-Malerei verfeinert. Hinzu kommen erste bemalte Holzreliefs und beidseitig bemalte Paravents. Teilnahme an der von Max Bill kuratierten Ausstellung *konkrete kunst – 50 jahre entwicklung* im Helmhaus in Zürich

1962
Erste internationale Einzelausstellung im Museo de Bellas Artes in Caracas

1965
Teilnahme an der gefeierten Ausstellung *The Responsive Eye* im Museum of Modern Art in New York City

1967
Es entstehen erste *Constellations*, mehrteilige Bildkompositionen, die Smiths Schaffen bis Mitte der 1970er-Jahren prägen werden.

1972
Gastprofessur an der University of California, Davis

1984
Die Neue Nationalgalerie in Berlin eröffnet mit *Leon Polk Smith – Collagen 1981–1983* die erste institutionelle Einzelausstellung des Künstlers in Europa.

1988
Eine Neuauflage seines bislang grössten mehrteiligen Gemäldes *Constellation Twelve Circles* auf Aluminium wird im Pharmaceutical Development Building von Ciba-Geigy (heute Novartis) in Summit, New Jersey, installiert.

1989
Erste Retrospektive im Wilhelm-Hack-Museum, Ludwigshafen am Rhein / Musée de Grenoble

1995
Die Retrospektive *Leon Polk Smith – American Painter* eröffnet im Brooklyn Museum

1996
Leon Polk Smith stirbt am 4. Dezember in New York City. Die von ihm und Robert Jamieson initiierte Leon Polk Smith Foundation wird mit einem kleinen Stiftungsrat gegründet, um Smiths Erbe zu verwalten, Forschung und Wissenschaft über Smith und seine Kunst zu fördern und seinen umfangreichen künstlerischen Nachlass zu verwalten.

Posthum wurden zahlreiche Einzelausstellungen ausgerichtet, von *Leon Polk im Arithmeum*, Universität Bonn (2001), bis hin zu *Leon Polk Smith: Hiding in Plain Sight*, Heard Museum, Phoenix, Arizona (2021).

1954
Inspired by pictures of baseballs and basketballs that he discovers in a sports equipment catalogue, Smith develops works on circular canvases, such as *First-One*. He is particularly interested in the round canvases' spatial effect.

1955
Starts his extensive series of collages made from torn colored paper.

1960
Begins his *Correspondence* series: two-color, organic, abstract works in which he refines his approach to Hard-edge Painting, which he primarily pursues for much of the 1960s. He also produces his first painted wood reliefs and folding screens painted on both sides. He participates in the exhibition *konkrete kunst – 50 jahre entwicklung* (concrete art: 50 years of development) curated by Max Bill at Helmhaus Zurich.

1962
First international solo exhibition is held at Museo de Bellas Artes in Caracas, Venezuela.

1965
Takes part in the celebrated exhibition *The Responsive Eye* at the Museum of Modern Art in New York City.

1967
Produces his first *Constellations*, which are multi-part, attached painting compositions that would dominate Smith's art until the mid-1970s.

1972
Takes a visiting professorship at the University of California, Davis.

1984
Neue Nationalgalerie in Berlin opens the artist's first solo museum exhibition in Europe: *Leon Polk Smith: Collages 1981–1983*.

1988
A new, enlarged version of his previously biggest multi-part painting *Constellation Twelve Circles* (1969) is realized on aluminum for the Ciba-Geigy Company (now Novartis) and installed in its pharmaceutical development building in Summit, New Jersey.

1989
His first retrospective is held at the Wilhelm-Hack-Museum, Ludwigshafen am Rhein, before traveling on to the Musée de Grenoble.

1995
The retrospective *Leon Polk Smith: American Painter* opens at the Brooklyn Museum in New York City.

1996
Leon Polk Smith dies on December 4th in New York City. The Leon Polk Smith Foundation, formed by Smith and Robert Jamieson, is established with a small board to oversee Smith's legacy, encourage research and scholarship about Smith and his art, and manage his sizable artistic estate.

Numerous gallery and museum solo exhibitions have been held since his death, spanning from *Leon Polk Smith in the Arithmeum* at the University of Bonn (2001) to *Leon Polk Smith: Hiding in Plain Sight* at the Heard Museum in Phoenix, Arizona (2021).

Autor:innen

David M. Roche ist ein national und international anerkannter Spezialist für die Kunst der Native Americans. Seit 2015 ist er Direktor und CEO am Heard Museum in Phoenix, Arizona, dem weltweit grössten privaten Museum, das sich der Kunst und Kultur der indigenen Bevölkerung Amerikas verschrieben hat. Davor war er 18 Jahre lang als Senior Specialist für dieses Themengebiet beim Auktionshaus Sotheby's in New York tätig. Er ist Mitglied der Association of Art Museum Directors (AAMD), hat sein Studium an der New York University als Master of Fine Arts abgeschlossen und seinen Bachelor of Arts an der University of Illinois in Urbana-Champaign gemacht. Er hat an Museen und Universitäten in den Vereinigten Staaten, in Grossbritannien und Frankreich Vorträge gehalten und an über 15 Publikationen mitgewirkt.

Sabine Schaschl, seit 2013 Direktorin des Museum Haus Konstruktiv in Zürich, ist Kunsthistorikerin und Kuratorin von Ausstellungen zur zeitgenössischen Kunst und zur klassischen Moderne sowie Autorin und Herausgeberin wissenschaftlicher Publikationen. Sie ist Mitglied zahlreicher Kommissionen und Jurys und wurde 2010 zum Chevalier de l'Ordre des Arts et des Lettres der Republik Frankreich ernannt. 2007 erhielt sie den Swiss Art Award, den Eidgenössischen Preis für Kunst und Kunstvermittlung.

Brandon Taylor ist emeritierter Professor für Kunstgeschichte an der University of Southampton, UK, und Dozent an der Ruskin School of Art, Oxford University. Er ist Autor mehrerer Bücher über moderne und zeitgenössische Kunst. Zuletzt erschienen *After Constructivism* (2013), *St Ives and British Modernism* (2015), *The Life of Forms in Art: Modernism, Organism, Vitality* (2020) und *Make It Modern: A History of Art in the Twentieth Century* (2022).

Margit Weinberg Staber lebt als Kunst- und Designpublizistin in Zürich. Sie hat an der von Max Bill mitgegründeten Hochschule für Gestaltung in Ulm studiert und ihr Diplom in der Abteilung Information gemacht. Von 1976 bis 1984 war sie Konservatorin am Kunstgewerbemuseum Zürich (Museum für Gestaltung) und von 1986 bis 1991 erste Kuratorin der Stiftung für konstruktive und konkrete Kunst Zürich (Träger Museum Haus Konstruktiv). Sie ist Autorin zahlreicher Künstlermonografien und kunstkritischer Texte sowie Verfasserin von Beiträgen zur Geschmacks- und Architekturgeschichte.

Authors

David M. Roche is a recognized national and international leader in the field of American Indian art. In 2015, he became the Director and CEO of the Heard Museum in Phoenix, Arizona, the largest private museum in the world dedicated to American Indian art and culture. Prior to that, he served as the Senior Specialist for American Indian art at Sotheby's Auction House in New York for 18 years. He is a member of the Association of Art Museum Directors (AAMD), has a Master of Fine Arts from New York University, and a Bachelor of Arts from the University of Illinois in Urbana-Champaign. He has lectured at museums and universities in the United States, United Kingdom, and France, and has contributed to more than 15 publications.

Sabine Schaschl, Director of Museum Haus Konstruktiv in Zurich since 2013, is an art historian and curator of exhibitions on contemporary art and classic modernism, as well as an author and editor of academic publications and catalogues. She is a member of numerous committees and juries and was named a Chevalier de l'Ordre des Arts et des Lettres by the French Republic in 2010. In 2007, she received the Swiss Federal Award for Art and Art Education at the Swiss Art Awards.

Brandon Taylor is Professor Emeritus in History of Art at the University of Southampton, UK, and a Tutor at the Ruskin School of Art, Oxford University. He is the author of several books on modern and contemporary art, most recently *After Constructivism* (2013), *St Ives and British Modernism* (2015), *The Life of Forms in Art: Modernism, Organism, Vitality* (2020), and *Make It Modern: A History of Art in the Twentieth Century* (2022).

Margit Weinberg Staber lives in Zurich as an art and design writer. She studied at the Ulm School of Design, co-founded by Max Bill, where she obtained her degree from the Information Department. She was a conservator at the Kunstgewerbemuseum Zurich (now Museum für Gestaltung) from 1976 to 1984 and the first curator at the Foundation for Constructivist and Concrete Art Zurich (which supports Museum Haus Konstruktiv) from 1986 to 1991. She is an author of numerous artist monographs and works of art criticism, as well as a writer of articles on the history of taste and architecture.

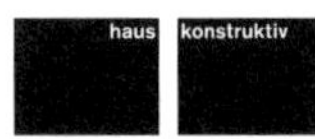

Museum Haus Konstruktiv
Selnaustrasse 25
8001 Zürich
Schweiz | Switzerland
www.hauskonstruktiv.ch

Direktorin und leitende Kuratorin |
Director and Head Curator
Sabine Schaschl

Kuratorin und Sammlungsleiterin |
Curator and Head of the Collection
Evelyne Bucher

Kuratorin | Curator
Eliza Lips

Leitung Administration, Finanzen und Personal |
Head of Office Management, Finances, and Personnel
Manuela Nüesch

Direktions- und Administrationsassistenz, Bibliothek |
Assistant to the Director, Office Management Assistant, Library
Friederike Müller

Verantwortliche Marketing und Kommunikation |
Head of Marketing and Communications
Ladina Hurst

Marketing und Kommunikation |
Marketing and Communications
Pascal Schlecht

Fundraising, Development
Joy Neri-Preiss

Kunstvermittlung | Art Education
Laura Flück, Felicitas Küng

Technische Leitung | Technical Managers
Kevin Aeschbacher, Pascal Sidler

Aufbau | Technical Support
Lucas Herzig, Silke Küste, David Kürsteiner, Thomas Moor

Leitung Museumsshop und Empfang, Editionen |
Museum Shop and Ticket Office Management, Editions
Martina Künzler

Leitung Museumscafé und Empfang |
Museum Coffee Shop and Ticket Office Management
Claudia Kammacher

Mitarbeiter:innen Empfang, Museumsshop und Museumscafé | Ticket Office, Museum Shop, and Museum Coffee Shop Staff
David Kürsteiner, Silke Küste, Pascal Schlecht, Anita Suter, Wu Xiaoqun

Führungen und Workshops |
Guided Tours and Workshops
Friederike Balke, Linda Christinger, Laura Flück, Felizitas Küng, Joy Neri-Preiss
Evelyne Bucher, Eliza Lips (Kuratorinnenführungen | Guided tours curatorial team)

Aufsicht | Museum Custodians
Lynn Bünger, Roy Felix, Emil Gut, Yoo Ja Kim, Silke Küste, Orlando Maglio, Mirjam Marti, Radhika Neelakandhan, Martin Zürcher

Ehrenamt (Aufsicht) | Volunteers (Museum Custodians)
Margrit Bäder, Barbara Dafft, Nancy van Dijk, Doris d'Hondt, Hans-Jakob Egli, Adriana Galli, Mercedes Gehrer, Ewa Hennel, Adrienne Herrmann, Beatrice Huldi, Annemarie Humm, Barbara Krizan, Patrick Macukic, Isabela Mateescu, Anni Mäder, Renée Müller, Barbara Rejman, Christina Sartorius, Herma Schmitt, Urs Thali, Hans-Jörg Tschachtli, Jakob Urech, Marta Varga, Ingrid Voit, Urs Vonlanthen, Verena Walser

Leihgeber | Lenders
Leon Polk Smith Foundation, Courtesy Lisson Gallery; Musée de Grenoble; Museum Ritter, Waldenbuch; Neues Museum Nürnberg; Städel Museum, Frankfurt am Main; Privatsammlung | Private collection, Berlin; Privatsammlung, Schweiz | Private collection, Switzerland; Nicole Schlégl-Helbling

Museum Haus Konstruktiv wird unterstützt von seinen Donator:innen, Gönner:innen, Club Fonds Konkret, Fördermitgliedern und Freund:innen, ausserdem von | Museum Haus Konstruktiv receives financial support from its donors, patrons, Club Fonds Konkret, sustaining members, and friends, as well as:

Stadt Zürich Fachstelle Kultur, Kanton Zürich, Zurich Insurance Company Ltd.

Die Realisierung der Ausstellung und der Publikation wurde grosszügig unterstützt von | This publication was made possible thanks to generous support from:

ART FOUNDATION
MENTOR LUCERNE

Weitere Unterstützung von | Further support from
Leon Polk Smith Foundation
Lisson Gallery

Diese Publikation erscheint anlässlich der Ausstellung |
This book is published on the occasion of the exhibition

Leon Polk Smith – Going Beyond Space

kuratiert von | curated by Sabine Schaschl

Museum Haus Konstruktiv
9. Februar – 7. Mai 2023 | February 9 – May 7, 2023

Herausgeberin | Editor
Sabine Schaschl, Stiftung für konstruktive, konkrete und konzeptuelle Kunst, Museum Haus Konstruktiv, Zürich

Redaktion | Managing Editors
Evelyne Bucher, Eliza Lips

Bildredaktion | Picture Editor
Friederike Müller

Lektorat | Copy Editing
Michelle Miles, michingo-translations.com (e)
Britta Schröder, schroeder-works.de (d/g)

Übersetzungen aus dem Deutschen ins Englische |
Translations from German into English
Simon Thomas, Berlin

Übersetzungen aus dem Englischen ins Deutsche |
Translations from English into German
Britta Schröder, schroeder-works.de

Grafische Gestaltung und Satz |
Graphic Design and Typesetting
Harald Pridgar, Frankfurt am Main

Schrift | Typeface
ES Allianz

Papier | Paper
Munken Print White, Arctic Volumen White

Projektmanagement Verlag | Project management
Valerie Hortolani, Hatje Cantz

Verlagsherstellung | Production
Thomas Lemaître, Hatje Cantz

Druck und Bindung | Printing and Binding
DZA Druckerei zu Altenburg

Fotonachweis | Photo Credits
Alle Ausstellungsaussichten von | All exhibition views by Stefan Altenburger, ausser | except
Eric Jobs S. | pp. 13, 23
George Darrell S. | p. 53
Mark Waldhauser S. | pp. 61, 109, 125

Erschienen im | Published by
Hatje Cantz Verlag GmbH
Mommsenstrasse 27
10629 Berlin
Deutschland | Germany
www.hatjecantz.com

Ein Unternehmen der Ganske Verlagsgruppe |
A Ganske Publishing Group Company

ISBN 978-3-7757-5471-2

Printed in Germany

Umschlagabbildungen | Cover Illustrations
Leon Polk Smith, *Constellation Twelve Circles*, 1968, Detail, Leon Polk Smith Foundation, Courtesy of Lisson Gallery, © 2023, ProLitteris, Zürich

Leon Polk Smith in seinem Atelier am | in his studio at Union Square in New York City, Schwarz-Weiss-Fotografie |Black and white photograph, nicht datiert | undated, Leon Polk Smith Foundation, © 2023, ProLitteris, Zürich

Vorsatzpapier | Endpapers
Leon Polk Smith beim Signieren von *Constellation Twelve Circles*, 1969–1988, nicht datiert | undated, Schwarz-Weiss-Fotografie | Black and white photograph, Novartis Art Collection, © 2023, ProLitteris, Zürich

Leon Polk Smith, Portrait, nicht datiert | undated, Schwarz-Weiss-Fotografie | Black and white photograph, Novartis Art Collection, © 2023, ProLitteris, Zürich

Leon Polk Smith beim Signieren von *Constellation Twelve Circles*, 1969–1988, Schwarz-Weiss-Fotografie | Black and white photograph, 1988, Novartis Art Collection, © 2023, ProLitteris, Zürich

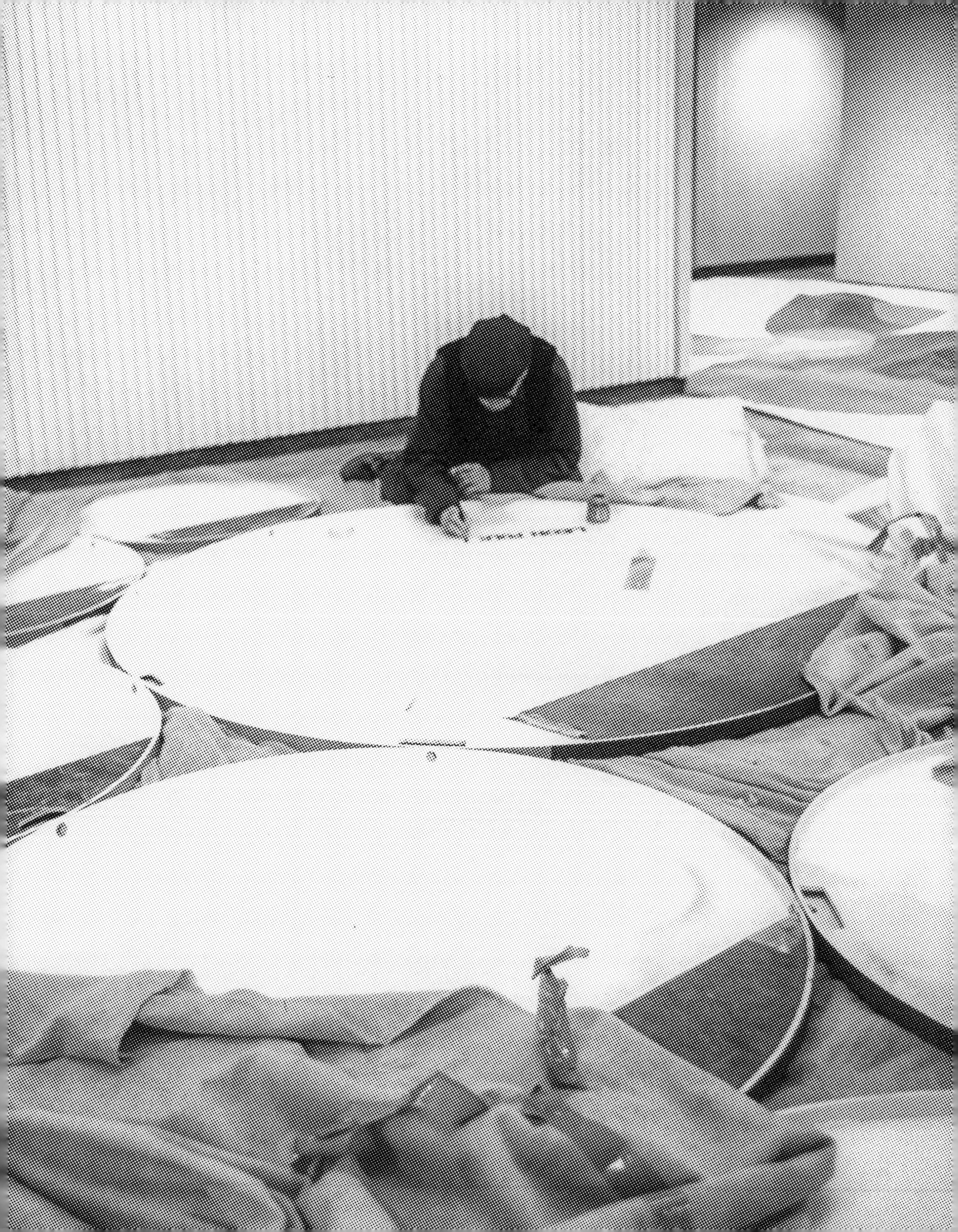

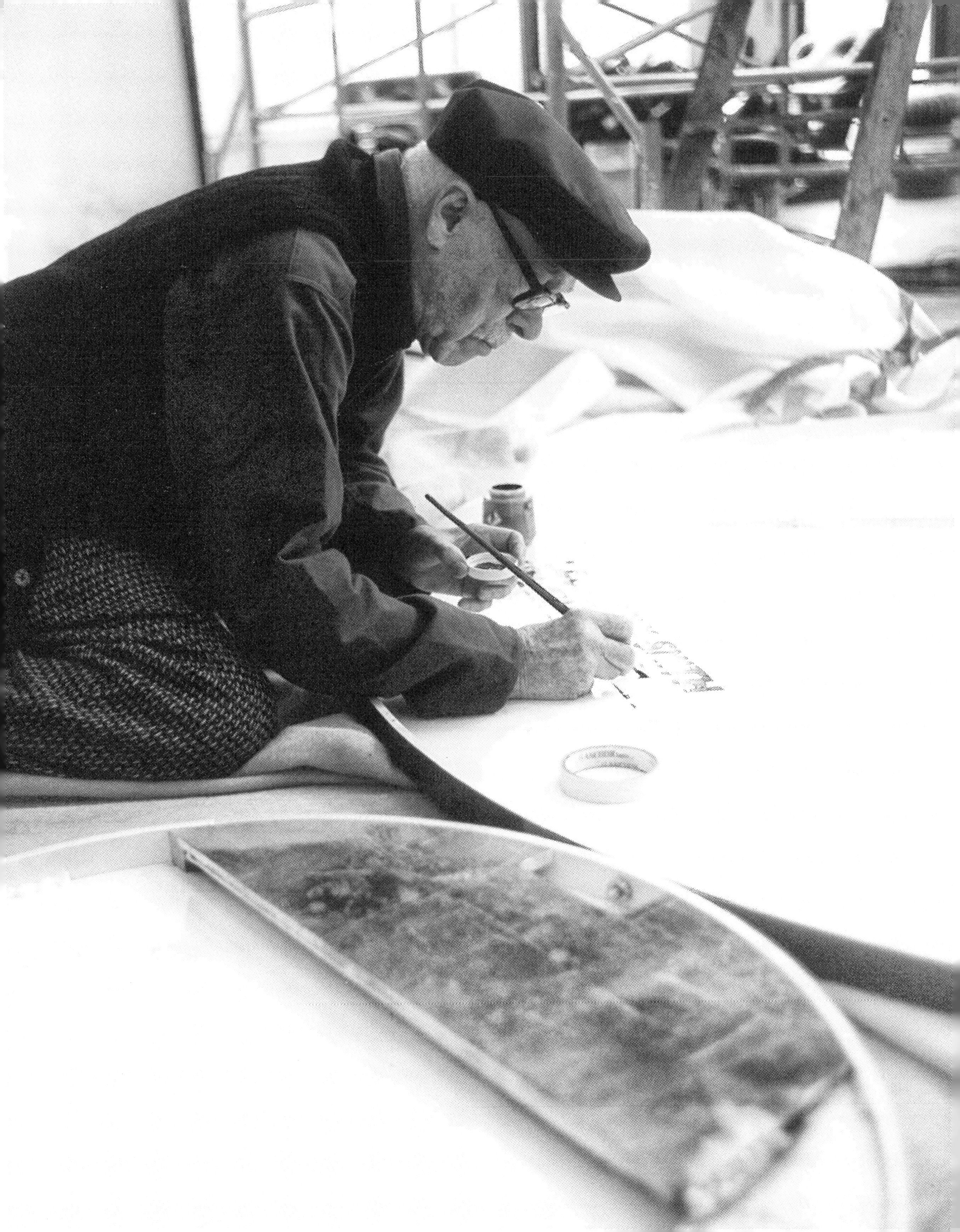